SOLVING THE MIGRAINE PUZZLE

The Successful Road To Recovery

by

L. Brooke Dubick

Judith E. Chiostri

Richard B. Chiostri—Editor/Graphic Designer

Solving The Migraine Puzzle

L. Brooke Dubick
Judith E. Chiostri

Editor: Richard Chiostri
Cover Design: Richard Chiostri

Second Edition – 2005

Publisher – C and D Solutions
Printed in the United States of America

For information contact us:
http://www.StopMigraineNow.com

ISBN 978-0-9772876-0-4
0-9772876-0-2

FORWARD

A TRUE STORY

This book grew out of the long and successful search for migraine relief of one of our authors, Brooke Dubick. Brooke did not have problems with migraine headaches as a young man. He was never seriously ill, could eat almost anything, and was a compulsive worker. At age 35, Brooke began having painful, disabling headaches. This sudden onset of headaches brought about fears of brain tumors or some chronic nervous disorder.

When Brooke was a high school teacher, he felt his headaches affected his job performance. His irritability made him short-tempered with his students. The bright lights from illustrating information for his students from an overhead projector brought pain. Besides the pain of the headache, Brooke's symptoms included: blurred vision, bouts of nausea and vomiting, constant nasal congestion, lack of energy, irritability, and trouble concentrating.

Brooke first went to a physician that specialized in ear, nose, and throat (ENT) problems. This physician felt Brooke might have a problem called Maxillary Sinusitis and prescribed antibiotics and surgery of the cheekbones to relieve pressure. When Brooke got a second opinion from another ENT physician before surgery, the second physician disagreed with the first physician's diagnosis. With conflicting opinions from two ENT physicians, Brooke decided to see an Allergist to explore other possible reasons for his suffering. All of the tests that the doctor performed indicated no allergies.

By a stroke of luck, Brooke heard about a lecture dealing with headaches. The lecture was going to be given by a physician specializing in neurology with a special interest in headaches. The headache specialist could have been describing Brooke and his symptoms during his lecture! At last, Brooke had found someone who really understood his problems.

Brooke made an appointment to see the specialist. The first step the doctor advised for Brooke was to keep a calendar to track the intensity and duration of headaches. At the second visit, Brooke received an examination to rule out any tumors or other medical reasons for his headaches. When the doctor found no physical abnormalities, he started Brooke on a regimen of deep relaxation techniques and dietary restrictions.

Brooke Dubick has suffered with migraine headaches for six long years. Like an alcoholic, he must take each day at a time. He controls his actions to avoid those conditions that may trigger a headache on a day-to-day basis. Through dedicated effort, Brooke is able to avoid developing migraine headaches. However, he must be vigilant about taking time for the deep relaxation and dietary restrictions. The occasional aspirin is sometimes needed, but this too is quite infrequent.

Brooke found the ideal treatment program for him. He did it by:

- Taking an active role in searching for the right diagnosis and treatment. Taking the lead role in the patient-physician team.
- Prodding and questioning his physicians.
- Reading about migraines to suggest new treatments to his physicians.
- Carefully tracking the success or failure of each treatment.
- Being aware of what was triggering his attacks, and avoiding those situations.
- Doggedly sticking to the regimen that worked for him.

That is what this book is all about: how to find your own ideal treatment program. You will learn:

- How migraines operate and what triggers them.
- How to keep records of your progress.*
- Simple precautions for everyday situations.*
- Simple relaxation exercises.*

- About biofeedback, hypnosis, and other treatments.
- About the use of drugs to treat migraines.
- How to identify and avoid the foods you are sensitive to.*

*These are things you can start doing right now. Read on.

Chapter 1

UNDERSTANDING MIGRAINES AND THEIR TREATMENT

Do You Have a Migraine?

Here are the symptoms:

- Pain on one side, both sides, or moving from the front towards the back of the head
- Loss of appetite
- Double vision, dizziness, or weakness
- Vertigo (spinning)
- Nausea
- Vomiting
- Spastic colon
- Diarrhea
- Confusion
- Swelling of hands and feet
- Tingling of face or hands
- Nasal congestion
- Intolerance to bright lights and loud sounds
- Blood shot and/or watery eyes (60)

These symptoms start most frequently in the early morning (between 5 and 10 A.M.). However, your migraine may start at other times of the day. The agony may last for 1 to 2 hours, or up to a week. You may suffer once or twice a week or every weekend.

The problems causing your headache might be related to other medical conditions. All headache sufferers should see a physician to be evaluated, especially those with daily headaches. Don't try to continuously self-medicate yourself without seeking medical advice as to the cause of your pain. (60)

Only a doctor can properly diagnose your problem. Other disorders have symptoms similar to migraines. And some of these disorders may be life threatening. So please see a doctor about your symptoms.

How Bad Does It Get?

Migraines affect up to 12 percent of the population and is three times more common in women than in men. Also, migraines are more common than diabetes or asthma. (13)

Everyone has had a headache at one time or another. Out of the 28 million Americans who suffer from migraine, 10 to 12 million have headaches so chronic, recurring, and painful that a doctor had to be seen at least once per year. A migraine attack may include severe pain, nausea, vomiting, dizziness, and tremors that can last for hours to a few days. Often, the person experiencing a migraine headache cannot work efficiently or is totally incapacitated.

Twenty four percent of females and 12 percent of males suffer from intense chronic migraine attacks. Chronic migraine is considered disabling when they occur on more than 15 days each month. (77)

Every year, absences due to migraine headaches deprive business of 112 million workdays at a cost to the economy of 50 billion dollars. Headache sufferers make eight million doctor's visits each year for treatment.

What Is A Migraine?

Migraine headaches have plagued people for at least 2000 years. Celebrities and historical figures with migraines were Vincent Van Gogh, Claude Money, Julius Caesar, Napoleon, Ulysses S. Grant, Robert E. Lee, Virginia Wolfe, Lewis Carroll, Mary Todd Lincoln, Elvis Presley, Loretta Lynn, and John F. Kennedy. The word "migraine" comes from the Greek to be "half-headed." This is appropriate since usually half of the head is affected with pain.

Certain foods, glaring lights and patterns, sounds and vibrations, and stressful situations may all trigger a migraine attack. They cause the body to release the amine, serotonin, into the bloodstream, which in turn causes the blood vessels to constrict.

This causes a reduced blood flow to the forehead, and results in the classic symptoms of double vision, weakness, and dizziness. Later, when the serotonin levels drop very low, the blood vessels in the scalp quickly expand, causing a throbbing pain in the forehead, face, or neck.

Treating Migraine

Doctors today have a huge arsenal of treatments for migraines, including drugs, diet, hypnosis, biofeedback, and relaxation therapy. Unfortunately, no single combination of these treatments will work for everyone, and there is no way to know which will work best for any individual. Each patient must experiment to find what works best.

This book is your guide to helping you find the best treatments for you. It tells you how to keep and use records of your migraines so you and your doctor can watch your progress. It allows you to start two treatments right now, on your own: diet modification and relaxation therapy. And it discusses other treatments for you to explore through your doctor.

The first chapters of this book will arm you with knowledge about your enemy, the migraine.

Chapter 1: Introduction.

Chapter 2: Explains how migraines operate.

Chapter 3: Discusses special cases such as children, sinusitis, and pregnancy.

The remaining chapters will guide you to establishing your ideal treatment program.

Chapter 4: Explains common migraine triggers and warning signs.

Chapter 5: Explains how to keep and use records for you and your doctor to monitor your progress.

Chapter 6: A compendium of simple precautions for everyday situations that you can begin using now.

Chapter 7: Simple relaxation exercises that you can begin using now.

Chapter 8: Discusses hypnosis, biofeedback, and other treatments that you can explore with your doctor.

Chapter 9: Discusses drugs and their effects.

Chapter 10: Lists foods that you can begin avoiding now.

Chapters 11- 19 present comprehensive diet plans you can begin using now.
Ch. 11/12 - Migraine reduction in 1200 to 2500 calorie diet plans
Ch. 13 - Food exchange lists
Ch. 14/15 - Cholesterol lowering diet
Ch. 16/17 - Diabetic control diet
Ch. 18/19 – Reduced sodium diet
Appendix A: Lists of migraine-safe foods
Appendix B: Recipes
Appendix C: Relaxation tapes
Appendix D: Headache centers and programs

Attitude

Anyone who has tried to lose weight, or stick to an exercise regimen, knows that a determined attitude will be important to following the diet and relaxation exercises described in this book.

But attitude has another role. The body's chemistry and blood flow respond continuously to what is happening around us, what we are doing, and our emotions. A positive attitude will help you to take control of managing your migraines and the conditions that trigger them.

This book asks you to make changes to your lifestyle, eliminate some favorite foods from your diet, and take time from your busy day to practice relaxing. With the right attitude, these are not very difficult sacrifices. Especially when you enhance your life by eliminating the pain and lost time of migraine attacks.

Chapter 2
KNOW THY ENEMY

Name That Migraine

There are four classes of migraine: Classic, Common, Cluster, and Complicated. The differences in treatment among these four classes is beyond the scope of this book, and inconsequential for most patients. This book describes therapies that are applicable to any of the four classes.

For those who insist on classifying and labeling . . .

Of the four types of migraine, the two most common types are migraine with Aura (Classic), and migraine without Aura (Common). Both of these involve vascular dilation during the headache phase. In the Classic type, initial vasoconstriction, or narrowing of the blood vessel, may occur and produce the pre-headache symptoms of flashing lights, blind spots, tingling or numbness, loss of strength, and difficulty in speaking. (60) In the Common migraine, pre-headache experiences do not occur, or at least are not readily recognized by the patient. (18)

Cluster headache diagnosis is often missed, so the exact incidence is unknown. Ninety percent of Cluster headache sufferers are males between the ages of 20 and 40. The pain usually lasts from a few minutes to four hours. This pain is severe, and it almost never occurs on both sides of the head simultaneously. The patient feels better rising and walking around. Most frequently, the headaches occur at night. There is no aura, nausea, or vomiting; and blurring of vision is rare. The patient may experience flushing of the face, tearing of the eyes, nasal congestion, and sweating of the neck. The attacks tend to be brief, and appear in groups or clusters over several weeks to several months. (18) Between clusters, the sufferers may free from headaches for weeks or months.

The last type is the Complicated, Hemiplegic, or Ophthalmoplegic headache. This type is a more severe form of the Classic migraine with neurological symptoms that persist after the headache itself is gone. (60) For instance, patients can experience both head pain, and a loss of sensation in the arms. Pain can be localized around the eye, often accompanied by various neurological disorders.

The Mechanics Of A Migraine

Blood vessels naturally constrict (contract) when exposed to certain chemicals, reducing the supply of oxygen to the brain. The blood vessels then dilate or expand to counteract the constriction and allow blood to flow normally again. If the blood vessels expand too much, pain-producing substances are released, leading to inflammation and swelling against nerve endings in the vessels. This inflammation and swelling in the blood vessels presses against the trigeminal nerve along the head, neck, scalp, and face, sending throbbing messages of pain to your brain.

Details

The pre-headache stage begins when the body is exposed to a stimulus or condition it can't handle. These include certain foods, glaring lights, or stress (all of which are discussed in other parts of this book). The body responds by over-producing the amine called serotonin. The serotonin, in turn, causes the brain's blood vessels to constrict, reducing blood flow to the forehead, and producing the classic symptoms of double vision, weakness, and dizziness. Serotonin can also stimulate activity in the intestines causing diarrhea, and prevent the release of water from the body, causing hands and feet to swell.

Later, when the serotonin levels drop very low, the blood vessels in the scalp quickly expand causing a throbbing pain in the forehead, face, or neck. At normal levels, serotonin combines with brain chemicals called endorphins to reduce pain. But, when serotonin levels are low, the endorphins don't work and pain results. (25)

If your migraine causes you to vomit, you often feel better afterwards. After vomiting, a very small amount of serotonin is released into the blood. This causes a slight constriction of the blood vessels, but not enough for a rebound effect. The constriction counteracts the over-dilation, taking pressure off the nerves, and reducing the pain. (25)

Amines are vasoactive chemicals (i.e., they affect blood vessels), and are naturally produced in the body. The most common vasoactive amines are: serotonin, tryptamine, tyramine, dopamine, and norepinephrine. All of them produce migraines in a manner similar to serotonin as described above. The active amine in food which causes the most problems is tyramine. Tyramine acts directly on blood vessels and, as a secondary effect, causes a release of even more amines into the blood stream.

Excessive amines often result from a malfunction in the metabolism which affects the breakdown of the amines in the body. For instance, tyramine and serotonin are normally absorbed into nerve cells with the help of an enzyme called monoamine oxidase (MAO), found in the gastrointestinal tract, liver, and kidneys. (19) In a migraine sufferer, there are fewer MAO enzymes available to metabolize the tyramine. The resulting excess tyramine causes more amines to be released, leading to a release of the neurotransmitter norephine and blood vessel constriction and the start of a migraine attack.

Chapter 3

MIGRAINE AND SPECIAL CIRCUMSTANCES

Migraine and Children

Most adults with migraines suffered their first attacks as children. It has been estimated that 10 percent of children have recurrent headaches, with the most common type being migraine. In addition, about 10 percent of all migraine sufferers are children. Somewhere between 70-90 percent of children with migraine headaches have parents with a history of migraines. Children can grow out of migraine problems as adults with symptoms returning in middle age. They can experience the same symptoms as adults such as swelling of the hands and feet, nausea, vomiting, increased urination, sweating, and being lethargic. However, children develop more abdominal migraine. A mild migraine can consist of motion sickness, unpredictable stomachaches, and vomiting when excited. (26)

Treatment is harder for children because it is not easy to know just what symptoms children really have. For instance, there is little evidence of visual disturbances such as the aura. Also, children get feelings that are hard for them to describe or explain. One good way to find out how bad the headaches are for the child is to have him to draw his feelings- Like the old saying: "A Picture Says A Thousand Words". The parents of the sufferer must cope with acute attacks, and prevent others from occurring. They need the children's cooperation, but must not increase their fears of future attacks. (27)

Ibuprofen and acetaminophen are safe and effective for acute migraine pain in children aged six years and older. Teens may also benefit from Imitrex nasal spray. The treatment for many health problems in children is not just drugs but often a lifestyle change.

To find help for your child, Appendix D contains two examples of pediatric headache clinics- one at the University of Maryland Hospital in Baltimore headed by Dr. Jack Gladstein, and the other in Little Rock, Arkansas founded by Dr. Joseph Elser.

Migraine and Pregnancy

During pregnancy, 80 percent of women find that their migraines either diminish in frequency and severity or disappear altogether by the end of the third month. Also, during the period of lactation (breast feeding), migraine improvement continues. Unfortunately, 20 percent of the women's migraines are more frequent and severe. However, the pattern of migraine can change from one pregnancy to the next. The change in your migraine pattern is basically due to the hormonal changes that occur.

Since it is advisable to stop all migraine medications once you know you are pregnant, the change in diet and the use of biofeedback can help to reduce any migraine problems.

Migraine and Hormonal Changes

In women, 60 percent of migraine attacks are related in some way to their menstrual cycle. When females start their menstrual period between the ages of 10-15, they develop more migraines due to their new hormonal balance. The migraine develops when the production of two hormones, estrogen and progesterone, decreases in the ovaries and the uterine lining begins to break down. Women with a history of migraines are twice as likely to have migraine headaches during the first three days of the menstrual period than at other times. (2)

However, these migraines were usually no worse than those occurring later in the menstrual cycle. When menopause begins, there can be a 50 percent reduction in the occurrence of migraine. If hormonal supplements are given to regulate menopause symptoms, a person can develop a migraine for the first time, or an existing migraine problem can worsen.

Migraine And The Pill

If a female has a family history of migraine, her first encounter with migraine can occur when oral contraceptive pills are first begun. If the migraine continues, there has should be a change in the brand of pill to lower the dose of estrogen. If this still doesn't work, the woman should go to another form of birth control.

Migraine and TMJ (Jaw And Facial Pain)

The Temporo-Mandibular Joint (TMJ) is located where the lower jaw (mandible) joins the temporal bone of the skull on each side of the ear. This joint gets a lot of use from chewing and talking. Like all joints, a piece of cartilage separates and protects the bones when the joint moves. However, excessive wear and tear on the cartilage, or if a misalignment of the jaw allows the cartilage to pop out of position, the bones may come in contact and grind against each other, exposing nerve endings and causing pain. The pain may be sharp and searing each time you talk, yawn, chew, or swallow; or the pain may be dull, constant, and boring. Muscles of the jaw, face, or skull may spasm. The pain may be felt the side of the head, the cheek, the jaw, and the teeth. Some people have attributed migraine, back pain, and shoulder pain to TMJ, but the most common symptom is ringing in the ears.

TMJ is often exacerbated by habitually clenching or grinding your teeth, or biting down forcibly. Many people carry out these nasty habits in their sleep, at work, or when concentrating or stressed. When properly diagnosed, TMJ can be treated by dentist specializing in TMJ with massage, hot compresses, mouth appliances (to prevent teeth clenching during sleep, etc.), muscle relaxants, or surgery.

Migraine and Allergies

Migraine and allergy appear to co-exist to a high degree. About one-third of migraine sufferers have allergies. Allergies themselves do not cause migraine, but they make you more susceptible. An allergist can diagnose and treat your allergy.

Migraine and Sinusitis

An attack of sinusitis or sinus infection can cause a headache, but is rarely the cause of migraine. Surgery to correct a deviated septum rarely cures migraine in most people. The sinus pain is usually relieved if the obstruction blocking the sinuses is drained. Nose drops, nasal spray, and steam inhalation may help to clear your nose. Antibiotics may have to be given to get rid of the infection.

Migraine and Stroke

Stroke is the third leading cause of death in this country. According to the New England Journal of Medicine, for women under the age of 45, 27 percent of strokes may be caused by migraine. Women who suffer from a migraine with aura are up to 10 times more likely to suffer a stroke. Auras affect about 15 percent of the estimated 28 million Americans who suffer migraines. Auras usually precede the migraine by up to 1 hour. The risk of stroke was 4 times higher in women who had migraines for more than 12 years. The risk was 10 times higher among women who continued to have migraines and aura more than once a month. Women under the age of 45 who take birth control pills have about 9 times the risk of getting a stroke. (85)

Migraine and Surgery

Patients undergoing a plastic surgery technique, which involves cutting muscles in the forehead, may reduce migraines. While 92 percent of the patients reported at least a 50 percent reduction in migraine frequency, duration, and intensity, 35 percent reported elimination of migraines. (14)

Melatonin Levels

Melatonin regulates sleep and people with migraines may have a low level of this chemical. If 3 milligrams of melatonin is taken over a 3 month period 30 minutes before bedtime, it may curb these headaches by 50 percent. (40)

Chapter 4

WHAT TRIGGERS A MIGRAINE ATTACK

This chapter discusses factors that trigger migraine attacks. While the later chapters on lifestyle, foods, and diet explain how to avoid these triggers, you must first learn to recognize them in your daily life.

You need to avoid only the triggers to which you are most sensitive. Look for the presence of these triggers whenever you have an attack. The record sheets described in the next chapter, Keeping Records, will help you identify which triggers affect you most.

Migraine Triggers In Our Foods

Of all of the factors that can trigger a migraine, food causes 50 percent of the problems. To emphasize the point about the effects of certain foods, a study was done that examined the medical histories of 500 migraine patients. The results were as follows:

Foods Associated with Migraines (37)

Food	**Out of 500 patients**	**Patients with migraine suffering relatives**
alcohol	29%	59%
chocolate	19%	30%
cheese	18%	25%
citrus fruit	11%	16%

Coffee, pork, eggs, and dairy products were reported by fewer than ten percent of the patients.

Of all the foods eaten, only certain ones have higher concentrations of amines. These foods add more amines into the body than is needed. This causes an imbalance between amines and the enzyme monoamine oxidase, triggering the abnormal constriction and dilation problems.

The amine in food which causes most problems is tyramine. It is formed by the restructuring of the amino acid, Tyrosine. In foods containing tyramine, the content varies because of differences in processing, contamination during handling, fermentation, ripening, degradation, or prolonged storage. The more these foods are aged, fermented, or spoiled, the larger the amount of tyramine present. (53)

Dr. B.J. McCabe suggests patients reduce their intake of tyramine below six milligrams per day. McCabe's detailed list of foods to avoid are presented in Appendix J. (53)

The summary below shows what can happen when the levels exceed a certain limit.

Tyramine Levels:

6 milligrams	may produce a mild crisis
10 to 25 milligrams	may produce severe headaches with intracranial hemorrhages

In contrast, Dr. Seymour Diamond recommends his patients avoid tyramine and other vasoactive substances completely. (19) Many of the foods restricted in Diamond's tyramine diet are also restricted in the diet given in this book.

A 1952 study found that by restricting those vasoactive foods for three months, 65 percent of their participants experienced complete relief, while 20 percent had partial relief. (60)

Other Triggers (18)

Your behavior and surroundings are sources of most triggers. For example, fasting or skipping a meal can lead to hypoglycemia, or low blood sugar, which causes dilation of blood vessels in the head and triggers an attack. Fortunately, you can avoid behaviors and surroundings that are potential triggers, if you learn to recognize them. Some common triggers are listed below. Environmental conditions, physical conditions, activities, and events can all trigger migraine attacks.

Source	Problem
Light	Strong direct or reflected light
	Flashing Lights
	Night driving: oncoming headlights and streetlights
Noise and Vibrations	Loud or continuous such as vacuum cleaner or lawn mower
	Low-frequency thump such as in loud music blaring from loudspeakers
Odors, Aromas, and Smells	Intense and penetrating odors such as fresh paint, solvents, and cleaning solvents
	First- or Second-hand smoke
Steam	Sensitivity in hot tubs, baths, and saunas
Poor Ventilation	Office buildings without opened windows and poor air circulation
	Indoor air pollution and dust
	Charged particles in indoor air
Sleep	Too much sleep
	Too little sleep two or more nights in a row
Lighting	Glare from bright lights
	Too little light
	Flicker
Computer/ Terminal Glare	Glare or eye fatigue from the glare of a CRT or monitor screen

Source	Problem
Motion	Nausea or dizziness from carnival rides
	Driving or riding in a car causes nausea or dizziness
	Reading or writing in a moving car causes nausea or dizziness
	Rocking in a chair causes nausea or dizziness
Outdoor Sports and Activities	Sun glare
Tennis and Badminton	Rapid eye movement and concentration on small objects
Jogging	Head bouncing
Gardening, Snow Shoveling, Bending over	Any bending or stooping in head-down position

Source	Problem
Clothing	Tight collars, waistbands, and hats
	Geometric patterns, pin stripes, and large prints
	Corduroy is uncomfortable to wear during an attack because skin is sensitive
	Leather is stiff and unyielding
Barometric Pressure	Long-Distance Flights over 35,000 Feet
	When air pressure falls below 30 inches, the arteries in the brain and scalp dilate
Cold and Wind	Prolonged exposure affects blood vessels
Heat	Hair dryers
	High Humidity

Warning Signs of an Attack

Let's start with the symptoms you should be aware of. Initial warning symptoms occur 8 to 48 hours before the onset of the headache. They may be neither striking nor disturbing. They often go unnoticed and are mainly minor discomforts for you. When you avoid treatments for your pre-headache conditions, more serious symptoms develop, leading up to the migraine.

Pre-headache warning symptoms (56):

hunger	yawning
fatigue-tired appearance	gooseflesh
shivering	dizziness
trembling hands	muscular aches
feeling of cold	numb hands and fingers
dryness of the mouth	sweating after minimal exercise
irritability	intolerant
hostility	

Many people experience some of these symptoms without experiencing migraine.

The next symptoms are known as "prodromes" since they occur a few minutes to a few hours before the actual headache:

- Feelings of swelling and tightness in the head
- Hands and fingers numb
- Change in manner of walking with a tendency to fall because of weakness in the legs
- Pain over one eye (usually reoccurring on the same side)
- Aura or flashing or watery light before the eyes causing blind spots in the field of vision
- Double vision

After the headache has gone on for a period of time, such as 4 or 5 hours, you most likely have already experienced weakness, irritability, and a great deal of tension, making concentration difficult. Even when you have finally gotten rid of the headache, you can still be exhausted for the next few days.

Following an attack, you should try very hard to determine what caused the headache (food or one of the other triggers), and what strategy should be used to avoid the situation again.

Chapter 5

KEEPING RECORDS

Doctor's Assessment Of Your Symptoms

Have yourself examined by a physician specializing in headache diagnosis, such as a neurologist. You must make certain there is no physical abnormality (such as an allergy, sinus condition, or tumor) causing your headaches.

This recommendation is not to scare you. We hope you will find that your doctor's examination will provide you with a chance to be reassured. Most headache sufferers do not have a brain tumor or other serious physical problem, but it is best to be safe and have it checked out.

Once your physician has determined there are no serious physical abnormalities, you must begin working with your physician to develop your ideal treatment program.

1. Take an active approach to your treatment. Read books on migraines. Take notes and discuss possible treatments with your physician.
2. Keep in close contact with the physician treating your headaches. Find a physician who will work with you. Seek second opinions, especially if surgery is recommended.
3. Maintain a positive attitude. Remember that the very next method you try could be the one that will work.
4. Be sure every doctor who prescribes you medicine is aware of all your medical problems.
5. Be aware of all side effects of medications taken. Look up medicines in an accepted reference book, such as the Physician's Desk Reference (66). If you are concerned about a drug's side affects, seek a second opinion.
6. Maintain the record sheets described in the next section. They are your key tool to determine your migraine triggers, and which treatments work best.

Assess What Triggers YOUR Migraine

Migraine triggers are not always immediate; they often do not produce a migraine until the next day. Humans that we are, it is tough to remember what we ate or did yesterday that triggered a migraine today. By keeping daily records, you can see not only which triggers you are most sensitive to, but also patterns in your behavior routinely causing your migraine attacks.

The Headache Calendar

Keep a calendar record of your headaches. A blank calendar is provided for you in **Figure 1** at the end of this chapter. Make several copies of it. Below is an example of how to make entries. Try to keep your calendar record for at least one month before you make any of the dietary or lifestyle changes suggested in this book. One month should be an ample amount of time to observe several patterns.

Make entries in your calendar record as follows:

Time:
Record the time of day your migraine started and its duration.

Severity:
Rate that day's migraine attack on a scale of 0 to 4 as defined in the severity key on the calendar. Be objective when rating a headache, as this provides important information that will aid your physician in making an accurate diagnosis. The scale is not a measure of the amount of pain you felt, but a measure of how the attack impacted your ability to function.

Suspected Trigger:
The most important entry on your calendar. When you have an attack, look back on the hours and days leading up to the attack, and try to identify what probably triggered it.

Meditation:
Record the amount of time you spent that day doing relaxation exercises.

Food/Medication:
Using the restricted food lists in Chapter 10 as a guide, list any foods you consumed that day that may trigger a migraine. List the foods even if you do not suffer a migraine that day, because your attack may not come for another 24 to 48 hours. Besides, if no attack occurs, you will then have proof that the food, in the quantity consumed, was safe for you.

List any medications you take that day, even if it is not for relief of migraine. Some drugs cause headaches as a side effect. If the medication was for migraine, record how much time past before it provided relief.

Exposure/Activities:
Using Chapter 6 as a guide, record any exposure to environmental factors (light, smoke, noise, etc.), or activities you participated in, which may trigger a migraine attack. List them even if you do not suffer a migraine that day, because your attack may come 24 to 48 hours later. Besides, if no attack occurs, you will then have proof that the activity, in the extent performed, was safe for you.

This way, you will have a record of just how many painful headaches that you used to have, and can measure your progress against it. The calendar could be taken when you go to see the neurologist, or use it to test the diet eliminations suggested later in this book.

Later on, you can keep track of any slip-ups in your diet. You may also wish to track the times you performed your daily deep relaxation on your calendars. If you start to slide away from the relaxation and diet recommendations, you will be able to see on your calendar just when it happened and also the headaches you got as a consequence.

You should also compare the calendar record to your daily or weekly routine. Perhaps you will discover links to your sleep patterns, such as staying up late for a favorite TV show; or to certain work or recreational activities, such as laundry day or rushing out the Friday reports.

Calendar Analysis: An Example

In **Figure 2** at the end of this chapter, one week of a calendar is filled out as an example. Please follow along with it as we analyze a week in the life of John Doe.

- On Sunday, John Doe felt fine and indulged in a slice of lemon pie after supper. On Monday morning, everything was fine, and John went jogging and practiced his relaxation exercises for 20 minutes. Around 3 p.m., John developed a migraine, yet he was still able to do his normal tasks. He took two Tylenol-tm, and the headache got better in about 2 hours. John blamed the lemon pie because of its citrus content.

- On Tuesday, no headache was experienced at all. While preparing briefs in the employee lounge, John was exposed to a lot of cigarette smoke. Supper was a sausage pizza.
- 5 a.m. Wednesday morning, a migraine kept John up. He took four Advil-tm during the day, and he tried meditation for 30 minutes. Finally, by evening, John felt well enough to go jogging. The sausage pizza (cheese, nitrates, onions) and the smoke were the apparent triggers.
- Thursday morning the migraine was gone. John did paperwork till 1 a.m.
- Friday. Again at 5 a.m. John suffered a migraine, this time with a stuffy nose and blurry eyes. John practiced biofeedback for 30 minutes and took two Allerest-tm. By 7:30 a.m., he felt better and went jogging. John was paying for staying up late Thursday.
- Saturday. John still felt a slight headache, so he practiced biofeedback again for 15 minutes. He also mowed the lawn in the mid-day sun.

Will Saturday's exposure to the sun affect John on Sunday? Is there a correlation between John's jogging and his attacks? If John meditates for longer periods, will attacks be reduced further, or is 15 minutes enough? We need a longer calendar than this example to answer these questions; and then we can only answer them for John. You need your calendar to to get the right answers for you. Why not start one today?

The Headache Record

Another form you will find indispensable in assessing your progress is the Headache Record Form (**Figure 3** at the end of this chapter). Use this form to track the symptoms of your headaches. Again, this is an important form to show your physician.

Any time you have a migraine attack, record the date, time, and duration. Check off the symptoms you experience. This will aid the physician in diagnosing your condition, and tracking the effectiveness of treatments.

Keeping and using good records is the key to finding your ideal treatment program.

MIGRAINE CALENDAR

Figure 1

Date:							
	Sunday	**Monday**	**Tuesday**	**Wednesday**	**Thursday**	**Friday**	**Saturday**
Time:							
Severity:							
Suspected Trigger:							
Meditation:							
Food/ Medication:							
Exposure/ Activities:							

Severity: 0 - No Headache 1 - Low level; hardly noticed 2 - Moderate; can perform tasks 3 - Severe; can't concentrate 4 - Intense; incapacitated

MIGRAINE CALENDAR

Figure 2

Date:	8	9	10	11	12	13	14
	Sunday	Monday	Tuesday	Wednesday	Thursday	Friday	Saturday
Time:		3 - 5 pm	5 - 7:30 am			5 - 7:30 am	
Severity:	0	2	0	3	0	2	0
Suspected Trigger:		Lemon Pie		pizza, smoke, stress		up late	
Meditation:		20 min.	15 min.	30 min.	20 min.	30 min.	15 min.
Food/ Medication:	lemon pie	2 Tylenol	sausage pizza	4 Advil		2 Allerest	lemon pie
Exposure/ Activities:		Jogging (am)	Briefing-smoky room	Jogging (pm)	up till 1 am	Jogging (pm)	Mowing in sun

Severity: 0 - No Headache 1 - Low level; hardly noticed 2 - Moderate; can perform tasks 3 - Severe; can't concentrate 4 - Intense; incapacitated

Figure 3

SYMPTOM RECORD

Check off the symptoms you experience every day.

Date	Time	Stuffy Nose	Pain Over Eye		Blurred Vision	Diarrhea	Stomach Cramps	Stuffy Ears	Other
			Left	Right					

Chapter 6

LIFESTYLES

The body's chemistry and blood flow respond continuously to what is happening around us, what we are doing, and our emotions. A positive attitude will help you help keep in control.

Beyond therapeutic treatments, there are many ordinary things you can do, not do, or change in your everyday life. Simple things like wearing sunglasses and avoiding pinstripes.

There is a lot of lore generated by migraine sufferers over the past 2000 years. Some of it, science has found time to prove or disprove. But science has not yet explored everything in the field of migraines. Some of the best advice is founded on just the claims of other sufferers and their experiences.

In this chapter, we have tried to collect some of the more widely useful tidbits.

Migraine Triggers And Prevention (25):

Source	Problem/Trigger	Prevention
Noise and Vibrations	Loud or continuous such as vacuum cleaner or lawn mower	Wear earplugs.
	Low-frequency thump such as in loud music blaring from loudspeakers	Avoid situations where noise and vibrations occur.

Source	Problem/Trigger	Prevention
Light	Strong direct or reflected light Flashing Lights Night driving: oncoming headlights and streetlights	Use light-polarizing sunglasses. Get sunglasses tinted green or gray. Ultra-Violet (UV) coatings also help. Such glasses will not seriously reduce daytime visibility. On prescription eyeglasses, get a 10% color tint and a UV coating.
Odors, Aromas, and Smells	Intense and penetrating odors such as fresh paint, solvents, and cleaning solvents First- or second-hand smoke	Have plenty of ventilation. Occasionally go outside for fresh air. Use non-smoking areas of restaurants. Do not smoke.
Steam	Sensitivity in hot tubs, baths, and saunas	Avoid saunas. Keep door open while bathing to avoid steam build-up.

Source	Problem/Trigger	Prevention
Poor Ventilation	Office buildings without opened windows and poor air circulation Indoor air pollution and dust Charged particles in indoor air	Open widows and run fans to circulate air. Install air filtration systems. Have furnace and air conditioning filters cleaned frequently. Try using negative ion generators.
Sleep	Too much sleep Too little sleep two or more nights in a row	Change your sleep pattern. That is, your bedtime and wake-up time. Keep your sleep pattern constant, even on weekends.
Lighting	Glare from bright lights Too little light Flicker	Replace standard light switches with dimmers. Do not turn on dimmers too low. Adjust the contrast and brightness of your television to reduce intensity. Use adequate reading light.

Source	Problem/Trigger	Prevention
Computer/Terminal Glare	Glare or eye fatigue from the glare of a CRT or monitor screen	Adjust the contrast and brightness of your computer monitor to reduce intensity. Install a glare guard (preferably polarized) on your computer monitor screen. On color computer monitors, try changing the foreground and background colors in your software. If you use a monochrome computer monitor, try a different color. Monochrome monitors come in green, amber, and white. Many people are sensitive to green monitors, but others are sensitive to amber or white. Choose what is right for you.

Source	**Problem/Trigger**	**Prevention**
Motion	Nausea or dizziness from carnival rides Driving or riding in a car causes nausea or dizziness Reading or writing in a moving car causes nausea or dizziness Rocking in a chair causes nausea or dizziness	Some people find the back seat of a car is less nauseating, but others prefer the front seat. Do not read or write while the car is moving. Let someone else take the kids on the carnival rides.
Outdoor Sports and Activities	Sun glare	Use glare-proof sunglasses.
Tennis and Badminton	Rapid eye movement and concentration on small objects	Avoid playing.
Jogging	Head bouncing	Walk instead.
Gardening, Snow Shoveling, Bending over	Any bending or stooping in head-down position	When lifting objects, bend your knees, keep your back straight and head erect. Use your leg muscles to lift. Use long-handled gardening tools. Use a shovel with a lever.

Source	Problem/Trigger	Prevention
Clothing	Tight collars, waistbands, and hats	Avoid wearing turtleneck sweaters and shirts. Wear collar spreaders to make collars more loose.
	Geometric patterns, pin stripes, and large prints	Wear soft colors such as blue, green, beige, and gray.
	Corduroy is uncomfortable to wear during an attack because skin is sensitive	Wear cotton for softness.
	Leather is stiff and unyielding	
Barometric Pressure	Long-Distance Flights over 35,000 Feet	Perform relaxation techniques.
	When air pressure falls below 30 inches, the arteries in the brain and scalp dilate	
Cold and Wind	Prolonged exposure affects blood vessels	Wear proper attire including hat and gloves.
Heat	Hair dryers	Put dryer on cold to warm settings.
	High Humidity	Drink plenty of fluids.

Eye Care

Vision can trigger a migraine attack, and a migraine attack can temporarily affect vision. Regular, thorough eye exams are essential. Your ophthalmologist or optometrist should be aware of your migraine problems, and can look for conditions associated with migraine.

If you are prone to a migraine, you shouldn't wear contact lenses. Your eyeballs bulge during an attack and when your eyes are closed the eyeball is pressed against the eyelids. The eyeball pushes the contacts against the eye causing irritation. However, if you have mild or infrequent attacks, you can wear contacts but you must take them out as soon as the migraine hits.

Travel

Even when you go on a trip, you should maintain regular eating and sleeping patterns. Take an extra pair of sunglasses and a copy of your prescription for eyeglasses with you. In addition, a letter confirming your migraine diagnosis should be carried with you. This is important because if you are stopped by the police and you appear drunk or on drugs, it just might be the symptoms of your pre-headache phase.

Health

1. Do not smoke.
2. Maintain your diet.
3. Exercise regularly. Choose mild to moderate exercises that are pleasant, easy, and non-stressful. If a person warms up for 10 minutes before strenuous exercise, delay reaction headaches could be prevented. When women (whom frequently have higher Nitric oxide levels than men) exercise, even for 30 seconds, many experience a 20 percents increase of Nitric oxide. This should be avoided, if possible, as Nitric oxide in large amounts may cause blood vessel inflammation. (11)
4. Stay active. Don't withdraw.
5. Avoid exhaustion.
6. Be sure every doctor who prescribes you medicine is aware of all your medical problems.
7. Be aware of all side effects of medications taken. Look up medicines in an accepted reference book.

Chapter 7
RELAXATION THERAPY

In this chapter, we will learn relaxation techniques. Relaxation and diet are highly effective treatments for many migraine sufferers. All of us know how to relax, in that we can blank out our mind, unwind our emotions, and make our body comfortable. But that is NOT the level of relaxation we are aiming for in this chapter. We want to relax the muscles, the blood flow, the nervous system, and the body's chemistry.

As Chapter 2 explains, migraines are produced when the body is stimulated to introduce excesses of certain chemicals into the bloodstream and the blood vessels respond by constricting or dilating. The body's chemistry and blood flow respond continuously to what is happening around us, what we are doing, and our emotions. A positive attitude and mastery of relaxation techniques will help you keep in control.

The knowledge of how to obtain the level of relaxation desired for controlling migraine is not something humans are born with, or that most of us learn while growing up. Like learning to play a piano, we have to DO something to learn it. Fortunately, the lessons are so easy, there is no excuse for anyone to not get an "A".

Relaxation training uses meditation, imaging, and breathing techniques to produce a tranquil state. We will cover two sets of relaxation exercises. The first set, Deep Relaxation, is an excellent introduction that will allow you to experience, and learn to recognize, a state of deep relaxation. The second set of exercises, Autogenic Training, is more practical to use day-to-day; but without prior experience with the deep relaxation state, Autogenic Training can be difficult to truly master. You may learn, even memorize the Autogenic exercises, but are you really achieving deep relaxation? Therefore, we recommend starting with the Deep Relaxation exercises.

WARNING: Relaxation exercises can leave you in a dazed afterglow. Somewhat like emerging from a theater after an engrossing movie, or having an alcohol-induced buzz, you may not be fully attuned to your surroundings. We know of one person who, right after meditating, inadvertently drove his car into a tree. Therefore, give yourself a little time after every relaxation session to fully "wakeup" before doing something dangerous like operating machinery.

Preparation:

Before you can do deep relaxation successfully, you must have an environment conducive to this process. Below are steps that you can follow at home to start reducing tensions.

1. Practice for a minimum of one 10-minute session per day. It is best to practice during a scheduled break in your day, not first thing in the morning or just before bed. Be sure to set a regular time for every day so you don't forget to practice.
2. When you practice, you should be in a quiet room away from other noisy areas of the house. Take the phone off the hook and tell all your family and friends you need some quiet time alone.
3. Pick a room with a comfortable bed or chair in which you can relax. If you find yourself falling asleep during practice sessions, switch to a chair with a more upright position.
4. The room should be a comfortable temperature and your clothes loose fitting and comfortable. Remove anything tight, constricting, or irritating in any way.
5. Even if you are doing the Deep Relaxation exercises, try practicing some of the exercises in the Autogenic Training. Try to include one hand warming and one muscle relaxation exercise in each practice session.

6. Be aware of your body and its sensations, and see if you can achieve the same sensations every time. If you find one exercise more helpful than others, it is all right to use only it, as long as you do both hand warming and muscle relaxation.

7. Do not make yourself tense over your practice sessions. These exercises and skills are like any other thing you try to learn. It is very rare to have instant success. Be patient with yourself. These exercises require a passive, relaxed attitude to be successful.

Deep Relaxation Exercises

The following steps for deep relaxation should be practiced daily. This relaxation technique can be used alone, or as an aid to biofeedback training (discussed in Chapter 8).

Have a friend read the steps to you as you relax. Or make an audio tape recording of these rules, and listen to it during your relaxation exercise. Go through the steps slowly, spreading them out over ten to thirty minutes.

If you prefer, you may use one or more professionally produced relaxation audiotapes. A list of deep relaxation tapes is found in Appendix C. For best results, the tapes should be used at the very first stage of a headache to eliminate or, at least, reduce the headache.

WARNING: Do NOT listen to the audio tape(s), whether professionally produced or home made, while operating a motor vehicle.

Steps For Deep Relaxation: (59)

1. Sit or lie down in a comfortable position with your eyes closed.
2. Do thirty or forty seconds of quiet deep breathing.
3. Continue your quiet deep breathing; lift your arms slowly high over your head.

4. Take a deep, deep breath and hold it. Now slowly lower your arms and hands.

5. As your arms and hands touch the bed or chair, breathe slowly out and go completely limp.

6. Repeat this step and continue your quiet deep breathing.

7. Lift your arms slowly high over your head and take a deep, deep breath. Hold it and slowly lower your arms and hands.

8. As they touch the bed or chair, breathe out slowly and go completely limp. Now hold your hands in front of you as if you were praying.

9. Press your palms together until your arm muscles tremble. Now breathe out slowly and go completely limp.

10. Now take a deep, deep breath and hold it. Slowly draw your hands toward your face as you touch your face- slowly breathe out.

11. Go completely limp. Your breathing should be deeper and deeper.

Continue for a few minutes . . .

12. Imagine the top of your head is being warmed by bright, bright sunshine. Feel the warmth on the top.

13. As you feel the warmth, imagine in your mind that your body is a hollow empty bottle- a hollow empty vessel within.

14. Slowly let the warmth flow like a warm fluid to fill your empty body. Let it flow down until it reaches your toes.

15. Notice the heavy warm feeling in the tips of your toes. Feel the warmth in your toes as it slowly begins to fill your entire body.

16. Feel your body get heavy and warm.

17. As the fluid level of the warmth begins to slowly rise, it fills the toes, feet, and legs, rising steadily and surely to your abdomen- now to your chest.

18. As the level of warm heaviness reaches your shoulder, let it flow naturally down your arms like warm broth until it reaches your fingers.

19. Feel the heavy warmth fill your fingertips as it overflows. The full heavy warm feeling in your body slowly fills your hands and arms. Your arms and body feel warm and heavy. Warm and wonderfully heavy, like a ton of warm sluggish molasses.

20. Continue this feeling, follow it, and let it happen.

Continue for a few minutes . . .

21. Notice once again your breathing- slow, regular, even, calm.

22. Keeping your eyes closed; roll your eyes so they look up to the top of your head.

23. Without straining, then just begin to notice what a warm pure sunlight is on the top of your head. The sunlight suddenly changes to a cool blue white light of a winter moon.

24. Let the coolness of the white blue light fill your mind as your eyes relax.

25. Let your mind flow with this cool blue white light- effortlessly unconcerned with your warm heavy body, and an alert cool head filled with blue white moonlight. Your hot heavy body filled with warmth, heaviness- quiet breathing, drifting, serene, pleasant, calm, effortless.

26. Float with the cool blue white light, filling your mind as your warm body sinks deeper and deeper.

27. Continue now your quiet time.

28. Now with your eyes closed, count slowly backwards- 4, 3, 2, 1- yawn and stretch.

29. Do this exercise twice a day for 15 minutes or do it whenever you have time to kill.

*** During the day, occasionally check your breathing. Always breathe slowly and regularly.

Autogenic Principles

To master Autogenic relaxation, it is helpful to know a little about the principles it is based upon. Autogenic relaxation has its roots in the Progressive Relaxation process. Progressive relaxation involves:

1. Learning to recognize excessive activity in a specific muscle or group of muscles.
2. Learning to reduce the activity of those muscles.

The patient starts by sitting or lying down with the eyes closed. First, the patient is told to contract the muscles and hold it to recognize the amount of tension that can be felt. Next, the patient is told to relax the muscles, and to keep doing so past the point at which the muscle feels relaxed. This process is continued for a period from 3 to 60 minutes, and is done 3 to 7 times per week. (48)

Jacobson believed that the patient could relax the muscles, storing into memory how it felt for later use. He was convinced that true muscle relaxation would also indirectly allow certain internal organ systems (Digestive and Circulatory) to be under voluntary control. (8)

In 1920, J. H. Schultz developed a system where patients repeated a series of phrases in order to relax. These mental exercises caused two types of body sensations that occur during a hypnotic state - feelings of heaviness in the extremities, and the feeling of warmth. (18) These exercises eventually became the Autogenic Relaxation method described below.

Autogenic Exercises

During the training session, six basic exercises are used. In each exercise, there are statements that accomplish certain goals. (See Table 1 at the end of this section.) For example, the statement, "My right arm is heavy," is an attempt to induce muscular relaxation, leading to increased peripheral blood flow, lowering of heart rate, lowering of respiration rate, and general sedation and drowsiness. Each statement is repeated and then "held mentally" for 30 to 60 seconds. The person can practice for about five minutes after lunch, after supper, and before going to sleep.

When the desired physiological changes in each exercise are reached, the person can go to the next exercise. (60)

After hours of practice in relaxing the muscles, exercises to induce warmth in those areas are introduced. The mastery of these body relaxation-warmth techniques can take from four to ten months.

Table 1
Autogenic Exercises

Exercises	Statements	Goals
1. Heaviness in the extremities	My right arm is heavy. My left arm is heavy. Both arms are heavy. My right leg is heavy. My left leg is heavy. Both legs are heavy. My right side is heavy. Everything is heavy.	Muscular relaxation
2. Warmth in the extremities	My right arm is warm. My left arm is warm. Both arms are warm. My right leg is warm. My left leg is warm. Both legs are warm. Both arms and legs are heavy and warm.	Vasodilation
3. Cardiac regulation	Heartbeat calm and regular.	Heart rate reduction
4. Respiration	Breathing calm and regular; it breathes me.	Deep, calm, and regular breathing
5. Abdominal warmth	My body is warm.	Muscular and central nervous system relaxation
6. Coolness of the forehead	My forehead is cool.	Sedation, drowsiness, and calming

Chapter 8

HYPNOSIS, BIOFEEDBACK, AND OTHER THERAPIES

In this chapter, we will discuss both common and experimental therapies not covered elsewhere in this book. The commonly used and proven therapies are biofeedback, hypnosis, and chants. Some less common and experimental therapies are discussed for your awareness, and because they offer some helpful insight.

Among these therapies, the combination of Biofeedback and Autogenic Training to alleviate the migraine was first suggested by Dr. Elmer Green of the Menninger Foundation. Green showed that the temperature in an arm or leg was directly related to the blood flow in that area. When a patient increased the blood flow to the hand, there was a spontaneous remission of the migraine. (18) Today, all headache treatment and research centers recommend non-drug therapies such as Relaxation Techniques, Biofeedback, and Psychotherapy, all of which are self-management in nature.

The therapies in this chapter all require at least training, if not continuous supervision, by a skilled professional. Your doctor can probably refer you to an appropriate professional in your area. If not, Appendix D offers a list of headache centers and programs.

Biofeedback Training

With biofeedback training, an individual can learn to control many body processes, such as heart rate and blood flow. To understand how, let's say a blind student wanted to learn to throw horseshoes. The student can throw horseshoes all day, but without knowing how close to the pole the horseshoes land, the student will not make any improvements. If, after each throw, the student is told the distance and direction from the pole where the horseshoe lands, the student can learn to become an accurate thrower. The instant feedback makes the learning possible.

Many body functions, such as heart rate, blood flow, and muscle tension are not easily observed and are therefore "involuntary processes." However, through the use of modern machines, the individual receives accurate feedback for these processes. Once control is learned, the monitoring machines become unnecessary.

This control of the mind is not new because, for centuries, Yogis and Zen masters in Eastern cultures have achieved self-awareness through physiological self-discipline. (8, 18) Tricks such as lying on beds of nails, slowing heartbeats and breathing to feign death, and walking on fire have been reported for centuries.

Only in the last 20 years have Western cultures realized that patients can learn to: (33)

1. Lower blood pressure
2. Increase or decrease temperature of the hands
3. Make the heart beat faster or slower
4. Increase or decrease stomach acid secretions
5. Alter the thickness of the stomach lining
6. Reduce harmful stress and stress related hormones
7. Increase the pleasurable relaxation related hormones.

By controlling these body functions, a patient can prevent or alleviate a migraine attack. For example, raising your hand temperature can divert blood flow away from the head, reducing pressure on nerve endings.

During a biofeedback training session, you may sit quietly in a chair, or lie on a cot, with sensors attached to your body. These sensors might measure forehead muscle tension or skin temperature. Depending on the type of machine, you might observe meters, light displays, tones, or numbers which constantly reflect changes in your body. (8)

The machine is set by the therapist to observe minute changes in your body. The therapist will instruct you to try to control the meter, thus raising your skin temperature. After practicing control with the machine at a highly sensitive setting, the therapist reduces the sensitivity, making it a little more difficult to control the meter. Thus, you will learn to exercise greater control over your body. (60)

By the time you complete your training, you can make the limbs tingle and feel heavy, and the hands feel warm. By controlling these sensations, you are not only inducing a state of relaxation, but controlling your blood circulation to reduce the incidence and severity of the migraine.

Hypnotherapy

Hypnotherapy is another, less used, treatment for migraines. Patients are given suggestions of imagery that lead to a relaxed, pleasant state, or to raise hand temperature and cool the head. Patients are instructed in autohypnosis for self-treatment.

In one case study, a 41 year-old nurse and migraine sufferer enjoyed classical music. Listening to classical music helped increase her capacity for imagery and relaxation. With classical music playing in the background, the nurse was told to relax by imagining going down stairs- "20 steps down the staircase, 19 steps down the staircase, etc. When she got to the bottom of the staircase, she was mentally placed in a special room. While in the "room", the nurse was given ego-strengthening suggestions.

The nurse was told to feel the coolness of ice packs, and to imagine seeing in full color the brain's arteries getting smaller, contracting to normal size. After nine months, the nurse had no more migraine headaches. This length of success was partly caused by the self-hypnosis that was practiced daily. She said she was "generally more relaxed, with better ability to cope with stress and was thinking things out more clearly". (55)

Chants

In 1975, Benson did research involving the use of imagination. He developed a method that was a variation of meditation and Yoga. The client would sit, silently repeating and concentrating on a simple word such as "ONE". Every time the word was repeated, the person would exhale deeply. This practice should be done 10 to 20 minutes twice daily, but not within 2 hours of eating or just before going to sleep. When done correctly, the breathing became relaxed, quiet, regular, and metabolic activity decreased. (60)

Electronic Pain Blockers

These are portable electronic stimulus devices that can send electrical impulses to the brain to stop pain from being felt.

Sleep Therapy

At the headache clinic of Mt. Sinai Medical Center in New York, medication is used to put a patient asleep for 3-4 hours when the migraine starts. After this deep sleep, the patient's headache is relieved.

The limited success, so far, of sleep therapy simply proves something we all know already: A good sleep is the best cure for an attack.

Acupuncture

Acupuncture, after 12 sessions, may provide lasting relief from the pain of chronic migraines. Sufferers reported experiencing 22 fewer days with headaches, used 15 percent less medication, made 25 percent fewer visits to the doctor, and took 15 percent fewer days off sick from work. (82)

Herb Treatments

Herbs have been used for hundreds of years to treat diseases. Feverfew, a member of the daisy family, can be taken as a tea or in capsule form. A capsule dose of 350 milligrams, 3 times per day may reduce the levels of serotonin, thus preventing vessel constriction. While this herb may cause allergic reactions and digestive tract irritations, it may possibly be used during pregnancy or with blood thinners. Please check with the doctor before starting any new herbs or medications. (65)

Butterfur, also known as Blatterdock, Flapperdock, or Langwort, taken as a dose of 75 milligrams, 2-3 times per day for a period of 12 weeks can reduce the frequency of migraines by 50 percent. In addition, a dosage of 50 milligrams may reduce the migraine frequency by 36 percent. You must contact your doctor before taking this herb as the root extract contains cancer-causing chemicals. (65)

Mineral/Vitamin Treatments

Migraine sufferers have been found to be deficient in the mineral Magnesium. When supplied with 600-800 milligram capsules of Magnesium, excitable brain cells may be stabilized. When 400 milligrams of vitamin B2 (riboflavin) are taken per day, fewer and milder migraines may exist, just as if a beta blocker is taken.

Yoga

Yoga is used to train people in proper breathing technique and to provide exercises to help relax muscles, maintain posture, and focus on the mind. This meditation technique increases flexibility, reduces stress, lowers blood pressure, and helps people with their asthma.

Chapter 9

DRUGS USED TO TREAT MIGRAINES

The goal of this book is to help you avoid or reduce the use of medications to control your migraine headaches by using biofeedback or some other relaxation technique. For those who must still use medications, the first step is often the use of over-the-counter pain relievers. These include aspirin, acetaminophen, and ibuprofen. As with any treatment, you should discuss these medications with your physician. Even over the counter medications can have slight side effects, or can interact with prescription medications. People who suffer from migraines may increase the frequency and severity of their headaches from medication overuse. These people have often not responded to treatment and, in an attempt to treat themselves, actually make the problem worse. Medication is considered to be overused for migraine relief if there is a use of opioids, triptans, or combination pain relievers for more than 10 days per month or simple pain relievers, such as aspirin or ibuprofen, for more than 15 days per month.

Your personal physician is your best resource for information about a medication. Some medications cannot be used when you are on other medications, or if you have a specific medical condition. Only you and your physician know the details of your medical history. The brief discussion that follows concerning some of the medication options is in no way intended as a substitute to the recommendations of your personal physician.

Ask your physician about any side effects when he prescribes a medication for you. If you want more information on the medication, there are a number of books available in libraries and bookstores which discuss side effects and modes of action of medications. Look for one that is easy for you to understand and yet appears to give the information you want. Discuss what you read in these books with your physician. Do not try to modify your medication dosage yourself.

We will discuss a few of the different medications available that your physician may recommend. At the end of this chapter is a list of medications and their common side effects. There are always new medications being introduced. Rather than attempting to cover every drug, the listing is only an introduction to some common classes of medications used to treat migraine headaches. (61, 74)

Some medications are recommended for use when a migraine is starting to occur. These medications are usually taken at the first sign of any migraine prodromes (symptoms preceding the onset of pain - e.g., double vision) or at the first onset of pain. Migraine medicine will not work once the headache has become severe because they do not address the sensitization that develops in the spinal cord. They work mainly in the first hour after the onset of an attack. (17)

A more extensive list of medications is used as prophylactics, meaning they are taken daily to prevent the development of the migraine headache, not just when a migraine headache occurs.

Some physicians may even recommend medications that are not currently approved by the FDA for use as a drug for treating migraine headaches. (18) These drugs may be approved for other uses, but your physician may have found that the medication has helped his other patients and may be of use to you. This area is beyond the scope of our discussion in this book.

Symptomatic Treatment:
for use when a migraine is starting

ERGOTAMINE compounds

Sample Brand Names: Bellergal, Cafergot, Wigraine

Action: constricts blood vessels

Some possible side effects: nausea, palpitations, weakness, and numbness, tingling, or pain in extremities

Prophylactic Treatment:

ERGOTAMINE compounds

Sample Brand Names: Bellergal, Cafergot, Wigraine

Action: constricts blood vessels

Some possible side effects: nausea, palpitations, weakness, and numbness, tingling, or pain in extremities

METHYSERGIDE MALEATE

Brand Name: Sansert

Action: inhibits serotonin

Some possible side effects: growth of fibrous tissue in pelvis, lung tissue, aorta, or heart valves with long term use, abdominal or extremity pain, nausea, vomiting, heartburn, insomnia, drowsiness, peripheral edema

MAO INHIBITORS

Sample Brand Names: Nardil, Marplan

Action: antidepressant

Some possible side effects: must follow dietary restrictions same as recommended for all migraine sufferers as listed in this book (low intake of tyramine and dopamine), hypertension, palpitations, dizziness, constipation, postural hypotension , drowsiness, weakness, edema, tremors, twitching, and patient must avoid many nonprescription drugs unless approved first by physician (included: cold tablets and liquids, nasal decongestants, hay fever medications, sinus medication, asthma inhalants, and weight loss pills)

CYPROHEPTADINE

Brand Name: Periactin

Action: inhibits serotonin

Some possible side effects: drowsiness, dizziness, nervousness, insomnia, tinnitus (ringing in the ears), blurred vision, hypotension, palpitations, anemia, nausea, vomiting, dryness of nose and throat, nasal stuffiness, fatigue, headache

BETA BLOCKERS

Sample Brand Names: Inderal (propanolol), Corgard (Nadolol),Tenormin (atenolol), Blocadren (timolol), Lopressor (metoprolol), Sectral (acebutolol), Visken (pindolol)

Action: inhibits serotonin and may limit blood vessel dilation.

Some possible side effects: hypotension, light headedness, depression, disorientation, nausea, vomiting, diarrhea, constipation, rash, sore throat, fatigue, memory problems

AMITRIPTYLINE

Brand Name: Elavil

Action: antidepressant

Some possible side effects: hypotension, hypertension, palpitations, arrhythmias, confusion, disorientation, nightmares, insomnia, anxiety, delusions, tremors, dry mouth, blurred vision, constipation, rash, bone marrow depression, nausea, anorexia, black tongue, dizziness

CLONIDINE

Brand Name: Catapres

Action: reduction of blood vessel dilation

Some possible side effects: dry mouth, drowsiness, sedation, constipation, dizziness, headache, fatigue, nightmares, rash, dry eyes

ISOMETHEPTENEMUCATE, DICHLORALPHENAZONE, ACETAMINOPHEN COMPOUND

Brand Name: Midrin

Action: prevents blood vessel dilation

Some possible side effects: transient dizziness, skin rash

CODEINE PHOSPHATE, BUCLIZINE HCL, ACETAMINOPHEN COMPOUND

Brand Name: Migraleve

Action: analgesic

Some possible side effects: nausea, sedation, dry mouth, constipation

CALCIUM CHANNEL BLOCKERS

Sample Brand Names: Adalat, Calan, Cardizem, Isoptin, Procardia

Action: may prevent initial blood vessel constriction before dilation that causes headache.

Some possible side effects: edema, headache, nausea, dizziness, skin rash, polyuria

NONSTEROIDAL ANTI-INFLAMMATORY AGENTS

Sample Brand Names: Anaprox, Clinoril, Indocin, Motrin, Naprosyn, Nalfon, Ponstel

Action: reduction in inflammation and pain by inhibiting prostaglandins

Some possible side-effects: nausea, heartburn, dizziness, skin rash, constipation, tinnitus, edema, diarrhea

Epilepsy drugs such as topiramate (brand name Topamax) helps prevent headaches without pain increases. Nearly half of the sufferers in a controlled study experienced at least a 50 percent reduction in migraine frequency. Frova, a triptan drug that includes Imitrex, Axert, and Zomig narrows the blood vessels in the brain and scalp helping to reduce pressure on pain-sensitive structures. (12)

The drug Atacand, one of the Angiotensin II receptor blockers (hypertension drug), may cut by almost 50 percent migraine attacks. The advantage over beta-blockers would be its improved safety since it doesn't lower pulse frequency. (51) People who suffer from migraines may increase the frequency and severity of their headaches from medication overuse. These people have often not responded to treatment and, in an attempt to treat themselves, actually make the problem worse. Medication is considered to be overused for migraine relief if there is a use of opioids, triptans, or combination pain relievers for more than 10 days per month or simple pain relievers, such as aspirin or ibuprofen, for more than 15 days per month.

Chapter 10

GENERAL NUTRITION INFORMATION

Introduction

Diet is for many people the most effective way to control migraine. Certain foodstuffs are potent migraine triggers in many people. At the end of this chapter, Lists #1 and #2 are suspected foods which the remaining chapters of this book will teach you how to avoid or limit in your diet.

Despite the seemingly endless number of restrictions in this migraine prevention diet, there are still many foods that you can eat. The food list in Appendix A list many of the foods that may be eaten, whether a fresh item or a commercially prepared convenience item. Based on their labels, the commercially prepared items listed as okay have none of the foods suspected of triggering migraine headaches. This is why some brands of an item are listed as okay, and another brand may not be listed. You should check the labels of brands you use to see if they contain any suspected ingredients.

Individuals who suffer from migraine and find relief with diet may, like the rest of the population, have other medical problems. These include: obesity, high blood pressure, diabetes, and high blood cholesterol. To help individuals with their special dietary concerns, these issues are discussed in later chapters with meal plans and menus.

If any of the suggestions contained in this book contradict what has been advised to you by your personal physician, you should, of course, follow your physician's advice. He/she knows your complete medical history and has specific reasons for recommending different aspects of your medical care.

Before starting this diet, please visit with your personal physician and show him this book to make sure it does not interfere with any other treatment you are following. If you feel you want more physician follow-up with your migraine headaches, ask your personal physician for a referral to a physician that specializes in headaches.

If you feel that you need more personalized help with implementing the dietary recommendations in this book, ask your physician for a referral to a Registered Dietitian or another reputable, highly trained nutrition counselor.

There are certain rules that everyone must follow to control migraine headaches. These rules are:

1. Eat at least every 4-5 hours during the day. Don't skip meals; divide your 3 meals into 5 smaller ones.

   Fasting, and the resulting low blood sugar (hypoglycemia) that develops, may trigger headaches in patients prone to migraines. Over 50 percent of those persons prone to migraines may have a migraine after 16 hours without food. When a person ingests an excess of carbohydrates, a migraine may occur in response to the rapid insulin secretion and, thus, lowering of blood sugar. To avoid problems, one should eat 3 well-balanced meals per day and avoid an overabundance of high sugar-laden foods. (58)

2. Never go more than 12 hours between the last meal or snack of the day and your next breakfast. (25)

   Avoid over-sleeping. Excessive sleep may alter the body's normal blood sugar level and cause hypoglycemia, resulting in a migraine. (18)

3. Don't get dehydrated.

4. Question what is in the food at a restaurant. Do not assume anything.

5. Don't eat foods heated in wines or sherries. (78)

6. Avoid all aged cheeses used in pasta dishes. (78)

7. When unsure about the contents of a food - don't eat it.

Keep one thought in mind: *Regardless of how good the food looks today, the headache tomorrow will not look or feel as good.*

Plan of Action

There are several different methods of utilizing the information in this book. You must decide which is the best method for you - there is no one right way to implement dietary change that works for everyone.

Plan A:

1. Eliminate all foods in List #1 from your diet for at least two to three months.
2. Continue to avoid all these foods permanently.

Plan B:

1. Eliminate all foods in List #1 from your diet for at least two to three months.
2. After 2-3 months, add back one type of food at a time (no more than one new food every 2 weeks) to see if you are sensitive to that food.

Plan C:

1. Eliminate only those foods which have been widely reported to cause reactions and have also been found to have a high active amine content. (See List #2.)
2. If headaches still persist, eliminate the "use caution" foods from List #2 one at a time (no more than one new food every two weeks) to see the effect.

For all of these plans, you will probably find it helpful to keep a record of when you had a migraine headache, when you had undergone stressful situations, when you may have eaten a non-recommended food, and when you deleted or added a specific food in your diet. A small pocket calendar which you can carry with you, or the Migraine Calendar from Chapter 5, are examples of items that can be used to keep a record and also provide a good visual demonstration of the individual relationship of diet, stress, and migraine headaches in you.

List #1:

Do Not Eat Any Of These Foods (even in a recipe or commercially made item), AVOID ALL OF THESE ITEMS!

1. Dairy Products:
    a. aged cheeses (OK for cottage, American, and cream cheese)
    b. all yogurts
2. Meat, Fish, and Poultry:
    a. smoked products (eg. bacon, ham, lox)
    b. chicken livers
    c. fermented sausages (eg.pepperoni, salami)
    d. all luncheon meats unless no nitrates or nitrites
    e. hot dogs
    f. pickled herring
3. Fruits:
    a. citrus fruits and juices: orange, lemon, and lime
    b. bananas
    c. canned figs
    d. nuts
4. Vegetables:
    a. avocado
    b. broad bean pods ("Italian" green beans and pea pods)
    c. onions
5. Beverages:
    a. all alcohol
    b. sodas with natural citrus juices and flavorings (e.g., Slice, 7up)
    c. coffee: regular or decaffeinated
    d. tea: all types including herbal
6. Desserts:
    a. anything with real chocolate
7. Seasonings:
    a. anything with MSG (monosodium glutamate)

Tyramine is found in cheese, especially aged, strong, and cheddar varieties. Phenylethylamine is present in chocolate, octopamine in citrus fruits, and histamine in red wine and beers. Phenylethylamine, theobromine, and caffeine in chocolate may alter the cerebral blood flow releasing norephinephrine. When caffeine is restricted from your diet, blood vessels dilate and an increase in cerebral blood flow may result in another headache. Alcohol has a vasodilator effect on cranial blood vessels because of the tyramine and histamine contained in the drink. Nitrites, formed by the reduction of nitrates in saliva or by bacteria in the intestines, act as a vasodilator. Foods with monosodium glutamate (MSG) can cause dizziness and tingling, usually within 15-60 minutes after eating. (58)

List #2:

Foods may be grouped into three categories:

1. Foods to avoid altogether;
2. Foods to be used with caution, in small amounts (less than 1/2 c. or 4 oz. is ok);
3. Foods you may or may not need to avoid. These may cause a migraine in you, but medical research linking these foods to migraine is incomplete.

AVOID FOODS:

cheese
stale meat or liver
broad bean pods
meat extracts
sauerkraut
aged sausages, such as pepperoni and salami
smoked or pickled fish
Chianti and vermouth wines
banana peel
yeast extracts/brewer's yeast
beer and ale

Note: All meat, fish, and poultry should be very fresh or else not used. When these protein products age, their active amine levels often increase.

CAUTION FOODS (no more than 1/2 cup or 4 oz.)

avocado
soy sauce
red and white wine
peanuts
unpasteurized cream or milk
raspberries
chocolate (no more than 1 oz.)
port wine (no more than 2 oz.)
yogurt
distilled liquors (no more than 1.5 oz.)

POSSIBLE PROBLEM FOODS

citrus fruits and juices	onions
hot dogs	canned figs
mushrooms	nuts
coffee	tea
cola sodas	MSG or monosodium glutamate

luncheon meats (not smoked but containing nitrates or nitrites)

Now, read through the following chapters to find out more about eating a healthy diet that also helps control your migraine headaches. Weight control menus are included in each "type" of diet discussed: general diets, diabetic diets, diets low in sodium, and diets for individuals with high blood cholesterol.

Chapter 11

THE GENERAL MIGRAINE REDUCTION DIET

Besides eliminating all foods associated with migraine headaches, a diet should provide an individual with all essential nutrients. All of the diets in this section, and in the specialized diet chapters, are examples of nutritionally balanced diets. These diets follow the recommendations of the National Cancer Institute, the American Heart Association, the American Diabetes Association, and the U.S. Dietary Goals.

The menus and meal plan outlines contained in this book are to be used as suggestions of how you could follow this migraine prevention diet. There is no one diet that is perfect for everyone.

Whenever possible, menu items requiring a special recipe are marked with an asterisk (*), and the recipe may be found in the Appendices. Not all of the recipes are appropriate for all of the specialized diets; however, those who do not need to follow any special restrictions may try any of the recipes.

When looking through the recipes, some which are listed as appropriate for people trying to lower their cholesterol or control their diabetes will appear to have a good deal of fat. There are two reasons these recipes were still included: ❶ a diet may still be low in fat for the day if one higher fat food is balanced by other lower fat foods throughout the day; and ❷ a higher fat food may be used infrequently for "special" occasions (the recipes in this book are modified to be lower in saturated fat even if the total fat is not very low in all recipes).

The goal level of fat in a recipe for every day use is as follows:

10 grams total fat for entrees and main dishes

5 grams total fat for side dishes, breads, and desserts

This chapter contains meal plans and sample menus for several calorie levels. Which calorie level you use depends on whether you are trying to gain, lose, or maintain your weight. None of the diets has less than 1200 calories; it is extremely difficult to get adequate amounts of nutrients when you eat less than this. So those who follow the lower calorie level diets (1200, 1500) that are included in this book should be careful to choose highly nutritious foods.

Individuals who need to consume 2000 or more calories daily will have fewer problems getting the nutrients they need because of the greater volume of food consumed. Such individuals should still consume nutritious foods and not just "empty" calories. Nutrient-poor foods (e.g., sodas, potato chips, and many traditional dessert items) are best consumed only occasionally, and then only after daily nutrient needs are met.

SAMPLE MEAL PATTERNS: The exchange size or portion is for each food group, and exactly what foods are included in each food group, may be found in Chapter 13, Food Exchange Lists.

1200 CALORIES

AMOUNT	FOOD GROUP
5 exchanges	Protein Foods
2 exchanges	Milk and Dairy
4 exchanges	Bread and Starches
3 exchanges	Vegetables
3 exchanges	Fruits
4 exchanges	Fats and Oils

1500 CALORIES

AMOUNT	FOOD GROUP
5 exchanges	Protein Foods
2 exchanges	Milk and Dairy
6 exchanges	Bread and Starches
4 exchanges	Vegetables
4 exchanges	Fruits
5 exchanges	Fats and Oils

2000 CALORIES

AMOUNT	FOOD GROUP
6 exchanges	Protein Foods
3 exchanges	Milk and Dairy
8 exchanges	Bread and Starches
4 exchanges	Vegetables
4 exchanges	Fruits
6 exchanges	Fats and Oils

Plus Miscellaneous item as desired to complete caloric needs

2500 CALORIES

AMOUNT	FOOD GROUP
7 exchanges	Protein Foods
3 exchanges	Milk and Dairy
9 exchanges	Bread and Starches
5 exchanges	Vegetables
5 exchanges	Fruits
8 exchanges	Fats and Oils

Plus Miscellaneous items or more Breads and Starches as desired to complete caloric needs.

SAMPLE MEAL PATTERNS AND MENUS

NUMBER OF SERVINGS PER CALORIE LEVEL

FOOD GROUP AND MEAL	1200	1500	2000	2500
BREAKFAST				
Protein Foods	0	0	0	0
Milk and Dairy	1	1	1	1
Bread and Starches	1	2	2	2
Fruits	1	2	2	2
Fats	0	1	1	2
LUNCH				
Protein Foods	2	2	3	3
Milk and Dairy	0	0	1	1
Breads and Starches	2	2	3	3
Vegetables	1	1	1	2
Fats and Oils	2	2	2	2
DINNER				
Protein Foods	3	3	3	4
Milk and Dairy	1	1	1	1
Breads and Starches	1	2	3	3
Vegetables	2	3	3	3
Fats and Oils	2	2	3	3
SNACKS				
Fruits	2	2	2	3
Breads and Starches	0	0	0	1
Miscellaneous Items	0	0	1	2
Fats and Oils	0	0	0	1

Chapter 12

MIGRAINE REDUCTION 7-DAY MENUS

SEVEN DAYS OF MENUS: These menus generally follow the meal plans, however, some variations from the meal plans are also included. The total number of exchanges for each calorie level is kept constant. Feel free to vary the meal plans to suit your individual needs but try to keep the total number of exchanges per day constant and consume either three meal and three snacks or six very small meals per day.

DAY #1

SIZE SERVING PER CALORIE LEVEL

FOOD AND MEAL	1200	1500	2000	2500
BREAKFAST				
Ready-to-eat Cereal with	3/4 c.	3/4 c.	3/4 c.	3/4 c.
Skim Milk	1/2 c.	1/2 c.	1/2 c.	1/2 c.
Whole Wheat Toast with	0	1 sl.	1 sl.	1 sl.
Margarine	0	1 tsp	1 tsp	1 tsp
Skim Milk (to drink)	1/2 c.	1/2 c.	1/2 c.	1/2 c.
Apple Juice	1/2 c.	1 c.	1 c.	1 c.
Pero or Postum	free	free	free	free
LUNCH				
Tuna (water-packed) with	2 oz.	2 oz.	3 oz.	3 oz.
Mayonnaise on	2 tsp	2 tsp	2 tsp	2 tsp
Rye Bread	2 sl.	2 sl.	2 sl.	2 sl.
Marinated Tomatoes*	0	0	0	1 c.
Diet Ginger Ale	free	free	free	free
Skim Milk	0	0	1 c.	1 c.

DAY #1

SIZE SERVING PER CALORIE LEVEL

FOOD AND MEAL	1200	1500	2000	2500
DINNER				
Crispy Oven Fried Chicken*	3 oz.	3 oz.	3 oz.	4 oz.
Parsley Potatoes*	1/2 c.	1/2 c.	1 c.	1 c.
Pumpernickel Bread with	0	1 sl.	1 sl.	1 sl.
Margarine	0	1 tsp	1 tsp	1 tsp
Steamed Broccoli with	1 c.	1 c.	1 c.	1 c.
Margarine	1 tsp	1/2 tsp	1 tsp	1 tsp
Sliced Beets	0	1/2 c.	1/2 c.	1/2 c.
Skim Milk	1 c.	1 c.	1 c.	1 c.
SNACKS (throughout the day: mid-morning, mid-afternoon, and evening)				
Apple	1	1	1	1
Bran Muffin*	0	0	0	1
Pretzels-hard Dutch type	0	0	1	3
Raw Carrot and Zucchini	1 c.	1 c.	1 c.	1 c.
Nectarine	1	1	1	1

DAY #2

SIZE SERVING PER CALORIE LEVEL

FOOD AND MEAL	1200	1500	2000	2500
BREAKFAST				
Hot Oatmeal with	1/2 c.	1 c.	1 c.	1 c.
Skim Milk	1/2 c.	1/2 c.	1/2 c.	1/2 c.
Apple Juice	1/2 c.	1/2 c.	1/2 c.	1/2 c.
Pero or Postum	free	free	free	free
LUNCH				
Meatless Chili*	1 c.	1 c.	1-1/2c.	1-1/2c.
Tossed Salad with	free	free	free	free
Vinegar and Oil	1 TBS	1 TBS	1 TBS	1 TBS
Toasted Wheat Bread with	1 sl.	1 sl.	2 sl.	2 sl.
Garlic Topping*	1 tsp	1 tsp	2 tsp	2 tsp
Diet Ginger Ale	free	free	free	free
Skim Milk	0	0	1 c.	1 c.

DAY #2

SIZE SERVING PER CALORIE LEVEL

FOOD AND MEAL	1200	1500	2000	2500
DINNER				
Sliced Roast Beef	3 oz.	3 oz.	3 oz.	4 oz.
Baked Potato	1 med.	1 lg.	1 lg.	1 lg.
Steamed Green Beans	1/2 c.	1 c.	1 c.	1 c.
Steamed Carrots	1/2 c.	1/2 c.	1/2 c.	1/2 c.
Margarine	2 tsp	2 tsp	3 tsp	3 tsp
Skim Milk	1 c.	1 c.	1 c.	1 c.
SNACKS (throughout the day: mid-morning, mid-afternoon, and evening)				
Apple	1	1	1	1
Pineapple Tidbits (canned)	1/2 c.	1 c.	1 c.	1 c.
Ready-to-eat-cereal with	2/3 c.	1-1/3c.	1-1/3c.	1-1/3c.
Skim Milk and	1/2 c.	1/2 c.	1/2 c.	1/2 c.
Sliced Peaches	0	0	0	1/2 c.
Hard Pretzels	0	0	2	3
Caffeine-free Cola	0	0	8 oz.	12 oz.

DAY #3

SIZE SERVING PER CALORIE LEVEL

FOOD AND MEAL	1200	1500	2000	2500
BREAKFAST				
Breakfast Shake*	1 c.	1 c.	1 c.	1 c.
Toasted Rye Bread with	1 sl.	1 sl.	1 sl.	1 sl.
Margarine and	1 tsp	1 tsp	1 tsp	1 tsp
Strawberry Preserves	0	0	1 tsp	2 tsp
Pero or Postum	free	free	free	free

DAY #3

SIZE SERVING PER CALORIE LEVEL

FOOD AND MEAL	1200	1500	2000	2500
LUNCH				
Chef Salad with lettuce,	free	free	free	free
American Cheese, and	1 oz.	1 oz.	1 oz.	1 oz.
Turkey Breast	1 oz.	1 oz.	2 oz.	2 oz.
Allowed Salad Dressing	1 TBS	1 TBS	1 TBS	1 TBS
Saltine Crackers	0	6	6	6
Diet Root-beer	free	free	free	free
Skim Milk	0	0	1 c.	1 c.
DINNER				
Spaghetti with	1 c.	1-1/2c.	2 c.	2 c.
Tomato Sauce* and	1/2 c.	1 c.	1 c.	1 c.
Meatballs*	3 oz.	3 oz.	3 oz.	4 oz.
Steamed Zucchini	1/2 c.	1/2 c.	1/2 c.	1/2 c.
Skim Milk	1 c.	1 c.	1 c.	1 c.
SNACKS (throughout the day: mid-morning, mid-afternoon, and evening)				
Fresh Pear	1	1	1	1
Toasted Rye Bagel	1/2	1/2	1	1
Cream Cheese	1 TBS	1 TBS	1 TBS	1 TBS
Raw Broccoli and	1 c.	1 c.	1 c.	1 c.
Cauliflower dipped in				
Allowed Salad Dressing	1 TBS	1 TBS	1 TBS	1 TBS
Vanilla Pudding	0	0	1/2 c.	1 c.

DAY #4

SIZE SERVING PER CALORIE LEVEL

FOOD AND MEAL	1200	1500	2000	2500
BREAKFAST				
Cinnamon Pancakes* with	2	3	3	3
Applesauce	1/2 c.	1/2 c.	1/2 c.	1/2 c.
Skim Milk	1 c.	1 c.	1 c.	1 c.
Pero or Postum	free	free	free	free
LUNCH				
Chicken Salad* with	1/3 c.	1/3 c.	1/2 c.	1/2 c.
Shredded Lettuce in	free	free	free	free
Small Pita Bread	1	1	1	1
Diet Ginger Ale or	free	free	free	free
Skim Milk	0	0	1 c.	1 c.
DINNER				
Baked Pork Chop*	3 oz.	3 oz.	3 oz.	4 oz.
Rice Pilaf*	1/2 c.	1/2 c.	1 c.	1 c.
Steamed Asparagus	1/2 c.	1 c.	1 c.	1 c.
Cucumber/Tomato Salad*	1/2 c.	1/2 c.	1/2 c.	1/2 c.
Skim Milk	1 c.	1 c.	1 c.	1 c.
SNACKS (throughout the day: mid-morning, mid-afternoon, and evening)				
Raisins	2 TBS	2 TBS	2 TBS	2 TBS
Apricots, canned halves	2	2	2	2
Crunchy Bread Sticks*	0	0	1	2
Marinated Zucchini Sticks*	1/2 c.	1/2 c.	1/2 c.	1/2 c.
Oat 'n Berry Cookies*	1	1	2	3

DAY #5

SIZE SERVING PER CALORIE LEVEL

FOOD AND MEAL	1200	1500	2000	2500
BREAKFAST				
Ready-to-eat Cereal with	3/4 c.	3/4 c.	3/4 c.	3/4 c.
Skim Milk and	1 c.	1 c.	1 c.	1 c.
Dates, Chopped	2 1/2	2 1/2	2 1/2	2 1/2
English Muffin with	0	1/2	1/2	1/2
Margarine and	0	0	1 tsp	1 tsp
Blackberry Preserves	0	1 tsp	1 tsp	1 tsp
Pero or Postum	free	free	free	free
LUNCH				
Cottage Cheese and	1/2 c.	1/2 c.	3/4 c.	3/4 c.
Mixed Fruit Plate(peach sl., pineapple, strawberries) on	1 c.	1 c.	1 c.	1 c.
Lettuce	free	free	free	free
Diet Root Beer	free	free	free	free
Skim Milk	0	0	1 c.	1 c.
DINNER				
Savory Chicken Stew*	1-1/2c.	1-1/2c.	1-1/2c.	2c.
Herb Biscuits*	1	1	2	2
Tossed Salad with	free	free	free	free
Allowed Salad Dressing	1 TBS	1 TBS	1 TBS	1 TBS
Diet Ginger Ale	free	free	free	free
SNACKS (throughout the day: mid-morning, mid-afternoon, and evening)				
Crunchy Bread Sticks*	1	2	2	2
Green Pepper Strips and Carrot Sticks dipped in	1 c.	1 c.	1 c.	1 c.
Allowed Diet Salad Dressing	free	free	free	free
Frosty Shake*	1-1/2c.	1-1/2c.	1-1/2c.	1-1/2c.
Apple	0	0	1 small	1 large
Gingerbread*	0	00	0	1 sl.

DAY #6

SIZE SERVING PER CALORIE LEVEL

FOOD AND MEAL	1200	1500	2000	2500
BREAKFAST				
Oatmeal cooked with	1/2 c.	1 c.	1 c.	1 c.
Dried Apricots	4 halves	4 halves	4 halves	4 halves
Skim Milk	1 c.	1 c.	1 c.	1 c.
Pero or Postum	free	free	free	free
LUNCH				
Sliced Fresh Turkey Breast	2 oz.	2 oz.	3 oz.	3 oz.
Lettuce	free	free	free	free
Mayonnaise	2 tsp	2 tsp	2 tsp	2 tsp
Pumpernickel Bread	2 sl.	2 sl.	2 sl.	2 sl.
Cherry Tomatoes	0	0	0	1/2 c.
Diet Root Beer	free	free	free	free
Skim Milk	0	0	1 c.	1 c.
DINNER				
Flounder Florentine*	3 oz.	3 oz.	3 oz.	4 oz.
Steamed Carrots	1/2 c.	1/2 c.	1 c.	1 c.
Whole Wheat Roll with	1	1	2	2
Margarine	1 tsp	1 tsp	2 tsp	2 tsp
Skim Milk	1 c.	1 c.	1 c.	1 c.
SNACKS (throughout the day: mid-morning, mid-afternoon, and evening)				
Applesauce	1/2 c.	1/2 c.	1/2 c.	1/2 c.
Butterscotch Pudding	0	0	1/2 c.	1 c.
Raw Cauliflower pieces and Carrot Sticks with Allowed Diet Salad Dressing	free	free	free	free
Strawberries, unsweetened	1 c.	1 c.	1 c.	1 c.

DAY #7

SIZE SERVING PER CALORIE LEVEL

FOOD AND MEAL	1200	1500	2000	2500
BREAKFAST				
Ready-to-eat Cereal with	3/4 c.	3/4 c.	3/4 c.	3/4 c.
Skim Milk	1 c.	1 c.	1 c.	1 c.
Toasted Bagel with	0	1/2	1/2	1/2
Cream Cheese and	0	1 TBS	1 TBS	1 TBS
Grape Jelly	0	0	1 tsp	1 tsp
Pineapple Juice	1/2 c.	1/2 c.	1/2 c.	1/2 c.
Pero or Postum	free	free	free	free
LUNCH				
Split Pea Soup*	1 c.	1 c.	1-1/2c.	1-1/2c.
Corn Bread* with	1 pc.	1 pc.	1 pc.	1 pc.
Margarine	1 tsp	1 tsp	1 tsp	1 tsp
Tossed Salad with	free	free	free	free
Allowed Diet Salad Dressing	free	free	free	free
Diet Cola	free	free	free	free
Skim Milk	0	0	1 c.	1 c.
DINNER				
Spinach Lasagna*	1-1/2 c.	2 c.	2-1/2c.	2-1/2c.
Marinated Zucchini*	1/2 c.	1/2 c.	1 c.	1 c.
Toasted Wheat Bread with	0	1 sl.	1 sl.	1 sl.
Garlic Topping*	0	1 tsp	1 tsp	1 tsp
Skim Milk	1 c.	1 c.	1 c.	1 c.
SNACKS (throughout the day: mid-morning, mid-afternoon, and evening)				
Baked Apple*	1	1	1	1
Spice Cookies*	1	1	2	3
Carrot/Raisin Salad*	1/2 c.	1/2 c.	2/3 c.	3/4 c.

Chapter 13

FOOD EXCHANGE LISTS

The following Food Exchange Lists are to be used for all of the different diets discussed in this book. The specialized diets (eg. weight loss, low sodium, low cholesterol, diabetic) use modified or limited versions of the lists. Each chapter on specialized diets has advice on which of the foods listed are better choices and those which should be avoided.

With the information in the Food Exchange Lists, you will develop your own "diet". Your diet may be based on an exchange system, counting calories, or counting grams of protein, fat, and carbohydrates. You may even make up your own diet based solely on the way that you eat now.

The suggested diet ideas in this book use the concept of "exchanges" in demonstrating a nutritionally balanced way of eating. An exchange is merely a measured portion of a food item.

Using an exchange system structures the diet by suggesting meals that include specified portions from the different food categories (e.g., so much vegetable, so much of dairy product, etc.). At the same time, it gives you freedom of choice of the foods you eat within each category (e.g., any type of vegetable preferred from the allowed list, any dairy product from the allowed list, etc.). However, individuals with a great deal of variety in the restaurants or foods they eat may find an exchange system restrictive.

A total calorie level is given for each of the example meal plans. The goal of each meal plan is to provide about 20 percent of the total calories from protein, at least 50 percent of the total calories from carbohydrates and no more than 30 percent of the calories from fats and oils. Alcohol, you will remember, is not a recommended item for many of you who suffer from migraine headaches.

In order to calculate the percent of calories from the carbohydrate, protein, or fat in your diet, you need to remember that you get approximately 4 calories from each gram of carbohydrate or protein, and 9 calories from each gram of fat. For each food group in the Food Exchange Lists the approximate protein, carbohydrate, and fat contents of the exchange portion are given. The average sodium content of each of the food groups is also provided. It must be emphasized that these are average amounts of sodium; the specific sodium content can be obtained from widely available resources. (35).

High fiber foods are emphasized in the Food Exchange Lists. Foods in their more natural forms (e.g., whole grains, fruits, and vegetables eaten with their skins) not only contain more fiber, but usually retain a higher vitamin and mineral content. Care should be taken to cook vegetables only until tender/crisp in a minimum of water to help prevent the loss of nutrients.

Individuals trying to lose weight should especially try to include food items with more fiber into their diets. The greater bulk and slower digestion of high fiber foods provide greater satisfaction with a diet by making you feel fuller longer. Foods with a high fiber content usually take longer to chew properly, adding to the sense of fullness.

Too much of a good thing should be avoided. If you do not eat many high fiber foods now, add these items to your diet gradually. Too much fiber too quickly may lead to problems with gas, diarrhea, or constipation.

Some people try just sprinkling some bran on their foods as their only way of getting more fiber. They are missing out on all the benefits of the additional vitamins and minerals in the other high fiber foods. They are also not getting the full benefits of eating a variety of fibers. Wheat bran fiber is not the same as oat bran fiber, which is not the same as the fiber in carrots, or in a potato eaten with its skin.

In the following chapters, we will show how these various food fibers have different health benefits. As with any other dietary recommendation, choosing a variety of good, whole foods will give you more benefit than just focusing on a few foods.

The seven food groups that we will use for the Food Exchange Lists are: Dairy Products, Fruits, Vegetables, Breads and Starches, High Protein Foods, Fats and Oils, and Other Miscellaneous Foods.

DAIRY PRODUCTS
(contain 12 grams carbohydrate, 8 grams protein, 2 or less grams fat, 80-100 calories, and 120 milligrams sodium)

ITEM	EXCHANGE PORTION
Skim or nonfat milk	1 cup
1% milk	1 cup
Nonfat dried milk powder	1/3 cup
Buttermilk from skim milk	1 cup

Two percent, and whole milk and milk products have more fat and calories than those products listed above. The higher fat dairy products may be used if desired when calories and cholesterol are not your primary concern. The lower fat items are especially well suited to diets where fats and calories need careful consideration: when trying to lose weight, when trying to control diabetes, and when trying to lower your blood cholesterol. The American Heart Association and U.S. Dietary Goals both stress the reduction of total fat and saturated fats (the primary type of fat found in milk products) in the diets of the American population as a whole.

Milk and milk products are excellent sources of protein, calcium, and vitamins A and D (usually added into skim and 1% milk because they are reduced when the milk fat is removed). Milk is not a good source of fiber in the diet.

FRUITS
(contain 15 grams carbohydrate, 60 calories, and a trace of sodium)

ITEM	EXCHANGE PORTION
Apple, raw	1 small
Apple cider	½ cup
Apple juice	½ cup
Applesauce (unsweetened)	½ cup
Apricots, raw, dried, or canned in water or juice	2 whole or 4 halves
Blackberries	¾ cup
Blueberries	¾ cup
Cantaloupe	1/3 small or 1 cup cubed
Cherries	12 whole
Dates	2-1/2 whole
Grapes	15 whole
Grape juice	1/3 cup
Honeydew melon	1/8 medium or 1 cup cubed

ITEM	EXCHANGE PORTION
Nectarine	1 small
Peach, raw, or canned in water or juice	1 whole or 2 halves
Pear, raw, or canned in water or juice	2 halves or ½ cup
Pineapple, raw, or canned in water or juice	1/2 cup or 2 slices
Pineapple juice	½ cup
Plums	2 medium
Prunes	3 medium
Prune juice	1/3 cup
Raisins	2 tablespoons
Strawberries	1-1/4 cup
Watermelon	1-1/4 cup

Fresh whole fruits are excellent sources of fiber. Fruit juices are poor sources of fiber. Different fruits have different vitamin and mineral contents; therefore, a variety of fruits should be consumed.

It is important to note the portion sizes listed for each exchange; they tend to be smaller than many people consider usual. If you are trying to count your calories or carbohydrates, you are only fooling yourself when you call a medium or large apple one serving when the correct exchange portion is a small.

VEGETABLES

(contain about 5 grams carbohydrate, 2 grams protein, 25 calories, and 25 milligrams sodium)

Items below marked * are higher in sodium; a low-sodium, fresh or frozen version (not regular canned types) should be used if you are trying to reduce sodium intake.

For each of the foods in this group, 1/2 cup cooked or 1 cup raw is considered to be one exchange portion.

Asparagus*	Green pepper	Rhubarb
Bean sprouts*	Greens	Rutabaga
Beets*	Beet*	String Beans*
Broccoli	Chard*	(green or yellow)
Brussels sprouts	Collards*	Summer Squash
Cabbage	Dandelion*	Tomato*
Carrots*	Kale*	Tomato juice*
Cauliflower	Mustard*	Turnips
Celery	Spinach*	Vegetable juice
Cucumbers	Turnip*	cocktail*
Eggplant	Okra*	Zucchini

The following vegetables may be used as desired:

Chinese cabbage	Lettuce
Chicory	Parsley
Endive	Radishes
Escarole	Watercress

Starchy Vegetables are found in the *Breads and Other Starches* group.

Vegetables are good sources of fiber, especially if eaten with their skins or peels whenever possible. The vitamin and mineral content of different vegetables varies greatly. The vitamin content of any one particular vegetable will also vary a great deal depending on how it was prepared.

Cutting, peeling, and then boiling a vegetable for a long time reduces the vitamin and mineral content. Some of the nutrients will leach out of the vegetable and into the cooking water; it is best to steam vegetables briefly, microwave them just until done, or stir-fry quickly in a very small amount of oil. The high heat of cooking also destroys some of the nutrients - another good reason to cook vegetables quickly.

The National Cancer Institute recommends the inclusion of raw vegetables into the diet. This does not have to be a typical iceberg lettuce and tomato salad; other choices include: carrot and raisin salad (watch the amount of added dressing!), or have some cut up raw broccoli, cauliflower, carrots, and green pepper strips with a low-fat dip or dip in diet salad dressing.

Also try some of the many different varieties of lettuces in your salad and sandwiches besides iceberg. The darker the color of the leaf, usually the more nutrients it has; try romaine, boston, red leaf, and green leaf varieties. Shredded green or red cabbage, shredded raw carrot, and small pieces of raw broccoli can all add interest and nutrients to your salads.

BREADS AND OTHER STARCHES

(contains 15 grams carbohydrate, 3 grams protein, a trace of fat, 80 calories, and 25 milligrams sodium).

Those items below marked with * have a higher sodium content of about 150 milligrams.

ITEM	EXCHANGE PORTION	ITEM	EXCHANGE PORTION
All breads- whole wheat, or whole grain preferable*	1 slice	Bread stick- 4"x1/2"*	2
English muffin*	1/2	Tortilla - corn or flour	1 small
Bagel*	1/2	Cereal, ready-to-eat, dry*	3/4 cup
Dinner roll*	1	Puffed cereals	1-1/2 cup
Frankfurter or hamburger roll*	1/2	Cooked cereal - prepared	1/2 cup
Pita bread*	1/2 large or 1 small	Rice - white or brown - cooked	1/3 cup

ITEM	EXCHANGE PORTION
Pasta - noodles, macaroni, or spaghetti - cooked*	1/2 cup
Popcorn - air popped	3 cups
Popcorn - oil or commercially popped*	1-1/2 cups
Animal crackers	8
Graham crackers	3 squares
Melba toast	5 slices
Saltine crackers*	6 squares
Oyster crackers	24
Rye crisp*	4 squares
Pretzels*	25 thin sticks or 1 thick Dutch twisted
Dried beans, peas and lentils - cooked	1/3 cup
Baked beans - no pork, canned*	1/4 cup
Corn	1/2 cup
Corn on the cob	1, 6" ear
Lima beans	1/2 cup
Parsnips	2/3 cup
Peas, green	1/2 cup
Potato, white, boiled	1 small

ITEM	EXCHANGE PORTION
Potato, white, baked	1/2 medium
Potato, white, mashed	1/2 cup
Pumpkin	3/4 cup
Winter squash, acorn or butternut	3/4 cup
Yam or sweet potato	1/3 cup

Whole wheat or whole grain bread and cereal products are good sources of fiber and many nutrients. Products made with enriched white flour are poor sources of fiber and the enriching process puts back only some of the nutrients lost in processing.

Contrary to popular belief, the foods in this group are good foods to add to the diet, including when trying to lose weight. Many of the calories associated with high carbohydrate foods come from fats or sauces added. An example is what can happen to a potato:

1 small boiled potato	70 calories
1 small potato with 2 tsp. butter	140 calories
1 small potato made into home fries	200 calories

For another good example, look in the Food Exchange Lists for starches at the difference in the portion size for popcorn that is air popped as opposed to popped in oil.

Quick breads (muffins, biscuits, pancakes, banana bread, etc.) have more fat and sodium in their recipes, and, therefore, the final product, than the starches included in the Breads and Other Starches food list. These types of foods may be included in the diet (for listing of these items, see Higher Fat Starches in the Miscellaneous Foods Section). However, those individuals who must limit total and saturated fats (for weight loss, diabetes, or high cholesterol) or sodium should either eliminate these foods as much as possible or prepare them at home using less total fat or salt in the recipes, substitute low-sodium baking powder for regular baking power, and substitute saturated fats (butter, vegetable shortening, lard) in the recipe with more unsaturated types (vegetable oils, margarine).

PROTEIN FOODS
(contains 7 grams protein, 3 or less grams fat, 55 calories, and 25 milligrams sodium).

Those foods below marked with * have a higher sodium content of 75 milligrams sodium or more and low-sodium version should be used if you are trying to reduce the amount of sodium in your diet.

<u>ITEM</u>	<u>EXCHANGE PORTION</u>
Meats - very lean only	
Beef- chipped*, round, flank	1 ounce
Lamb - loin, shoulder	1 ounce
Pork, fresh- loin	1 ounce
Veal- loin, shoulder	1 ounce
Poultry - without skin only	
White or dark meat - chicken, Turkey, cornish hen	1 ounce
Fish - any fresh or frozen 1-ounce	
Water packed, canned*: tuna, salmon,crab, lobster, shrimp	1/4 cup
Clams, oysters, scallops, shrimp*	6 whole
Crab, lobster*	2 ounce
Cottage or Farmer's cheese - made from skim or 1% milk*	1/4 cup
Dried beans, peas, or lentils - cooked	1/3 cup
Egg -	
whites are fat and cholesterol free	3
yolks have fat and high cholesterol	1

All meat, fish, and poultry, cheeses and eggs are poor sources of fiber. Dried beans, peas, and lentils are good sources of fiber. All of the protein sources listed above, except the cheeses, provide not only protein but iron, zinc, and other nutrients as well.

For those individuals trying to limit the amount of cholesterol in their diets, a more in-depth discussion of ways to accomplish this may be found in the chapter dealing with low cholesterol diets (Chapter 14). For the information of those readers who may not review that chapter, the cholesterol contents of all red meats, fish, and poultry are somewhat similar. Most recommendations you may have heard about eating less red meat and more fish and poultry are to help you reduce the amount of saturated fats you consume, not necessarily that much less cholesterol. The excess consumption of saturated animal fats can lead to an elevated blood cholesterol in some individuals. Extremely lean red meats may have as little fat as a skinless piece of chicken. The key word though is LEAN.

One way to reduce not only your cholesterol intake but your saturated fat intake is to include some meatless meals in your diet. Some example of some meals which would give you some good protein but not any cholesterol would be:

Split pea soup and Garlic toast	Large tossed salad with 1/2 cup kidney beans along with a plate of spaghetti with marinara tomato sauce

A discussion of ways to get meals with good complete protein will also be found in the chapter on low cholesterol diets. Many diabetics will find that adding some low-fat vegetarian meals can improve their control of their blood glucose levels, too.

FATS AND OILS
(contains 5 grams of fat, 45 calories, and trace amounts sodium).

Those foods below marked with * have a higher sodium content of about 50 milligrams, a lower sodium version may be used.

ITEM	EXCHANGE PORTION
Unsaturated Fats	
Avocado	1/8 medium
Margarine*	1 teaspoon
Margarine, diet*	1 Tablespoon
Mayonnaise*	1 teaspoon
Mayonnaise, low-cal*	1 Tablespoon
Oil (canola, corn, cottonseed, olive, soybean, safflower, sunflower)	1 teaspoon
Salad dressing*	1 Tablespoon
Salad dressing, low-cal*	2 Tablespoons
Saturated Fats	
Butter*	1 teaspoon
Coconut, shredded	2 Tablespoons
Coffee whitener, powder	4 teaspoons
Cream (light, coffee, table)	2 Tablespoons
Cream, sour	2 Tablespoons
Cream (heavy, whipping)	1 Tablespoon
Cream cheese*	1 Tablespoon

The foods in this group are divided into unsaturated and saturated groups. This was done to help you differentiate between these types of fats. Both the American Heart Association and the American Diabetes Association recommend a reduction in the diet of saturated fats. Some of these types of fats may be replaced with unsaturated types. Caution must be used, though, even in the use of unsaturated fats; a healthy, well-balanced diet is low in total fats as well as saturated fats.

The foods in this group are not good sources of fiber, and should be used sparingly to control calories.

MISCELLANEOUS OTHER FOODS
(these contain a variety of levels of carbohydrates, protein, fat, calories, and sodium)

Those foods below that are higher in sodium are marked with *.

FREE ITEMS:

Fat-free bouillon or broth*
Sugar-free, caffeine-free, citrus-free sodas*
Carbonated water
Club soda*
Sugar-free Gelatin dessert
Sugar substitutes
Mustard*
Vinegar
Herbs, spices and extracts (except onion or MSG)

SUGARS AND SWEETS

Sugar- white or brown	1 teaspoon=16 calories
Jelly and jam	1 Tablespoon=55 calories
Honey	1 Tablespoon=61 calories
Maple syrup	1 Tablespoon=50 calories
Jelly beans	6 pieces=60 calories
Marshmallow	1 large=25 calories
Gum drops	28 pieces=97 calories
Caffeine-free, citrus-free sugar swtn. sodas*	12 oz.=140 calories
Fruit sorbet	1 cup=180 calories
Sherbet*	1 cup=250 calories
Ice milk*	1 cup=200 calories
Ice cream-regular*	1 cup=270 calories
Ice cream-rich*	1 cup=340 calories
Gelatin-sugar sweetened	1 cup=160 calories
Pudding-instant made with skim milk*	1 cup=300 calories
Pudding-instant made with whole milk*	1 cup=350 calories

HIGHER FAT STARCHES

(these foods count in the diet as 1 bread serving and 1 fat serving)

Biscuit*	2-1/2" diameter
Chow mein noodles	1/2 cup
Corn bread*	2" cube
Cracker, butter type*	6
French fried potatoes	10, 2" to 3-1/2" long
Muffin, plain*	1 small
Pancake*	2, 4" diameter
Stuffing, prepared	1/4 cup
Taco shell	1, 6" across
Waffle*	1, 4-1/2" square

Foods from the *Sugars*, and the *Higher Fat Starches* sections should be avoided or only used occasionally by those who need to limit their caloric intakes, and those who are diabetic. Those foods marked with * should be homemade without any added salt. Also, higher sodium products such as baking powder and baking soda should be replaced in the recipe with a sodium-free product.

Chapter 14

CHOLESTEROL LOWERING DIET INFORMATION

The cholesterol lowering menus that are listed in these chapters are very similar to the sample general diets in the previous chapter. A cholesterol lowering diet is simply a good, well-balanced diet with a special emphasis on keeping saturated fats and cholesterol containing foods to a minimum. Your dietary efforts to reduce the incidence of your migraine headaches, and to lower your blood cholesterol, does not prevent you from having a healthy and varied diet.

Your cholesterol level and risk for developing heart disease is affected not only by your diet,but other factors as well. High cholesterol levels often run in families. You may have an inherited tendency towards higher cholesterol levels. There are many different metabolic reasons for a high blood cholesterol level; therefore, each individual's blood cholesterol reacts in an individual manner to dietary changes. Other risk factors for the development of heart disease include: lack of exercise, being over your ideal weight, smoking, and high blood pressure. Except for your possibly inherited tendency towards a high blood cholesterol, each of the other risk factors is ones that you can control:

- Eat a low-fat and low-cholesterol diet,
- Exercise regularly,
- Maintain your ideal body weight,
- Stop smoking, and
- Have your blood pressure taken regularly and treated, if necessary, by your physician.

Before we continue any further in this chapter, some definitions are probably in order:

CHOLESTEROL A waxy, fat-like substance that is found in animals but is not found in plants. Therefore, you will not find any cholesterol in completely vegetable based products (e.g., all vegetable oils). CHOLESTEROL in your blood stream travels in small particles called lipoproteins (lipo means fat so a lipoprotein is a particle that is part fat and part protein). All of your cholesterol lipoproteins are partly made up of cholesterol, fat, and protein. The proteins in the lipoprotein help the cholesterol and fat flow through the your watery blood. After all, oil and water don't mix! Your physician can perform a blood test to determine if your blood cholesterol is too high. Current recommendations of the National Cholesterol Education Program, sponsored by the National Institutes of Health, suggest that a cholesterol level of less than 200 mg/dl is most desirable. If you do not know the exact level of your blood cholesterol, ask your doctor to give this specific information.

LIPOPROTEINS There are several types of cholesterol lipoproteins in your blood stream. The main types of lipoproteins that are concerned with cholesterol are called high-density lipoprotein (HDL), and low-density lipoprotein (LDL).

HDL Also known by many as your "good" cholesterol, HDL is thought to be a protective factor against the development of heart disease if it is present in your blood in sufficient amounts. So, you want your HDL to be as high as possible. HDL can be measured by your physician through a blood test and he/she can tell you if you have the right amount of HDL considering your age and sex. Some ways you can encourage your body to produce as much HDL as it can are: exercise regularly, maintain ideal body weight, and follow a low-fat, well-balanced diet.

LDL Also known as your "bad" cholesterol, high LDL levels in the blood stream are thought to mean that you have an increased risk of developing heart disease. So, you want your LDL levels to be as low as possible. Once again, your physician can tell you if your LDL levels are too high from a blood test.

All fats and oils in your foods are a mixture of what are called saturated, mono-unsaturated, and poly-unsaturated fats. All that these terms mean is that each of the types of fats has a different type of physical/chemical arrangement which makes them act differently in the body and have different characteristics (liquid versus solid). These different types of fats are closely related, and all provide approximately nine calories per gram.

When someone says that beef fat is a saturated fat or that corn oil is a polyunsaturated fat, what they really mean that these fats and oils are either predominately saturated or polyunsaturated. Corn oil still has some small amounts of saturated fat and beef fat has some small amounts of polyunsaturated fat. Fatty acids, mainly linoleic and oleic acids, may be involved in the start of vascular headaches. This reaction may be due to a rise in the blood levels of the fatty acids with a simultaneous release of serotonin from blood platelets and an abnormal dilation of cranial arteries. The aura that is a precursor to a migraine is characterized by blind spots and cranial artery constriction followed by dilation. (58)

The type of fat that you consume can have a dramatic effect on your blood cholesterol levels:

SATURATED FATS Are usually the predominate type of fat in any type of animal or dairy product. However, there are some vegetable fats that contain a high proportion of saturated fat; these are: coconut oil (often used in shortening, non-dairy creamers and commercially made baked goods), palm oil (same uses as coconut), cocoa butter from chocolate, and any hydrogenated fat (hydrogenated means that a fat was made more saturated even if it started off as a highly unsaturated fat like sunflower or canola oil).

UNSATURATED FATS (Polyunsaturated and Monounsaturated) are usually the predominate type of fat in any type of vegetable product (except palm, coconut, vegetable shortening, and cocoa butter which are more saturated). Therefore, the natural fats and oils found in vegetables, grains, and seeds are mostly unsaturated.

Why should you care what type of fats you are consuming? Both unsaturated and saturated fats can affect your blood cholesterol levels. Remember that your cholesterol lipoproteins are not only protein and cholesterol but also part fat. The type of fat you consume effects how your lipoprotein particles are metabolized.

By just lowering the amount of saturated fat in your diet, you can usually lower your blood cholesterol. If you consume, on a regular basis, some unsaturated fats, this can also help lower your cholesterol. The most effective therapy for lowering blood cholesterol levels includes, then, not just reducing the amount of cholesterol consumed but also keeping saturated fats at a minimum and consuming some small amounts of unsaturated fats daily.

The total amount of fat in the diet should also be kept low. A decrease in fat intake to a maximum of 20 grams per day may cause a significant decrease in frequency, intensity, and duration of a migraine. Foods high in omega-3 fatty acids have been found to prevent migraines by stabilizing the effect on nerve cell membranes and making them more resistant to the mechanisms that cause migraine. (58) Just because having a little of the unsaturates can help lower blood cholesterol, adding a lot is not necessarily better. Too much added polyunsaturates could lower your HDL, which you want to be as high as possible. Also, a higher total fat diet may be linked with increased incidence of some types of cancer.

There are several things you can do to reduce the amount of dietary cholesterol that you consume:

- Keep portions of meat, fish, and poultry small,
- Keep egg yolks as low as possible in the diet (egg whites are okay), and

- Use low-fat dairy products like skim milk and part-skim unaged cheeses

Another way to lower your blood cholesterol level is to consume adequate amounts of what are called soluble fibers. These types of fibers are found in raw fruits and vegetables, legumes (e.g., kidney beans, split peas, navy beans, lentils), and whole oats (e.g., oatmeal and oat bran cereal).

Another way to help lower blood cholesterol levels is to include some vegetarian (meatless) type of meals. A meal using legumes as the main source of protein (e.g., meatless chili, or homemade split pea soup) has two advantages over a "traditional" meal with some type of meat, fish, or poultry:

1. The meal will contain much less saturated fat and cholesterol; and
2. Will be high in soluble fibers.

Vegetable sources of protein usually have a low level of one or more of the essential amino acids or protein building blocks that humans need. These proteins are then called "incomplete". Animal sources of protein usually have sufficient amounts of all the amino acids humans need. These proteins are then called "complete".

Because a vegetable protein is not "complete" does not mean that you cannot get all the amino acids you need from a vegetarian meal. Different types of vegetable sources of protein have different amino acids that they have in insufficient levels. The correct combination or "complement" of vegetable proteins can be consumed at a meal to correct this.

The following table summarizes how to combined different types of vegetable proteins to get good "complete" protein in a meal.

MATCH A FOOD FROM COLUMN "A" WITH A FOOD FROM COLUMN "B" FOR COMPLETE PROTEIN

Column A	Column B
Legumes	
Black Beans	Non-fat and Low-fat Dairy Products
Garbanzo Beans (Chickpeas)	Grain Products
Great Northern Beans	Egg Whites
Kidney Beans	
Lentils	
Lima Beans	
Pinto Beans	
Mung Beans	
Soy Beans	
Tofu	
Black-eyed Peas	
Cow Peas	
Field Peas	
Split Peas	
Whole Grains	
Barley	Non-fat and Low-fat Dairy Products
Corn (cornbread, grits)	Legumes
Oats	Egg Whites
Rice	
Rye	
Wheat (bulgar, wheat germ, sprouts)	

As you probably noticed from looking at the above table, having some type of non-fat or low-fat (1% milk fat or less) dairy product with one of the vegetable sources of protein will "complete" the protein in that meal. The dairy protein is already a complete protein and has all the amino acids to complement your legumes and grains.

Some caution should be used in choosing your dairy product to complete your protein. Do not use American cheese unless it is a low-fat, diet type. If you use cottage cheese, use 1% or skim milk types. All other cheeses are not only high in saturated fats but are not allowed because of their possible effect in initiating migraine headaches. A glass of skim milk will complete the proteins eaten at any vegetarian meal, especially if your are not sure you consumed complete protein from your meal.

Please notice in the following sample menus that while an emphasis is made to include mostly poultry and fish, some red meats have been included. The cholesterol content of beef, pork, and lamb is very close to that of chicken or turkey. The emphasis on the poultry and fish is usually made in cholesterol lowering diets as a way to reduce the amount of total and saturated fats. Very lean cuts of red meats are acceptable on a cholesterol lowering diet. Many individuals use more veal in their meal planning when trying to lower their cholesterol; please note that veal is actually slightly higher in cholesterol than regular beef. Veal tends to be leaner than beef but that is its only advantage.

Some evidence has been found that the consumption of fish may help to reduce the risk of heart disease. Most of the studies have centered on the incidence of heart disease in several different population (e.g., Eskimos). Researchers studied the amount of fish oils these groups consumed from fish in their diets.

Very little information has actually been reported on the effectiveness of the different fish oil capsules; also unknown is exactly what the correct effective dosage of these fish oil pills is, especially from individual to individual. What effect there may be after consuming these concentrated forms of fish oil over long periods of time is also unknown.

The use of the fish oil capsules may or may not be of benefit. Some benefit has been noted, however, when as little as the equivalent of an ounce of fish per day is consumed (7 oz. per week). This could be a couple of tuna sandwiches over the course of the week for lunch or a tuna or salmon sandwich for lunch one day and filet of flounder for dinner one evening. So, try to eat at least two or three meals per week where the entree is some type of fish.

Chapter 15

CHOLESTEROL LOWERING 7-DAY MENUS

SEVEN DAYS OF MENUS:

These menus closely resemble those found in the General Diets section (Chapter 12). They have been altered somewhat to help to keep the amount of cholesterol lower. These menus also have an increased emphasis on inclusion of soluble fiber sources. Otherwise, please notice that the menus of a low cholesterol diet do not vary much from a varied, well-rounded, healthy diet. The number and distribution of the food exchanges are the same as found in the general diets.

DAY #1

SIZE SERVING PER CALORIE LEVEL

FOOD AND MEAL	1200	1500	2000	2500
BREAKFAST				
Ready-to-eat Cereal with	3/4 c.	3/4 c.	3/4 c.	3/4 c.
Skim Milk	1/2 c.	1/2 c.	1/2 c.	1/2 c.
Whole Wheat Toast with	0	1 sl.	1 sl.	1 sl.
Margarine	0	1 tsp.	1 tsp.	1 tsp.
Skim Milk (to drink)	1/2 c.	1/2 c.	1/2 c.	1/2 c.
Apple Juice	1/2 c.	1 c.	1 c.	1 c.
Pero or Postum	free	free	free	free
LUNCH				
Tuna (water-packed) with	2 oz.	2 oz.	3 oz.	3 oz.
Mayonnaise on	2 tsp.	2 tsp.	2 tsp.	2 tsp.
Rye Bread	2 sl.	2 sl.	2 sl.	2 sl.
Marinated Tomatoes*	0	0	0	1 c.
Diet Ginger ale	free	free	free	free
Skim Milk	0	0	1 c.	1 c.

DAY #1

SIZE SERVING PER CALORIE LEVEL

FOOD AND MEAL	1200	1500	2000	2500
DINNER				
Crispy Oven Fried Oat Chicken*	3 oz.	3 oz.	3 oz.	4 oz.
Parsley Potatoes*	1/2 c.	1/2 c.	1 c.	1 c.
Pumpernickel Bread with	0	1 sl.	1 sl.	1 sl.
Margarine	0	1 tsp.	1 tsp.	1 tsp.
Steamed Broccoli with	1 c.	1 c.	1 c.	1 c.
Margarine	1 tsp.	1/2 tsp.	1 tsp.	1 tsp.
Sliced beets	0	1/2 c.	1/2 c.	1/2 c.
Skim Milk	1 c.	1 c.	1 c.	1 c.
SNACKS (throughout the day: mid-morning, mid-afternoon, and evening)				
Apple	1	1	1	1
Oatbran Muffin*	0	0	0	1
Pretzels-hard Dutch type	0	0	1	3
Raw Carrot and Zucchini	1 c.	1 c.	1 c.	1 c.
Nectarine	1	1	1	1

DAY #2

SIZE SERVING PER CALORIE LEVEL

FOOD AND MEAL	1200	1500	2000	2500
BREAKFAST				
Hot Oatmeal with	1/2 c.	1/2 c.	1/2 c.	1/2 c.
Skim Milk	1/2 c.	1/2 c.	1/2 c.	1/2 c.
Apple Juice	1/2 c.	1/2 c.	1/2 c.	1/2 c.
Pero or Postum	free	free	free	free

DAY #2

SIZE SERVING PER CALORIE LEVEL

FOOD AND MEAL	1200	1500	2000	2500
LUNCH				
Meatless Chili*	1 c.	1 c.	1-1/2c.	1-1/2c.
Tossed Salad with	free	free	free	free
Vinegar and Oil	1 TBS	1 TBS	1 TBS	1 TBS
Toasted Wheat Bread with	1 sl.	1 sl.	2 sl.	2 sl.
Garlic Topping*	1 tsp.	1 tsp.	2 tsp.	2 tsp.
Diet Ginger ale	free	free	free	free
Skim Milk	0	0	1 c.	1 c.
DINNER				
Sliced Lean Roast Beef	3 oz.	3 oz.	3 oz.	4 oz.
Baked Potato with	1 med.	1 lg.	1 lg.	1 lg.
Low Cholesterol Sour Cream*	(1TBS=free)			
Steamed Green Beans	1/2 c.	1 c.	1 c.	1 c.
Steamed Carrots	1/2 c.	1/2 c.	1/2 c.	1/2 c.
Margarine	2 tsp.	2 tsp.	3 tsp.	3 tsp.
Skim Milk	1 c.	1 c.	1 c.	1 c.
SNACKS (throughout the day: mid-morning, mid-afternoon, and evening)				
Apple	1	1	1	1
Pineapple Tidbits (canned)	1/2 c.	1 c.	1 c.	1 c.
Oat-bran Cereal with	1/2 c.	1 c.	1 c.	1 c.
Skim Milk and	1/2 c.	1/2 c.	1/2 c.	1/2 c.
Sliced Peaches	0	0	0	1/2 c.
Hard Pretzels	0	0	2	3
Caffeine-free Cola	0	0	8 oz.	12 oz.

DAY #3

SIZE SERVING PER CALORIE LEVEL

FOOD AND MEAL	1200	1500	2000	2500
BREAKFAST				
Breakfast Shake*	1 c.	1 c.	1 c.	1 c.
Toasted Oat Bread* with	1 sl.	1 sl.	1 sl.	1 sl.
Margarine and	1 tsp.	1 tsp.	1 tsp.	1 tsp.
Strawberry Preserves	0	0	1 tsp.	1 tsp.
Pero or Postum	free	free	free	free
LUNCH				
Chef Salad with Lettuce	free	free	free	free
Low-fat American Cheese, and	1 oz.	1 oz.	1 oz.	1 oz.
Turkey Breast	1 oz.	1 oz.	1 oz.	1 oz.
Allowed Salad Dressing	1 TBS.	1 TBS.	1 TBS.	1 TBS.
Saltine Crackers	0	6	6	6
Diet Root Beer	free	free	free	free
Skim Milk	0	0	1 c.	1 c.
DINNER				
Spaghetti with	1 c.	1-1/2 c.	2 c.	2 c.
Tomato Sauce* and	1/2 c.	1 c.	1 c.	1 c.
Turkey Meatballs*	3 oz.	3 oz.	3 oz.	4 oz.
Steamed Zucchini	1/2 c.	1/2 c.	1/2 c.	1/2 c.
Skim Milk	1 c.	1 c.	1 c.	1 c.
SNACKS (throughout the day: mid-morning, mid-afternoon, and evening)				
Fresh Pear	1	1	1	1
Toasted Rye Bagel	1/2	1/2	1	1
Margarine	1 tsp.	1 tsp.	2 tsp.	2 tsp.
Raw Broccoli and	1/2 c.	1/2 c.	1/2 c.	1/2 c.
Cauliflower dipped in	1/2 c.	1/2 c.	1/2 c.	1/2 c.
Allowed Salad Dressing	1 TBS.	1 TBS.	1 TBS.	1 TBS.
Vanilla Pudding (Skim-milk based)	0	0	1/2 c.	1 c.

DAY #4

SIZE SERVING PER CALORIE LEVEL

FOOD AND MEAL	1200	1500	2000	2500
BREAKFAST				
Low-cholesterol Cinnamon Pancakes*	2	3	3	3
Applesauce	1/2 c.	1/2 c.	1/2 c.	1/2 c.
Skim Milk	1 c.	1 c.	1 c.	1 c.
Pero or Postum	free	free	free	free
LUNCH				
Chicken Salad* with	1/3 c.	1/3 c.	1/2 c.	1/2 c.
Shredded Lettuce in	free	free	free	free
Small Pita Bread	1	1	1	1
Diet Ginger ale	free	free	free	free
Skim Milk	0	0	1 c.	1 c.
DINNER				
Baked Veal Chop*	3 oz.	3 oz.	3 oz.	4 oz.
Rice Pilaf*	1/2 c.	1/2 c.	1 c.	1 c.
Steamed Asparagus	1/2 c.	1 c.	1 c.	1 c.
Cucumber/Tomato Salad*	1/2 c.	1/2 c.	1/2 c.	1/2 c.
Skim Milk	1 c.	1 c.	1 c.	1 c.
SNACKS (throughout the day: mid-morning, mid-afternoon, and evening)				
Raisins	2 TBS.	2 TBS.	2 TBS.	2 TBS.
Apricots, canned halves	2	2	2	2
Crunchy Oat Sticks*	0	0	1	2
Marinated Zucchini Sticks*	1/2 c.	1/2 c.	1/2 c.	1/2 c.
Oat 'n Berry Cookies*	1	1	2	3

DAY #5

SIZE SERVING PER CALORIE LEVEL

FOOD AND MEAL	1200	1500	2000	2500
BREAKFAST				
Oat-bran Cereal with	1/2 c.	1/2 c.	1/2 c.	1/2 c.
Skim Milk and	1 c.	1 c.	1 c.	1 c.
Dates, chopped	2-1/2	2-1/2	2-1/2	2-1/2
English Muffin with	0	1/2	1/2	1/2
Margarine and	0	0	1 tsp.	1 tsp.
Blackberry Preserves	0	1 tsp.	1 tsp.	1 tsp.
Pero or Postum	free	free	free	free
LUNCH				
Low-fat Cottage Cheese and	1/2 c.	1/2 c.	3/4 c.	3/4 c.
Mixed Fruit Plate (peaches, pineapple, strawberries) on	1 c.	1 c.	1 c.	1 c.
Lettuce	free	free	free	free
Diet Root Beer	free	free	free	free
Skim Milk	0	0	1 c.	1 c.
DINNER				
Savory Chicken Stew*	1-1/2 c.	1-1/2 c.	1-1/2 c.	2 c.
Low Sat Fat Herb Biscuits*	1	1	1	1
Tossed Salad with	free	free	free	free
Allowed Salad Dressing	1 TBS.	1 TBS.	1 TBS.	1 TBS.
Diet Ginger ale	free	free	free	free
SNACK (throughout the day: mid-morning, mid-afternoon, and evening)				
Crunchy Oat Sticks*	1	2	2	2
Green Pepper Strips and	1/2 c.	1/2 c.	1/2 c.	1/2 c.
Carrot Sticks dipped in	1/2 c.	1/2 c.	1/2 c.	1/2 c.
Allowed Diet salad dressing	free	free	free	free
Frosty Fiber Shake*	1-1/2c.	1-1/2c.	1-1/2c.	1-1/2c.
Apple	0	0	1 small	1 large
Gingerbread, low-cholesterol*	0	0	0	1 sl.

DAY #6

SIZE SERVING PER CALORIE LEVEL

FOOD AND MEAL	1200	1500	2000	2500
BREAKFAST				
Oatmeal cooked with	1/2 c.	1 c.	1 c.	1 c.
Dried Apricots	4 halves	4 halves	4 halves	4 halves
Skim Milk	1 c.	1 c.	1 c.	1 c.
Pero or Postum	free	free	free	free
LUNCH				
Sliced Turkey Breast	2 oz.	2 oz.	3 oz.	3 oz.
Lettuce	free	free	free	free
Mayonnaise	2 tsp.	2 tsp.	2 tsp.	2 tsp.
Pumpernickel Bread	2 sl.	2 sl.	2 sl.	2 sl.
Cherry Tomatoes	0	0	0	1/2 c.
Diet Root Beer	free	free	free	free
Skim Milk	0	0	1 c.	1 c.
DINNER				
Flounder Florentine*	3 oz.	3 oz.	3 oz.	4 oz.
Steamed Carrots	1/2 c.	1/2 c.	1 c.	1 c.
Whole Wheat Roll with	1	1	2	2
Margarine	1 tsp.	1 tsp.	2 tsp.	2 tsp.
Skim Milk	1 c.	1 c.	1 c.	1 c.
SNACK (throughout the day: mid-morning, mid-afternoon, and evening)				
Applesauce	1/2 c.	1/2 c.	1/2 c.	1/2 c.
Butterscotch Pudding (made with skim milk	0	0	1/2 c.	1/2 c.
Raw Cauliflower and	1/2 c.	1/2 c.	1/2 c.	1/2 c.
Carrot Sticks dipped in	1/2 c.	1/2 c.	1/2 c.	1/2 c.
Allowed Diet Dressing	free	free	free	free
Strawberries (unsweetened)	1 c.	1 c.	1 c.	1 c.

DAY #7

SIZE SERVING PER CALORIE LEVEL

FOOD AND MEAL	1200	1500	2000	2500
BREAKFAST				
Ready-to-eat Cereal with	3/4 c.	3/4 c.	3/4 c.	3/4 c.
Skim Milk	1 c.	1 c.	1 c.	1 c.
Toasted Bagel with	0	1/2	1/2	1/2
Cottage Cheese Spread* and	0	1 TBS	1 TBS	1 TBS
Grape Jelly	0	0	1 tsp	1 tsp
Pineapple Juice	1/2 c.	1/2 c.	1/2 c.	1/2 c.
Pero or Postum	free	free	free	free
LUNCH				
Split Pea Soup*	1 c.	1 c.	1-1/2c.	1-1/2c.
Low-chole.Corn Bread* with	1 pc.	1 pc.	1 pc.	1 pc.
Margarine	1 tsp	1 tsp	1 tsp	1 tsp
Tossed Salad with	free	free	free	free
Allowed Diet Salad Dressing	free	free	free	free
Diet Cola	free	free	free	free
Skim Milk	0	0	1 c.	1 c.
DINNER				
Spinach Lasagna*	1-1/2 c.	2 c.	2-1/2 c.	2-1/2 c.
Marinated Zucchini*	1/2 c.	1/2 c.	2 c.	2 c.
Toasted Oat Bread* with	0	1 sl.	1 sl.	1 sl.
Garlic Topping*	0	1 tsp	1 tsp	1 tsp
Skim Milk	1 c.	1 c.	1 c.	1 c.
SNACK (throughout the day: mid-morning, mid-afternoon, and evening)				
Baked Apple*	1	1	1	1
Oat 'n Berry Cookies*	1	1	2	3
Carrot/Raisin Salad*	1/2 c.	1/2 c.	1/2 c.	1/2 c.

Chapter 16

DIABETIC CONTROL DIET INFORMATION

There are two main types of diabetes, insulin-dependent and noninsulin-dependent. Individuals with insulin-dependent diabetes usually do not produce enough insulin in their bodies; this means that a daily injection of insulin is required. The body uses glucose (sugar) for energy to nourish the many cells in the body so that it functions correctly. Insulin is necessary within the body so that the glucose or sugar in the blood may be used. This lack of adequate insulin for the amount of food consumed (and later broken down to glucose in the blood) is the main reason for the high blood sugar found in an individual with insulin-dependent diabetes.

Noninsulin-dependent diabetes is a somewhat different situation. This type of diabetes does not require a daily injection of insulin. In fact, with this type of diabetes, an individual may be producing normal amounts of insulin in his body but cannot efficiently use this insulin. Alternately, with noninsulin-dependent diabetes, an individual may be producing some insulin but just not enough to cover the blood glucose produced from their usual, unregulated diet (or excess weight, if applicable). All of these different individuals with noninsulin-dependent diabetes may be able to control their blood sugars by diet (avoiding sugary and fatty foods, and consuming high fiber foods) and exercise. Some individuals with this type of diabetes need a pill type of medication which, while not insulin, helps their bodies maintain an acceptable blood sugar level, along with the diet and exercise.

Before anyone with diabetes makes any changes in diet or exercise, he should consult his physician as to what effect it may have on insulin or medication doses. Many physicians recommend that their patients perform at-home blood glucose monitoring to help insure they are under adequate blood glucose control.

If your physician has never discussed at-home blood glucose monitoring with you, ask him about it. It requires only a drop of blood from your finger and a special test tape and/or meter. The results from this type of test gives you more sensitive information than the traditional at-home urine test for sugar. Often, no sugar will spill into the urine until the blood sugar levels are at 200mg/dl or greater. Normal, more optimal blood glucose levels are between 70 and 120mg/dl. Your blood glucose levels could be running at a less than optimal level, of perhaps 170mg/dl, and your urine would not indicate this. Information from a record of your blood sugars at different times of the day may help your physician tailor your insulin, medication, diet, and exercise schedule for better diabetes control and treatment.

An individual with diabetes, successfully following a diet to control blood sugars, is likely to experience fewer complications in the progression of his disease. These complications can include: elevated blood cholesterol and triglycerides, peripheral neuropathy (pains in the hands, arms, legs, and feet), and diabetic retinopathy (progressive blindness due primarily to changes in the blood vessels in the retina of the eye).

Fasting and the resulting low blood sugar (hypoglycemia) that develops may trigger headaches in patients prone to migraines. Over 50 percent of those persons prone to migraines may have a migraine after 16 hours without food. When a person ingests an excess of carbohydrates, a migraine may occur in response to the rapid insulin secretion and, thus, lowering of blood sugar. To avoid problems, one should eat 3 well-balanced meals per day and avoid an overabundance of high sugar-laden foods. (58)

In many ways, a diet for controlling diabetes is consistent with a healthy, well-rounded diet. The addition of limitations discussed in Chapter 10 will attempt to limit migraine headaches. The migraine sufferer and the diabetic must each try to spread their food intake out over the day to maintain as even a blood sugar as possible.

This chapter lists some sample menus similar to those in Chapter 12, except that more emphasis has been made to reduce the amounts of simple carbohydrates (sugars) and to increase the amount of fiber. The rolel of fiber in moderating blood sugar levels has been of increasing interest for many years.

The main categories of fiber are: water-insoluble and water-soluble types. Water-insoluble fibers are the typical types of fiber you think of when you think of fiber. These are called cellulose and hemi-cellulose and are found in the tough, structural components of grains and vegetable matter. Water-soluble fibers tend to form gels or are thickeners. These are called gums, pectins, and mucilages and are found in fresh fruits and vegetables, oats, and legumes (dried beans and peas, like kidney beans). Both types of fiber are desirable in the diet. Their actions include bulking of the stools to prevent constipation (especially the insoluble types), and appear to lower blood glucose and cholesterol levels (especially the soluble types).

Fiber should be added to the diet slowly to avoid any discomfort. You should also be sure to drink plenty of fluids or else your fiber may become constipating instead of acting to loosen the stools for easier bowel movements.

Strategies for ensuring enough fiber in the diet include:

- Have raw fruits and vegetables as snacks or at meals,
- Use only whole grain breads, crackers, and pastas, when possible,
- Include legumes daily in meal planning (chili, kidney beans on your salad), and
- Use whole-grain breakfast cereals - especially oats (oatmeal, oat bran cereal, Cheerio(tm)-type cereals).

Chapter 17

DIABETIC CONTROL 7-DAY MENUS

SEVEN DAYS OF MENUS: These menus closely resemble those found in the General Diets section (Chapter 12). They have been altered somewhat to decrease the amount of sugar, (a small amount of sugar within a meal is acceptable) and increase the amount of soluble fiber. Otherwise, please notice that the menus of a diabetic diet do not vary much from any varied, well-rounded, healthy diet. The number and distribution of the food exchanges are the same as found in the general diets.

DAY #1

SIZE SERVING PER CALORIE LEVEL

FOOD AND MEAL	1200	1500	2000	2500
BREAKFAST				
Ready-to-eat Cereal with	3/4 c.	3/4 c.	3/4 c.	3/4 c.
Skim Milk	1/2 c.	1/2 c.	1/2 c.	1/2 c.
Whole Wheat Toast with	0	1 sl.	1 sl.	1 sl.
Margarine	0	1 tsp.	1 tsp.	1 tsp.
Skim Milk (to drink)	1/2 c.	1/2 c.	1/2 c.	1/2 c.
Apple Juice	1/2 c.	1 c.	1 c.	1 c.
Pero or Postum	free	free	free	free
LUNCH				
Tuna (water-packed) with	2 oz.	2 oz.	3 oz.	3 oz.
Mayonnaise on	2 tsp.	2 tsp.	2 tsp.	2 tsp.
Rye Bread	2 sl.	2 sl.	2 sl.	2 sl.
Marinated Tomatoes*	0	0	0	1 c.
Diet Ginger ale	free	free	free	free
Skim Milk	0	0	1 c.	1 c.

DAY #1

SIZE SERVING PER CALORIE LEVEL

FOOD AND MEAL	1200	1500	2000	2500
DINNER				
Crispy Oven Fried Oat Chicken*	3 oz.	3 oz.	3 oz.	4 oz.
Parsley Potatoes*	1/2 c.	1/2 c.	1 c.	1 c.
Pumpernickel Bread with	0	1 sl.	1 sl.	1 sl.
Margarine	0	1 tsp.	1 tsp.	1 tsp.
Steamed Broccoli with	1 c.	1 c.	1 c.	1 c.
Margarine	1 tsp.	1/2 tsp.	1 tsp.	1 tsp.
Sliced Beets	0	1/2 c.	1/2 c.	1/2 c.
Skim Milk	1 c.	1 c.	1 c.	1 c.
SNACKS (throughout the day: mid-morning, mid-afternoon, and evening)				
Apple	1	1	1	1
Oatbran Muffin*	0	0	0	1
Pretzels-hard Dutch type	0	0	1	3
Raw Carrot and Zucchini	1 c.	1 c.	1 c.	1 c.
Nectarine	1	1	1	1

DAY #2

SIZE SERVING PER CALORIE LEVEL

FOOD AND MEAL	1200	1500	2000	2500
BREAKFAST				
Hot Oatmeal with	1/2 c.	1/2 c.	1/2 c.	1/2 c.
Skim Milk	1/2 c.	1/2 c.	1/2 c.	1/2 c.
Apple Juice	1/2 c.	1/2 c.	1/2 c.	1/2 c.
Pero or Postum	free	free	free	free

DAY #2

SIZE SERVING PER CALORIE LEVEL

FOOD AND MEAL	1200	1500	2000	2500
LUNCH				
Meatless Chili*	1 c.	1 c.	1-1/2c.	1-1/2c.
Tossed Salad with	free	free	free	free
Vinegar and Oil	1 TBS	1 TBS	1 TBS	1 TBS
Toasted Wheat Bread with	1 sl.	1 sl.	1 sl.	1 sl.
Garlic Topping*	1 tsp.	1 tsp.	1 tsp.	1 tsp.
Diet Ginger ale	free	free	free	free
Skim Milk	0	0	1 c.	1 c.
DINNER				
Sliced Lean Roast Beef	3 oz.	3 oz.	3 oz.	4 oz.
Baked Potato with	1 med.	1 lg.	1 lg.	1 lg.
Low Cholesterol Sour Cream*	(1TBS=free)			
Steamed Green Beans	1/2 c.	1 c.	1 c.	1 c.
Steamed Carrots	1/2 c.	1/2 c.	1/2 c.	1/2 c.
Margarine	2 tsp.	2 tsp.	3 tsp.	3 tsp.
Skim Milk	1 c.	1 c.	1 c.	1 c.
SNACKS (throughout the day: mid-morning, mid-afternoon, and evening)				
Apple	1	1	1	1
Pineapple Tidbits (canned)	1/2 c.	1 c.	1 c.	1 c.
Oat Bran Cereal with	1/2 c.	1 c.	1 c.	1 c.
Skim Milk and	1/2 c.	1/2 c.	1/2 c.	1/2 c.
Sliced Peaches	0	0	0	1/2 c.
Hard Pretzels	0	0	2	3
Caffeine-free Cola, Diet	free	free	free	free

DAY #3

SIZE SERVING PER CALORIE LEVEL

FOOD AND MEAL	1200	1500	2000	2500
BREAKFAST				
Breakfast Shake*	1 c	1 c	1 c	1 c
Toasted Oat Bread* with	1 sl.	1 sl.	1 sl.	1 sl.
Margarine	1 tsp.	1 tsp.	1 tsp.	1 tsp.
Pero or Postum	free	free	free	free
LUNCH				
Chef Salad with Lettuce	free	free	free	free
Low-fat American cheese, and	1 oz.	1 oz.	1 oz.	1 oz.
Turkey Breast	1 oz.	1 oz.	1 oz.	1 oz.
Allowed Salad Dressing	1 TBS.	1 TBS.	1 TBS.	1 TBS.
Saltine Crackers	0	6	6	6
Diet Root Beer				
Skim Milk	0	0	1 c.	1 c.
DINNER				
Spaghetti with	1 c.	1-1/2c.	2 c.	2 c.
Tomato Sauce* and	1/2 c.	1 c.	1 c.	1 c.
Turkey Meatballs*	3 oz.	3 oz.	3 oz.	4 oz.
Steamed Zucchini	1/2 c.	1/2 c.	1/2 c.	1/2 c.
Skim Milk	1 c.	1 c.	1 c.	1 c.
SNACKS (throughout the day: mid-morning, mid-afternoon, and evening)				
Fresh Pear	1	1	1	1
Toasted Rye Bagel	1/2	1/2	1	1
Margarine	1 tsp.	1 tsp.	2 tsp.	2 tsp.
Raw Broccoli and	1/2 c.	1/2 c.	1/2 c.	1/2 c.
Cauliflower dipped in	1/2 c.	1/2 c.	1/2 c.	1/2 c.
Allowed Salad Dressing	1 TBS.	1 TBS.	1 TBS.	1 TBS.
Vanilla Pudding (Skim-milk based and Artif. Swt.)	0	0	1/2 c.	1/2 c.

DAY #4

SIZE SERVING PER CALORIE LEVEL

FOOD AND MEAL	1200	1500	2000	2500
BREAKFAST				
Low-cholesterol Cinnamon Pancakes*	2	3	3	3
Applesauce	1/2 c.	1/2 c.	1/2 c.	1/2 c.
Skim Milk	1 c.	1 c.	1 c.	1 c.
Pero or Postum	free	free	free	free
LUNCH				
Chicken Salad* with	1/3 c.	1/3 c.	1/2 c.	1/2 c.
Shredded Lettuce in	free	free	free	free
Small Pita Bread	1	1	1	
Diet Ginger ale	free	free	free	free
Skim Milk	0	0	1 c.	1 c.
DINNER				
Baked Veal Chop*	3 oz.	3 oz.	3 oz.	4 oz.
Rice Pilaf*	1/2 c.	1/2 c.	1 c.	1 c.
Steamed Asparagus	1/2 c.	1 c.	1 c.	1 c.
Cucumber/Tomato Salad*	1/2 c.	1/2 c.	1/2 c.	1/2 c.
Skim Milk	1 c.	1 c.	1 c.	1 c.
SNACKS (throughout the day: mid-morning, mid-afternoon, and evening)				
Raisins	2 TBS.	2 TBS.	2 TBS.	2 TBS.
Apricots, canned halves	2	2	2	2
Crunchy Oat Sticks*	0	0	1	2
Marinated Zucchini Sticks*	1/2 c.	1/2 c.	1/2 c.	1/2 c.
Oat 'n Berry Cookies*	1	1	2	3

DAY #5

SIZE SERVING PER CALORIE LEVEL

FOOD AND MEAL	1200	1500	2000	2500
BREAKFAST				
Oat Bran Cereal with	1/2 c.	1/2 c.	1/2 c.	1/2 c.
Skim Milk and	1 c.	1 c.	1 c.	1 c.
Dates, chopped	2-1/2	2-1/2	2-1/2	2-1/2
English Muffin with	0	1/2	1/2	1/2
Margarine	0	0	1 tsp.	1 tsp.
Pero or Postum	free	free	free	free
LUNCH				
Low-fat Cottage Cheese and	1/2 c.	1/2 c.	3/4 c.	3/4 c.
Mixed Fruit Plate (peaches, pineapple, strawberries) on	1 c.	1 c.	1 c.	1 c.
Lettuce	free	free	free	free
Diet Root Beer	free	free	free	free
Skim Milk	0	0	1 c.	1 c.
DINNER				
Savory Chicken Stew*	1-1/2 c.	1-1/2 c.	1-1/2 c.	2 c.
Low Sat Fat Herb Biscuits*	1	1	2	2
Tossed Salad with	free	free	free	free
Allowed Salad Dressing	1 TBS.	1 TBS.	1 TBS.	1 TBS.
Diet Ginger ale	free	free	free	free
SNACKS (throughout the day: mid-morning, mid-afternoon, and evening)				
Crunchy Oat Sticks*	1	2	2	2
Green Pepper Strips and	1/2 c.	1/2 c.	1/2 c.	1/2 c.
Carrot Sticks dipped in	1/2 c.	1/2 c.	1/2 c.	1/2 c.
Allowed Diet Salad Dressing	free	free	free	free
Frosty Fiber Shake*	1-1/2c.	1-1/2c.	1-1/2c.	1-1/2c.
Apple	0	0	1 small	1 large
Gingerbread*	0	0	0	1 sl.

DAY #6

SIZE SERVING PER CALORIE LEVEL

FOOD AND MEAL	1200	1500	2000	2500
BREAKFAST				
Oatmeal cooked with	1/2 c.	1 c.	1 c.	1 c.
Dried Apricots	4 halves	4 halves	4 halves	4 halves
Skim Milk	1 c.	1 c.	1 c.	1 c.
Pero or Postum	free	free	free	free
LUNCH				
Sliced Turkey Breast	2 oz.	2 oz.	3 oz.	3 oz.
Lettuce	free	free	free	free
Mayonnaise	2 tsp.	2 tsp.	2 tsp.	2 tsp.
Pumpernickel Bread	2 sl.	2 sl.	2 sl.	2 sl.
Cherry Tomatoes	0	0	0	1/2 c.
Diet Root Beer	free	free	free	free
Skim Milk	0	0	1 c.	1 c.
DINNER				
Flounder Florentine*	3 oz.	3 oz.	3 oz.	4 oz.
Steamed Carrots	1/2 c.	1/2 c.	1 c.	1 c.
Whole Wheat Roll with	1	1	2	2
Margarine	1 tsp.	1 tsp.	1 tsp.	1 tsp.
Skim Milk	1 c.	1 c.	1 c.	1 c.
SNACKS (throughout the day: mid-morning, mid-afternoon, and evening)				
Applesauce	1/2 c.	1/2 c.	1/2 c.	1/2 c.
Butterscotch Pudding (made with Skim Milk, Artif. Swt)	0	0	1/2 c.	1 c.
Raw Cauliflower and	1/2 c.	1/2 c.	1/2 c.	1/2 c.
Carrot Sticks dipped in	1/2 c.	1/2 c.	1/2 c.	1/2 c.
Allowed Diet Dressing	free	free	free	free
Strawberries (unsweetened)	1 c.	1 c.	1 c.	1 c.

DAY #7

SIZE SERVING PER CALORIE LEVEL

FOOD AND MEAL	1200	1500	2000	2500
BREAKFAST				
Ready-to-eat Cereal with	3/4 c.	3/4 c.	3/4 c.	3/4 c.
Skim Milk	1 c.	1 c.	1 c.	1 c.
Toasted Bagel with	0	1/2	1/2	1/2
Cottage Cheese Spread*	0	1 TBS	1 TBS	1 TBS
Pineapple Juice	1/2 c.	1/2 c.	1/2 c.	1/2 c.
Pero or Postum	free	free	free	free
LUNCH				
Split Pea Soup*	1 c.	1 c.	1-1/2c.	1-1/2c.
Corn Bread* with	1 pc.	1 pc.	1 pc.	1 pc.
Margarine	1 tsp	1 tsp	1 tsp	1 tsp
Tossed Salad with	free	free	free	free
Allowed Diet Salad Dressing	free	free	free	free
Diet Cola	free	free	free	free
Skim Milk	0	0	1 c.	1 c.
DINNER				
Spinach Lasagna*	1-1/2c.	2 c.	2-1/2c.	2-1/2c.
Marinated Zucchini*	1/2 c.	1/2 c.	1 c.	1 c.
Toasted Oat Bread* with	0	1 sl.	1 sl.	1 sl.
Garlic Topping*	0	1 tsp	1 tsp	1 tsp
Skim Milk	1 c.	1 c.	1 c.	1 c.
SNACKS (throughout the day: mid-morning, mid-afternoon, and evening)				
Baked Apple*	1	1	1	1
Oat 'n Berry Cookies*	1	1	2	3
Carrot/Raisin Salad*	1/2 c.	1/2 c.	2/3 c.	2/3 c.

Chapter 18

REDUCED SODIUM DIET INFORMATION

Sodium is a mineral that a healthy person must have in certain amounts. Most Americans, however, consume more sodium than their bodies really need. The average person can excrete in the urine any excess sodium. Those people who cannot excrete the excess sodium due to various medical conditions often develop a condition called edema. Edema is the accumulation of extra water in the body; this fluid collects because the body is trying to dilute the extra sodium it was unable to excrete.

If you have a problem of excessive fluid collection in the body, your physician may have suggested that you reduce the amount of salt or sodium in your diet. Typical conditions where this dietary recommendation is given is if you have high blood pressure (too much fluid pressure in the blood vessels), congestive heart failure, and premenstrual fluid retention.

Most Americans consume from 2500 to 7000 milligrams of sodium each day. A low sodium diet usually restricts sodium intake to 1000 to 2000 milligrams per day. Your physician can best prescribe for you the appropriate level of sodium restriction necessary. The menus in this chapter list diets that contain approximately 2000 milligrams of sodium per day. This is considered a mild sodium restriction.

Even though many people will say both "low salt" and "low sodium" to mean the same thing, they are not exactly the same. Salt is a compound that is about forty percent sodium, and about sixty percent chloride (another mineral). Not every food high in sodium is necessarily high in table salt.

Most foods naturally have some sodium in them. You can get all the sodium that your body needs from your foods without adding any additional salt. Some foods have more sodium than others, but that does not necessarily mean that you must exclude that food. For example, milk is relatively high in sodium compared to most fruits and vegetables. This does not mean that you should cut out all milk from your diet. Milk contains many very important nutrients and several glasses of milk each day can still be consumed while keeping the sodium content of the diet within 2000 mg. per day.

Eliminating salt from your cooking and not adding salt at the table will help reduce the amount of sodium that you are consuming. You must also check the labels of your food products to check for any added sodium. Check for any ingredient that lists sodium as part of its name (e.g., monosodium glutamate); also check for ingredients that are high in sodium but sodium is not part of their names (e.g., baking soda, baking powder).

The United States Food and Drug Administration (FDA) has set-up guidelines for food manufacturers to follow concerning sodium. These definitions are:

SODIUM FREE: 5 mg or less sodium per serving,

VERY LOW SODIUM: 35 mg or less per serving,

LOW SODIUM: 140 mg or less per serving,

REDUCED SODIUM: One serving has no more than 75 percent of the amount of sodium in the regular product, and

NO SALT ADDED, UNSALTED, OR WITHOUT ADDED SALT: No salt was added during the processing; this term can only be used for foods that usually have salt added.

There are several different salt substitutes on the market. In genera, it is best not to use these without discussing it with your physician first. Many people find that by two months after eliminating added salt in the diet and eliminating high sodium foods, that they do not miss the flavoring salt adds to foods. At first, your food may taste somewhat bland, but this will pass. The use of other spices and herbs will help you enjoy your foods without the salt.

ALLOWED SPICES AND CONDIMENTS:

- Allspice
- Almond Extract
- Anise Seed
- Baking powder
- Basil
- Bay Leaf
- Bouillon (low-sodium type only)
- Caraway Seed
- Cardamon
- Celery Seed
- Chili Powder
- Cinnamon
- Cloves
- Coconut
- Cumin
- Curry
- Dill
- Fennel
- Garlic, garlic juice or powder
- Ginger
- Horseradish
- Ketchup (low-sodium type and no onion)
- Maple Extract
- Marjoram
- Mint
- Mustard, dry or Mustard Seed
- Nutmeg
- Oregano
- Paprika
- Parsley
- Pepper-green, red, or black
- Peppermint Extract
- Pimientos
- Poppy Seed
- Rosemary
- Saffron
- Sage
- Savory
- Sesame Seed
- Sorrel
- Tarragon
- Thyme
- Tumeric
- Vanilla Extract
- Vinegar
- Walnut Extract

NON-ALLOWED SPICES AND CONDIMENTS:

- Baking Powder (regular types)
- Baking Powder
- Barbeque, chili, or steak sauce
- Bouillon (regular types)
- Celery Salt
- Chili Sauce
- Cooking Wine
- Cured, salted meats (i.e., bacon)
- Garlic Salt
- Hydrolyzed Vegetable Protein
- Lemon Juice, extract or pee
- Meat Extracts
- Meat Sauces
- Meat Tenderizers
- Monosodium Glutamate
- Mustard, prepared
- Olives
- Onion Salt, juice, powder, or fresh
- Orange Juice, extract or peel
- Pickles
- Relishes
- Salt at the Table
- Season Salt
- Sodium Compounds (i.e., sodium benzoate, hydroxide, nitrate, nitrite, phosphate)
- Soups, canned or dried mix
- Soy Sauce
- Worcestershire Sauce

General Guidelines for Reducing the Sodium in the Diet:

1. Do not use salt in cooking or at the table. Use the spices and condiments listed as okay above.

2. Read the ingredient label of processed foods. Try to buy only those foods that contain little or no salt or sodium. Also remember to be on the watch for any ingredients that may initiate migraine headaches.

3. Use reduced-sodium or unsalted margarines.

4. Use only fresh or frozen vegetables, without any added salt. Canned vegetables usually have too much salt added in their processing for them to be used in a low-sodium diet. However, some markets carry low-sodium or no added salt canned vegetables, and these may be used.

5. Avoid hidden sources of sodium:

   - Some antacids (those containing sodium bicarbonate, citrate, or phosphate)
   - Aspirin
   - Certain medications (ask your physician or pharmacist)
   - Some laxatives (those containing sodium bicarbonate, citrate, or phosphate)
   - Some sleeping aids (those containing sodium citrate)

6. Avoid baked goods that are made with large amounts of salt or sodium containing ingredients (muffins, biscuits, some cakes, cookies, and crackers).

7. Avoid dessert items that are higher in sodium (puddings, ice cream)

The Food Exchange Lists in Chapter 13 highlights those foods that tend to be higher in salt or sodium. The Reduced Sodium Menus that follow are based on those in the General Diets Chapter but have been adjusted to reduce the amount of sodium. The recipes are also adjusted to reduce the sodium content of that item.

Chapter 19

REDUCED SODIUM 7-DAY MENUS

SEVEN-DAY MENUS: These menus are based on those in the General Diets Chapter. Just because you are trying to reduce the amount of sodium in your diet, does not mean you cannot have a variety of delicious foods. If a regular recipe was altered to reduce the sodium content, the letters LS (Low Sodium) appear in the name of the recipe.

DAY #1

SIZE SERVING PER CALORIE LEVEL

FOOD AND MEAL	1200	1500	2000	2500
BREAKFAST				
Puffed Cereal with	1 c.	1 c.	1 c.	1 c.
Skim Milk	1/2 c.	1/2 c.	1/2 c.	1/2 c.
Whole Wheat Toast with	0	1 sl.	1 sl.	1 sl.
Margarine	0	1 tsp	1 tsp	1 tsp
Skim Milk (to drink)	1 tsp	1 tsp	1 tsp	1 tsp
Apple Juice	1/2 c.	1 c.	1 c.	1 c.
Pero or Postum	free	free	free	free
LUNCH				
Tuna, low-sodium, with	2 oz.	2 oz.	3 oz.	3 oz.
Mayonnaise on	2 tsp	2 tsp	2 tsp	2 tsp
Rye Bread	2 sl.	2 sl.	2 sl.	2 sl.
Marinated Tomatoes*	0	0	0	1 c.
Diet Ginger ale	free	free	free	free
Skim Milk	0	0	1 c.	1 c.

DAY #1

SIZE SERVING PER CALORIE LEVEL

FOOD AND MEAL	1200	1500	2000	2500
DINNER				
Crispy Oven Fried Chicken*	3 oz.	3 oz.	3 oz.	4 oz.
Parsley Potatoes*	1/2 c.	1/2 c.	1 c.	1 c.
Pumpernickel Bread with	0	1 sl.	1 sl.	1 sl.
Margarine	0	1 tsp.	1 tsp.	1 tsp.
Steamed Broccoli with	1 c.	1 c.	1 c.	1 c.
Margarine	1 tsp.	1 tsp.	1 tsp.	1 tsp.
Sliced Beets	0	1/2 c.	1/2 c.	1/2 c.
Skim Milk	1 c.	1 c.	1 c.	1 c.
SNACKS (throughout the day: mid-morning, mid-afternoon, and evening)				
Apple	1	1	1	1
Oatbran Muffin*	0	0	0	1
Pretzels-unsalted, Dutch	0	0	1	3
Raw Carrot and Zucchini	1 c.	1 c.	1 c.	1 c.
Nectarine	1	1	1	1

DAY #2

SIZE SERVING PER CALORIE LEVEL

FOOD AND MEAL	1200	1500	2000	2500
BREAKFAST				
Hot Oatmeal with	1/2 c.	1 c.	1 c.	1 c.
Skim Milk	1/2 c.	1/2 c.	1/2 c.	1/2 c.
Apple Juice	1/2 c.	1/2 c.	1/2 c.	1/2 c.
Pero or Postum	free	free	free	free
LUNCH				
Meatless Chili LS*	1 c.	1 c.	1-1/2c.	1-1/2c.
Tossed Salad with	free	free	free	free
Vinegar and Oil	1 TBS	1 TBS	1 TBS	1 TBS
Toasted Wheat Bread with	1 sl.	1 sl.	1 sl.	1 sl.
Garlic Topping*	1 tsp.	1 tsp.	1 tsp.	1 tsp.
Diet Ginger ale	free	free	free	free
Skim Milk	0	0	1 c.	1 c.

DAY #2

SIZE SERVING PER CALORIE LEVEL

FOOD AND MEAL	1200	1500	2000	2500
DINNER				
Sliced Roast Beef	3 oz.	3 oz.	3 oz.	4 oz.
Baked Potato	1 med.	1 lg.	1 lg.	1 lg.
Steamed Green Beans	1/2 c.	1 c.	1 c.	1 c.
Steamed Carrots	1/2 c.	1/2 c.	1/2 c.	1/2 c.
Margarine	2 tsp.	2 tsp.	3 tsp.	3 tsp.
Skim Milk	1 c.	1 c.	1 c.	1 c.
SNACKS (throughout the day: mid-morning, mid-afternoon, and evening)				
Apple	1	1	1	1
Pineapple Tidbits (canned)	1/2 c.	1 c.	1 c.	1 c.
Puffed Cereal with	1 c.	1 c.	1 c.	1 c.
Skim Milk and	1/2 c.	1/2 c.	1/2 c.	1/2 c.
Sliced Peaches	0	0	0	1/2 c.
Pretzel-unsalted, Dutch	0	0	2	3

DAY #3

SIZE SERVING PER CALORIE LEVEL

FOOD AND MEAL	1200	1500	2000	2500
BREAKFAST				
Breakfast Shake*	1 c	1 c	1 c	1 c
Toasted Rye Bread with	1 sl.	1 sl.	1 sl.	1 sl.
Margarine and	1 tsp.	1 tsp.	1 tsp.	1 tsp.
Strawberry Preserves	9	9	1 tsp.	1 tsp.
Pero or Postum	free	free	free	free
LUNCH				
Chef Salad with Lettuce	free	free	free	free
LS American Cheese and	1 oz.	1 oz.	1 oz.	1 oz.
Turkey Breast	1 oz.	1 oz.	2 oz.	2 oz.
Allowed Salad Dressing	1 TBS.	1 TBS.	1 TBS.	1 TBS.
LS Saltine Crackers	0	6	6	6
Diet Root Beer	free	free	free	free
Skim Milk	0	0	1 c.	1 c.

DAY #3

SIZE SERVING PER CALORIE LEVEL

FOOD AND MEAL	1200	1500	2000	2500
DINNER				
Spaghetti with	1 c.	1-1/2c.	2 c.	2 c.
Tomato Sauce LS*	1/2 c.	1 c.	1 c.	1 c.
Meatballs*	3 oz.	3 oz.	3 oz.	4 oz.
Steamed Zucchini	1/2 c.	1/2 c.	1/2 c.	1/2 c.
Skim Milk	1 c.	1 c.	1 c.	1 c.
SNACKS (throughout the day: mid-morning, mid-afternoon, and evening)				
Fresh Pear	1	1	1	1
Toasted Rye Bagel with	1/2	1/2	1	1
Cream Cheese	1 TBS	1 TBS	2 TBS	2 TBS
Raw Broccoli and Cauliflower dipped in	1 c.	1 c.	1 c.	1 c.
Allowed Salad Dressing	1 TBS.	1 TBS.	1 TBS.	1 TBS.
Strawberry Sorbet	0	0	1/2 c.	1 c.

DAY #4

SIZE SERVING PER CALORIE LEVEL

FOOD AND MEAL	1200	1500	2000	2500
BREAKFAST				
Cinnamon Pancakes LS* with	2	3	3	3
Applesauce	1/2 c.	1/2 c.	1/2 c.	1/2 c.
Skim Milk	1 c.	1 c.	1 c.	1 c.
Pero or Postum	free	free	free	free
LUNCH				
Chicken Salad* with	1/3 c.	1/3 c.	1/2 c.	1/2 c.
Shredded Lettuce in	free	free	free	free
Small Pita Bread	1	1	1	
Diet Ginger ale	free	free	free	free
Skim Milk	0	0	1 c.	1 c.

DAY #4

SIZE SERVING PER CALORIE LEVEL

FOOD AND MEAL	1200	1500	2000	2500
DINNER				
Baked Pork Chop*	3 oz.	3 oz.	3 oz.	4 oz.
Rice Pilaf LS*	1/2 c.	1/2 c.	1 c.	1 c.
Steamed Asparagus	1/2 c.	1 c.	1 c.	1 c.
Cucumber/Tomato Salad*	1/2 c.	1/2 c.	1/2 c.	1/2 c.
Skim Milk	1 c.	1 c.	1 c.	1 c.
SNACKS (throughout the day: mid-morning, mid-afternoon, and evening)				
Raisins	2 TBS.	2 TBS.	2 TBS.	2 TBS.
Apricots, canned halves	2	2	2	2
Crunchy Bread Sticks LS*	0	0	1	2
Marinated Zucchini Sticks*	1/2 c.	1/2 c.	1/2 c.	1/2 c.
Oat 'n Berry Cookies LS*	1	1	2	3

DAY #5

SIZE SERVING PER CALORIE LEVEL

FOOD AND MEAL	1200	1500	2000	2500
BREAKFAST				
Puffed Cereal with	1 c.	1 c.	1 c.	1 c.
Skim Milk and	1 c.	1 c.	1 c.	1 c.
Dates, chopped	2-1/2	2-1/2	2-1/2	2-1/2
English Muffin with	0	1/2	1/2	1/2
Margarine and	0	0	1 tsp.	1 tsp.
Blackberry Preserves	0	1 tsp.	1 tsp.	1 tsp.
Pero or Postum	free	free	free	free
LUNCH				
Cottage Cheese LS and	1/2 c.	1/2 c.	3/4 c.	3/4 c.
Mixed Fruit Plate (peaches, pineapple, strawberries) on	1 c.	1 c.	1 c.	1 c.
Lettuce	free	free	free	free
Diet Root Beer	free	free	free	free
Skim Milk	0	0	1 c.	1 c.

DAY #5

SIZE SERVING PER CALORIE LEVEL

FOOD AND MEAL	1200	1500	2000	2500
DINNER				
Savory Chicken Stew*	1-1/2 c.	1-1/2 c.	1-1/2 c.	2 c.
Herb Biscuits LS*	1	1	2	2
Tossed Salad with	free	free	free	free
Allowed Salad Dressing	1 TBS.	1 TBS.	1 TBS.	1 TBS.
Diet Ginger ale	free	free	free	free
SNACKS (throughout the day: mid-morning, mid-afternoon, and evening)				
Crunchy Oat Sticks*	1	2	2	2
Green Pepper Strips and				
Carrot Sticks dipped in	1 c.	1 c.	1 c.	1 c.
Allowed LS Diet Salad	free	free	free	free
Dressing	free	free	free	free
Frosty Shake*	1-1/2c.	1-1/2c.	1-1/2c.	1-1/2c.
Apple	0	0	1 small	1 large
Gingerbread*	0	0	0	1 sl.

DAY #6

SIZE SERVING PER CALORIE LEVEL

FOOD AND MEAL	1200	1500	2000	2500
BREAKFAST				
Oatmeal cooked with	1/2 c.	1 c.	1 c.	1 c.
Dried Apricots	4 halves	4 halves	4 halves	4 halves
Skim Milk	1 c.	1 c.	1 c.	1 c.
Pero or Postum	free	free	free	free
LUNCH				
Sliced Fresh Turkey Breast	2 oz.	2 oz.	3 oz.	3 oz.
Lettuce	free	free	free	free
Mayonnaise	2 tsp.	2 tsp.	2 tsp.	2 tsp.
Pumpernickel Bread	2 sl.	2 sl.	2 sl.	2 sl.
Cherry Tomatoes	0	0	0	1/2 c.
Diet Root Beer	free	free	free	free
Skim Milk	0	0	1 c.	1 c.

DAY #6

SIZE SERVING PER CALORIE LEVEL

FOOD AND MEAL	1200	1500	2000	2500
DINNER				
Flounder Florentine LS*	3 oz.	3 oz.	3 oz.	4 oz.
Steamed Carrots	1/2 c.	1/2 c.	1 c.	1 c.
Whole Wheat Roll	1	1	2	2
Margarine	1 tsp.	1 tsp.	1 tsp.	1 tsp.
Skim Milk	1 c.	1 c.	1 c.	1 c.
SNACKS (throughout the day: mid-morning, mid-afternoon, and evening)				
Applesauce	1/2 c.	1/2 c.	1/2 c.	1/2 c.
Raspberry Sorbet	0	0	1/2 c.	1 c.
Raw Cauliflower Pieces and				
Carrot Sticks with	1 c.	1 c.	1 c.	1 c.
Allowed LS Diet Dressing	free	free	free	free
Strawberries (unsweetened)	1 c.	1 c.	1 c.	1 c.

DAY #7

SIZE SERVING PER CALORIE LEVEL

FOOD AND MEAL	1200	1500	2000	2500
BREAKFAST				
Puffed Cereal with	1 c.	1 c.	1 c.	1 c.
Skim Milk	1 c.	1 c.	1 c.	1 c.
Toasted Bagel with	0	1/2	1/2	1/2
Cream Cheese and	0	1 TBS	1 TBS	1 TBS
Grape Jelly	0	0	1 tsp	1 tsp
Pineapple Juice	1/2 c.	1/2 c.	1/2 c.	1/2 c.
Pero or Postum	free	free	free	free

DAY #7

SIZE SERVING PER CALORIE LEVEL

FOOD AND MEAL	1200	1500	2000	2500
LUNCH				
Split Pea Soup LS*	1 c.	1 c.	1-1/2c.	1-1/2c.
Corn Bread LS* with	1 pc.	1 pc.	1 pc.	1 pc.
Margarine	1 tsp	1 tsp	1 tsp	1 tsp
Tossed Salad with	free	free	free	free
Allowed LS Diet Salad Dressing	free	free	free	free
Diet Cola	free	free	free	free
Skim Milk	0	0	1 c.	1 c.
DINNER				
Spinach Lasagna LS*	1-1/2c.	2 c.	2-1/2c.	2-1/2c.
Marinated Zucchini*	1/2 c.	1/2 c.	1 c.	1 c.
Toasted Wheat Bread with	0	1 sl.	1 sl.	1 sl.
Garlic Topping*	0	1 tsp	1 tsp	1 tsp
Skim Milk	1 c.	1 c.	1 c.	1 c.
SNACKS (throughout the day: mid-morning, mid-afternoon, and evening)				
Baked Apple*	1	1	1	1
Spice Cookies LS*	1	1	2	3
Carrot/Raisin Salad*	1/2 c.	1/2 c.	2/3 c.	2/3 c.

Appendix A

MIGRAINE-SAFE FOOD LIST

This appendix contains a list of food products that are free of substances that could trigger migraines. When making up this migraine-safe food list, foods containing any of the ingredients found on the restricted list were eliminated, regardless of how little a product contained. This was done to keep even small amounts of the unwanted chemicals from building up in the body, thus reducing, as much as possible, the chance of getting a headache solely from the foods eaten.

Under each type of food, a list of brand names and varieties are given.

For example:

Biscuits- Hungry Jack- Buttermilk Flaky- 1869 Brand (buttermilk)

When looking at this list, keep in mind that there are brands not listed and products that could be added. You can find other safe foods to eat, by comparing the ingredients to the restricted food lists in Chapter 10.

Certain brands listed below are found in one food store - Safeway. These brands are: Mrs. Wright's, Lucerne, CragMont, Town House, Country Pure, Scotch Buy, Empress, Crown Colony, NuMade, Sea Trader, Bel-air, Busy Baker, and Party Pride. Your local store may have other brands.

1. Apple Butter
   a. Piedmont - Safeway
   b. White House
   c. Polaner (Smooth, Chunk)

2. Apple Sauce
   a. White House (Regular)
   b. Mott's
   c. Town House (Regular)
   d. Musselman's
   e. Seneca (Cinnamon, McIntosh)
   f. Country Pure (No Sugar)
   g. Del Monte - Fruit Naturals (small container)-Mixed Fruit, Diced Peaches, Pineapple Tidbits, Diced Pears

3. American Pasteurized Process Cheese Food
   a. Lact-Aid- Lactose Reduced
   b. Weight Watchers
   c. Fisher - Cheez-ola - Low Cholesterol
   d. Beatrice - Mun-chee
   e. Borden (Vera - Shar, Lite-Line - American Flavor)
   f. Kraft (Old English Sharp, Deluxe American)
   g. Cooper - C-V slices - Sharp
   h. Sargento – Imitation - Mozzarella
   i. Formage - American

4. Bacon Bits - Imitation
   a. McCormick (Imitation Bacon Bits)
   b. Betty Crocker (Bacos)
   c. Crown Colony (Imitation Bacon Bits)

5. Bagels - Frozen
   a. Bagel Master, Inc. (Plain) CharLeft 1, 0
   b. Lender's (Plain, Egg, Raisin'n Honey, Blueberry, Cinnamon Raisin)
   c. Sara Lee Bagel Time (Cinnamon + Raisin, Poppy Seed, Plain)
   d. Whatsa Bagel - Safeway (Plain, Sesame, Cinnamon)

6. Baked Apples - Lucky Leaf - Dutch style

7. Bakery
   a. Cake - Safeway (Angel Food)
   b. Pie

(1) Pumpkin - Safeway
(2) Peach, Blueberry, Cherry, Apple - Hostess

c. Buns - Honey, Honey Dip
d. Turnovers - Blueberry, Apple, Cherry
f. Bagels - Poppy Seed, Plain, Raisin, Pumpernickel
g. Rolls
   (1) Safeway (Hard, Club, Sandwich, Hoagie, Kaiser, Rye)
h. Bread - Raisin, Cinnamon Apple, Jewish Rye, Pumpernickel

8. Bakery Products - to be made in oven
   a. Apple Danish - Pillsbury's
   b. Oatmeal Raisin Cookies - Pillsbury's
   c. Sugar Cookies - Pillsbury's
   d. Cinnamon Raisin Danish Rolls with Icing - Pillsbury's
   e. Cinnamon Rolls - Pillsbury's
   f. Crescent Dinner Rolls - Pillsbury's
   g. Hungry Jack - Buttermilk- Flaky Biscuits - Pillsbury's
   h. Hungry Jack - Butter Tastin' Flaky Biscuits- Pillsbury's
   i. Hungry Jack - Flaky Biscuits- Pillsbury's
   j. 1869 Brand- Buttermilk Biscuits- Pillsbury's
   k. Southern Style - Big Country Biscuits- Pillsbury's
   l. Big Country Biscuits - Pillsbury's
   m. Good'n Buttery Big Country Biscuits - Pillsbury's
   n. Big Deluxe Heat'n Eat Biscuits - Pillsbury's
   o. All Ready Pie Crusts - Pillsbury's
   p. Pipin' Hot- White loaf - Pillsbury's
   q. Soft Bread Sticks - Pillsbury's
   r. Crusty French Loaf - Pillsbury's
   s. Buttermilk Biscuits
   t. Texas Style- Butter Biscuits - Mrs. Wright's
   u. Mrs. Butter-worth's - Cinnamon Sweet Rolls
   v. Pepperidge Farm - Apple Crisp, Cinnamon Rolls

9. Baking Powder
   a. Rumford
   b. Calumet
   c. Hearth Club -Safeway

10. Baking Soda - Arm and Hammer

11. Beef Patties - Frozen
   a. Grand Duchess

b. Safeway

12. Biscuits- Baking Powder - Safeway

13. Bran- Unprocessed - Quaker

14. Breads
    a. Pita
        (1) Thomas' - Sahara style
        (2) Q.P.S. Bakery (White, Whole Wheat)
    b. Hawaiian Bread - King's
    c. Bake and Serve - Safeway (Regular, Cinnamon)
    d. White
        (1) Mrs. Wright's (Regular, Sandwich, Buttermilk)
        (2) Wonder (Thin with Buttermilk)
        (3) Schmidt's - Blue Ribbon (Family and King loaves, Less, Hollywood - light and dark)
        (4) Arnold (Brick Oven, Very Thin, Country White)
        (5) Pepperidge Farm (Very Thin White, Sandwich Style)
        (6) Monastary (Thin Style)
    e. Wheat
        (1) Mrs. Wright's (Regular)
        (2) Schmidt's (Less, Old Tyme Split Top)
        (3) Arnold (Brick Oven Whole, Honey Wheat Berry, Milk and Honey)
        (4) Home Pride
        (5) Pepperidge Farm (Very Thin Whole, Honey Wheat Berry)
    f. Rye
        (1) Mrs. Wright's (Soft Deli, Jewish Seeded)
        (2) Schmidt's (Delicatessen)
    g. Pumpernickel
        (1) Manischewitz
        (2) Iverson (Light)
    h. Raisin- Arnold
    i. French
        (1) Vie de France (Regular, Mini Baguettes)
        (2) Colombo (Extra Sour)
    j. Italian
        (1) Pepperidge Farm
        (2) Schmidt's
        (3) F and S Marento (Vienna Style)
        (4) Mrs. Wright's

    k. Roman Meal - Schmidt's

l. Oatmeal
   (1) Columbia Union College
   (2) Pepperidge Farm
m. Oat - Arnold (Bran'nola)
n. Cinnamon
   (1) Pepperidge Farm
   (2) Mrs. Wright's
o. Honey Bran - Pepperidge Farm
p. Sourdough - Mrs. Wright's
q. Honey Oatberry - Mrs. Wright's
r. Black- Mrs. Wright's
s. Corn Bread - Aunt Jemima

15. Bread Crumbs/Cubes
   a. Mrs. Wright's - Unseasoned
   b. Devonsheer - Plain

16. Bread/Dough - Frozen
   a. Rich's (Enriched White Breads Dough, Enriched Homestyle Roll Dough)
   b. Thomas' (Protogen Protein Bread)
   c. Bellacicco - Safeway (Garlic)
   d. Bridgford - White
   e. Mrs. Butterworth's - White, Honeywheat, Dinner Rolls
   f. Mamma Bella - Garlic Bread
   g. Cole's - Garlic
   h. New York Brand - Breadsticks (garlic), Garlic bread

17. Bread Mixes
   a. Washington (Spoon Bread, Popover, Buttermilk Biscuit, Corn Bread, Corn Muffin, Bran Muffin, Raga Muffins (Blueberry, Apple and Cinnamon, Strawberry)
   b. Flako (Corn)
   c. Jiffy (Corn, Baking Mix)
   d. Pillsbury (Cranberry, Date, Hot Roll)
   e. Aunt Jemima (Corn)
   f. Bisquick (Buttermilk)
   g B + M (Brown Bread with Raisins)
   h Gingerbread
      (1) Washington
      (2) Betty Crocker
      (3) Nabisco (Dromedary)

18. Bread Sticks
    a. Angona's (Plain, Sesame, Whole Wheat)
    b. Flavor tree (Sesame)

19. Breakfast- frozen
    a. Swanson - Breakfast Blast- French Toast Sticks, Mini French Toast, Waffle Sticks
    b. Farm Rich - French Toast Sticks - Origina, Cinnamon
    c. Aunt Jemima - French Toast Sticks, French Toast, Morning Bites
    d. King's Hawaiian - French Toast

20. Breath Mints
    a. Warner-Lambert - Certs (Peppermint, Cinnamon, Wintergreen, Spearmint, Fruit)
    b. Ragold - Velamints (Spearmint, Peppermint)
    c. Nabisco - Breath Savers (Peppermint, Wintergreen), Life Savers (Peppermint, Wint O Green, Wild Cherry, Cryst O Mint, Butterscotch, Five Flavors)

21. Bulk Foods - Each store has different distributors for their bulk products. Therefore, read the labels just to be safe.
    a. Candy
        (1) Pastel Mints
        (2) Strawberry Licorice Sticks
        (3) Smarties
        (4) Gummy Cola Bears
        (5) Candy Corn
        (6) Gummy Bears
        (7) Pineapple Chunks
        (8) German Raspberries
        (9) Jelly Beans
        (10) Swedish Fish
        (11) Gum Drops
        (12) Spicettes
        (13) Bubble Gum Balls
    b. Fruits
        (1) Whole Prunes
        (2) Pitted Prunes
        (3) Dried Figs
        (4) Dried Pears
        (5) Apricot Halves
        (6) Pitted Dates

(7) Seedless Dark Raisins

c. Cereals
   (1) Bran
   (2) Bite Size Shredded Wheat
   (3) Corn Flakes
   (4) Quick Oats
   (5) Wheat Bran
   (6) Rolled Oats

d. Mixes
   (1) Buttermilk Pancake Mix
   (2) Biscuit Mix
   (3) Bran Muffin Mix
   (4) Corn Muffin Mix

e. Toppings
   (1) Pancake Syrup
   (2) Honey

f. Beans
   (1) Lentils
   (2) Pinto Beans
   (3) Great Northern Beans
   (4) Red Kidney Beans

g. Rice
   (1) Long Grain White Rice
   (2) Brown Rice
   (3) Long Grain and Wild Rice

h. Noodles
   (1) Whole Wheat Elbow Macaroni
   (2) Elbow Macaroni
   (3) Shells
   (4) Cut Ziti
   (5) Rigatoni
   (6) Rotini
   (7) Wide Egg Noodles
   (8) Spinach Noodles
   (9) Chow Mein Noodles

i. Snacks
   (1) Petite Pretzlers
   (2) Pretzel Nibs
   (3) Popcorn
   (4) Sesame Bread Sticks
   (5) Sesame sticks - Harmony Foods
   (6) Oriental Rice Crackers - Harmony

22. Butter
    a. Safeway
    b. Land O' Lakes (Regular, Country Morning Blend Lightly Salted, Unsalted)
    c. Blue Bonnet
    d. Breakstone (Whipped-Sweet, Lightly Salted)
    e. Lucerne (Sweet Cream, Unsalted- Whipped)

23. Candy (Avoid any Lemon, Lime, or Orange- Natural Flavors)
    a. Y and S – Twizzlers - Licorice (Black, Red)
    b. Switzer (Licorice Bites -Black-, Good and Plenty)
    c. Kraft (Caramels, Marshmallows)
    d. Goetze's (Caramel Creams)
    e. Spangler's (Dum Dum Pops)
    f. Nabisco (Life Savers Lollipops, Chuckles, JuJubes, Bonkers)
    g. Charms (Blow Pop)
    h. Mars (Skittles, Starburst)
    i. Vernell's (Buttermints)
    j. Heide (Gummi Bears, Juicy Fruits)
    k. Pearson (Carmel Nip)
    l. Brach's (Starlight Mints, Sparkles, Cinnamon Imperials)
    m. Pennsylvania Dutch - Candy Drops (Horehound, Wild Cherry)
    n. Werther's (Butter Flavor Drops)
    o. Ce De Candy - Smarties (All Flavors)
    p. Atkinson's (Mint Twists)
    q. Necco - Canada (Wintergreen, Original)
    r. Richardson (Pastel Mints, Jelly Center Mints)
    s. Borden - Campfire- Marshmallows
    t. Callard and Bowser (Butterscotch, Licorice Toffees, English Toffees)
24. Capers
    a. Crosse and Blackwell
    b. Bonavita (in Vinegar and Brine)
    c. Progresso

25. Cauliflower - Sweet Pickled - Heckman

26. Cereals - Dry
    a. Quaker (Puffed Wheat and Rice, Life (Regular, Cinnamon), Cap'n Crunch, Crunch Berries, Corn Bran, 100% Natural Oats and Honey, Oast, Honey, and Raisin)
    b. Ralston (Chex (Wheat, Rice, Corn, Bran), Cabbage Patch Kids, Sun Flakes, Multi-Bran, Urkelos, Double Chex)

c. Kellogg's (Fruitful Bran, Nutri-Grain -Wheat and Raisins, Wheat-, Corn Pops, Frosted Mini-Wheats, Cracklin'Oat Bran, Bran Buds, All-Bran, Bran Flakes, Apple Raisin Crisp, Product 19, Honey Smacks, Apple Jack, Crispix, Special K, Corn Flakes, Frosted Flakes, Rice Krispies, Common Sense- Oat Bran, Complete Bran Flaakes, Raisin Squares, Raisin Bran, Cinnamon Mini Buns, Frosted Bran)
d. Post (Alpha-Bits, Honey-Comb, Smurf-Berry Crunch, Super Golden Crisp, Fruit Pebbles, Grape-nuts -Raisin, Regular Flakes-, Natural Bran Flakes, Regular and Natural Raisin Bran, Fruit and Fibre, Honey Bunches of Oats)
e. Safeway (Frosted Flakes, Corn Flakes)
f. Nabisco (Shredded Wheat Team Flakes, Toasted Wheat and Raisins, Shredded Wheat'n Bran, Frosted Wheat Squares, Fruit Wheats)
g. General Mills (Fiber One, Crispy Wheat'n Raisins, Total, Golden Grahams, Honey Buc Wheat Crisp, Kix, Lucky Charms, Cinnamon Toast Crunch, Pac-Man, Trix, Cheerios, Wheaties, Triples, Berry Berry Kix, Apple Cinnamon Cheerios, Total- Raisin Bran)
h. Malt-O-Meal (Puffed Wheat, Sugar Puffs)
i. Town House (Crunchy Nuggets, Raisin Bran, Magic Stars, crispy Rice, Corn Flakes, Toasted Oats)
j. Health Valley (100% Natural Bran, Brown Rice Lites, Golden Corn Lites, Oat Bran Flakes, Organic Fiber 7 Flakes, Raisin Bran Flakes)
k. Good Shepherd - Wheat Bran
l. Kashi - Breakfast Pilaf
m. Kolln (Fruit'n Oat Bran Crunch, Oat Bran Crunch)
n. New Morning (Oatios, Crispy Rice, Corn Flakes, Natural Raisin Bran, Multi-Bran)

27. Cereals- Hot
a. Quaker (White Hominy Grits -Regular, Instant-, Instant Oatmeal -Maple and Brown Sugar, Apple and Cinnamon, Raisins and Spice, Peaches and Cream, Regular, Cinnamon Toast, Oat Bran)
b. Pillsbury (Farina)
c. Maypo Oatmeal
d. Wheatena (Bran and Wheat Germ)
e. Ralston (Whole Wheat - Instant)
f. Nabisco (Cream of Wheat - Regular, No Salt or Sugar Added-, Mix'n Eat-Cream of Wheat- Apple'n Cinnamon, Brown Sugar Cinnamon, Cream of Rice)
g. Mother's (Oat Bran, Whole Wheat)
h. Kretschner (Wheat Germ, Toasted Wheat Bran)
i. Date Tree (Brewer's Yeast)

j. Safeway (Quick Oats)
k. Town House (Hot Wheat, Instant Oatmeal- Apples and Cinnamon, Maple and Brown Sugar-, Quick Oats)

28. Chicken - Frozen
   a. Banquet (Chicken Nugget, Hot'n Spicy Chicken Nuggets, Breaded Chicken Patties)
   b. Weaver (Dutch Frye- Fried Chicken Breasts- Pieces with Ribs)

29. Chips
   a. Utz (Regular, Home Style, Tortilla, -Ripples)
   b. Cape Cod- Natural
   c. Nibble With Gibble's
   d. Lays - Regular
   e. Ruffles - Regualr
   f. Eagle (Thins, Ridged)
   g. Keeble - O'Boisies - Original
   h. Santitas - Tortilla
   i. Tostitos - White Corn Tortilla
   j. Sun Chips - Original

30. Cookies
   a. Keebler (Soft Batch -Sugar, Oatmeal Raisin-, Oatmeal Cremes, French Vanilla Creme, Cinnamon Sugar, Mini Middles-Oatmeal)
   b. Little Debbie (Raisin Creme Pie)
   c. FFV (Ginger Boy)
   d. Ripppin'Good (Coconut Bars, Granola Creme, Macaroon Creme, Creme Sandwich, Iced Spice, Sugar, Macaroon, Oatmeal)
   e. Le Petit - Beurre (Butter Biscuit)
   f. Nabisco (Lorna Doone, Brown Edge Wafers, Almost Home- Iced Oatmeal-, Animal Crackers, Oatmeal, Vanilla, Nilla Waffers, Ginger Snaps)
   g. Duncan Hines (Oatmeal Raisin, Oatmeal Cinnamon)
   h. Pepperidge Farm (Ginger Man, Sugar, Oatmeal Raisin, Molasses Crisp, Bordeaux Style, Raisin Bran, Chessman Butter, Irish Oatmeal, Shortbread)
   i. Archway (Sugar, Date or Apple Filled Oatmeal, Oatmeal, Old Fashioned Molasses, Coconut Macaroon, Gingersnaps)
   j. Stella D' Oro (Angel Wings, Sesame, Dietetic- Apple Pastry, Egg Biscuits, Anisette Toast, Anisette Sponge, Breakfast Treats)
   k. Carr's - Hob-nobs (Oatmeal, Honey Wheat Graham, Wheatmeal Biscuits)
   l. Murray (Goldi's Honey Bears, Sugar Wafers)

m. Sunshine - Oatmeal
n. Betty Crocker (Dunkaroos, Graham Cookies - Vanilla Frosting)

31. Cooking Spray
    a. PAM - Vegetable Oil (Regular, Butter Flavor)
    b. Mazola (Corn Oil)
    c. Baker's Joy (Soybean Oil)

32. Corn Meal
    a. Quaker (Yellow, Masa Harina - De Maiz)
    b. Indian Head (Yellow, White)
    c. Washington (White)
    d. Mrs. Wright's
    e. Town House
    f. Arrowhead Mills

33. Corn Starch
    a. Argo
    b. Cream

34. Corn Tortillas
    a. Baja
    b. Mariachi
    c. Mexicalli (don't use seasoning packet)

35. Cottage Cheese
    a. Lucerne
    b. Breakstone (Regular, Pineapple)

36. Crackers
    a. Paterson's (All Butter Shortbread)
    b. Pepperidge Farm (English Water Biscuits, Goldfish- Pretzel Flavor-, Cracked Wheat, Sesame, Hearty Wheat, English Water, Butter Thins)
    c. Red Oval Farms (Stoned Wheat Thins)
    d. Keebler (Sea Toast; Toasteds -Sesame, Rye, Buttercrisp; Wheat Snacks; Stones Creek -Sour Dough; Honey and Cinnamon Crisp Graham; Tuc; Waldorf- Low Sodium; Club; Zesta; Town House)
    e. Milk Lunch (New England Biscuits)
    f. Busy Baker (Wheatstone, Pumperknickel, Sesame, Graham)
    g. Chico San Inc.(Rice Cakes - Salted, Unsalted)
    h. Devonssheer (Melba Toast -Sesame, Wheat, Rye, Plain-, Melba Rounds - Plain, Garlic)

i. General Mills (Bugles)
j. FFV (Sesame Crisp Cracker and Wafer, Ocean Crisp)
k. Ralston (Natural Ry Krisp -Regular, Seasoned)
l. Nabisco (Oysterettes; Uneeda Biscuit; Social Tea Biscuits; Graham - Cinnamon Treats, Regular, Honey Maid; Premium Saltine- Salted, Low Salt; Ritz -Regular, Low Salt; Escort; Waverly; Wheat Thins; Wheatworth; Triscuit -Regular, Rye, Low Salt; Sociables, Mr. Phipps-original, fat free)
m. O.T.C. (Chowder and Oyster)

37. Cranberry Sauce
   a. Town House (Jellied)
   b. Ocean Spray (Jellied, Cran Raspberry, Whole Berry)

38. Cream Cheese – Block - with:
   a. Chives - Kraft- Philadelphia Brand
   b. Pimentos - Kraft
   c. Strawberries - Kraft
   d. Pineapple - Kraft
   e. Olive and Pimento - Kraft

39. Cream Cheese - Soft and Blocks
   a. Kraft - Philadelphia Brand (Regular)
   b. Lucerne

40. Creamers - Non-Dairy- Frozen
   a. Lucerne (Coffee Whitener)
   b. Rich's (Coffee Rich, Poly Rich)

41. Croissants
   a. Pepperidge Farm (All Butter)
   b. Vie de France (Butter)

42. Croutons - Safeway (Toasted Cubes)

43. Cucumber Slices - Sweet- Heckman

44. Delicatessen
   a. Meat - Turkey Breast, Chicken Breast
   b. Cheese- American - White, Yellow
   c. Packaged Meat
      (1) Oscar Mayer - Oven Roasted Turkey Breast

(2) Weaver - Chicken White Meat Roll

45. Desserts
   a. Duncan Hines (Oatmeal Raisin Cookie)
   b. Aunt Jemima (Coffee Cake)
   c. Cakes
      (1) Betty Crocker (Applesauce Raisin, Pound, Stir'n Frost -yellow(omit Frosting Mix), Date Bar, Super Moist - Yellow)
      (2) Duncan Hines (Angel Food, Spice, White, Yellow, Golden, Strawberry Supreme, French Vanilla)
      (3) Pillsbury Plus (White, Carrot'n Spice, Butter Recipe, Yellow, Streusel Swirl Cinnamon)
      (4) Mrs. Wright's (Yellow, Spice, Lemon- Artificial flavor-, White, Pound)
      (5) Washington (Yellow, White, Spice)
      (6) Nabisco – Dromedary - (Pound, Gingerbread)
      (7) Little Debbie (Donut Sticks, Holiday Snack Cakes, Apple Delights)
      (8) Hostess (Mini Coffee Cakes, Twinkies- regular, lights
   d. Pie Mixes- Box - Jello (Coconut Cream)
   e. Pudding and Pie Filling
      (1) Jello (Vanilla, Butterscotch, Tapioca- Box and refrigerated cups)
      (2) Royal (Vanilla)
      (3) Thank You - Rice, Tapioca
   f. Instant Pudding
      (1) Jello (French Vanilla, Coconut Cream, Vanilla, Vanilla Tapioca, Egg Custard Rice Pudding)
      (2) Royal (Vanilla)
      (3) Del Monte (Pudding Cup- Vanilla)
      (4) Hunt's - Snack Pack (Vanilla, Butterscotch, Tapioca)
      (5) Minute - Tapioca (Vanilla)
      (6) Town House (Vanilla, Butterschotch, Tapioca- Snack Cup)
   g. Gelatin Desserts
      (1) Jello (Strawberry -Regular, Sugar Free-, Black Raspberry, Peach, Apricot, Cherry and Raspberry -Regular, Sugar Free)
      (2) Town House (Strawberry, Cherry, Raspberry)
   h. Pie - Entenmann's - Coconut Custard, Homestyle Apple

46. Desserts - Accessories
   a. Sauces - Evans (Butterscotch, Pineapple)
   b. Cone Cups
      (1) Tem-T Double Heder Cones, Sugar Cones
      (2) Party Pride -Safeway

47. Dessert Decorations
   a. Frostings
      (1) Washington (Creamy White)
      (2) Betty Crocker (Fluffy White, Creamy Vanilla, Creamy Deluxe Vanilla, Cream Cheese)
      (3) Duncan Hines (Vanilla)
      (4) Pillsbury (Vanilla)
      (5) Mrs. Wright's (White)
   b. Candies - Cake Mate (Red, Green, Mixed, Cinnamon, Fruit Flavored)
   c. Icing
      (1) Cake Mate (Yellow, Red, Pink, Blue)
      (2) Pillsbury (Yellow, Green, Red)
   d. Coconut
      (1) Baker's
      (2) Town House
   e. Marshmallow Cream - Little Crow
   f. Whipped Topping Mix - Dream Whip

48. Desserts- Frozen
   a. Croissants
      (1) Vie de France (Butter)
      (2) Sara Lee (All Butter)
   b. Pies/Cobblers
      (1) Chef Pierre (Fully Baked Fresh Apple, Pumpkin)
      (2) Mrs. Smith's - "Pie in Minutes"(Cherry, Apple), Bake and Serve(Apple, Cherry, Dutch Apple Crumb, Pumpkin Custard, Natural Juice- Apple, Cherry)
      (3) Weight Watchers (Apple)
      (4) Sara Lee (Dutch Apple, Apple)
      (5) Marie Callender's (Peach, Apple, Cherry Cobbler)
   c. Buns- Morton (Honey)
   d. Donuts - Morton- Mini donuts (Sugar'n Spice)
   e. Cake - Sara Lee (Butter Streusel Coffee Cake, Original Pound Cake)
   f. Pastries
      (1) Pillsbury (Toaster Strudel- Blueberry, Apple, Strawberry, Breakfast Pastries)
      (2) Peppperidge Farm (Apple and Cherry Turnovers, Apple Fruit Square)
   g. Pie Crusts/Shells
      (1) Pepperidge Farm (Puff Pastry, Pie-Rolled Sheet)
      (2) Bel-air
      (3) Pet Ritz

h. Non-Diary Topping
    (1) Cool Whip
    (2) Party Whip Pride (Safeway)
i. Ice Cream
    (1) Heidi (Vanilla Cups)
    (2) Lact Aid - Lactose Reduced- Vanilla
    (3) Dairy Kiss (Vanilla)
    (4) Breyers (Vanilla, Strawberry)
    (5) Haagen Dazs (Vanilla, Strawberry, Honey Vanilla)
    (6) Lucerne (Vanilla, Peach, Wild Blackberry Marble, Strawberries and Cream)
    (7) Louis Sherry (Vanilla)
    (8) Edy's (Vanilla, Pumpkin)
    (9) Homestyle- Peach
j. Frozen Pops
    (1) Lucerne (Fruit Juice Bars-all artificial)
    (2) Jello - Gelatin Pops (Strawberry, Variety Pops-not Orange)
    (3) Dole (Fruit'n Juice, Peach, Strawberry)
k. Cream Bars - Dole (Peach, Strawberry, Raspberry)
l. Juice Bars - Dole (Strawberry, Pineapple, Raspberry)
m. Sherbert
    (1) Lucerne (Pineapple, Raspberry)
    (2) Dole- Fruit Sorbet (Pineapple)
n. Fruit Ice
    (1) Mama Tish's - Gourmet Sorbetto (Strawberry)
    (2) Dole (Strawberry)
o. Ice Milk
    (1) Lucerne (Vanilla)
    (2) Sweet'n Low (Frozen Dietary Dairy Dessert- Vanilla)
p. Fruit
    (1) Bel-air (Red Raspberries, Strawberries, Blueberries, Dark Sweet Cherries, Peach)
    (2) Brady (Blueberries)
    (3) Birds Eye (Strawberries)

49. Dietetic Foods
    a. Syrup - Cary's - Artificially Sweetened
    b. Preserves/Jelly - Polaner (Strawberry, Grape)
    c. Tuna - Chicken of the Sea (Low Sodium)
    d. Juices
        (1) Diet Delight (Tomato - Low Sodium)
        (2) Ocean Spray (Cranberry Juice Cocktail)

   e. Tomatoes - Diet Delight (Low Sodium)
   f. Vegetable Juice - V-8 (No Salt Added)
   g. Canned Fruit
      (1) Diet Delight (Bartlett Pears, Cling Peaches, Fruits for Salad, Fruit Cocktail)
      (2) White House (Unsweetened Apple Sauce)
   h. Soups- Campbell's (Chicken Broth -Low Sodium-, Cream of Mushroom - Low Sodium)
   i. Sweetners - Sugar Replacement
      (1) Sugar Twin (Brown Sugar, Regular)
      (2) Equal (Regular)
      (3) Sweet'n (Regular)
   j. Gelaltin - D-Zerta (Raspberry, Strawberry)
   k. Whipped Topping Mix - D-Zerta
   l. Candy- Estes Drops (Licorice, Fruit Assortment)
   m. Cookies - Estes (Vanilla Creme Filled Wafers, Coconut Cookies, Vanilla Thin, Wheat Wafers, Oatmeal Raisin)
   n. Diet Meals - Sego (Strawberry, Vanilla)

50. Dough Wrappers for Vegetables
   a. Won Ton - Nemco
   b. Egg Roll - Nemco

51. Drinks - Frozen in Cans
   a. Apple Juice
      (1) Seneca
      (2) Bel-air
   b. Grape Juice
      (1) Seneca
      (2) Welch's
      (3) Bel-air
   c. Cranberry Apple cocktail - Welch's
   d. Cranberry Juice Cocktail - Welch's
   e. Fruit Punch - Minute Maid
   f. Cranberry Raspberry Juice Cocktail - Welch's
   g. Cranberry Cherry Juice Cocktail - Welch's

52. Drinks - Powdered and Liquid
   a. Package, Box
      (1) Grape
         (a) Kool-Aid
         (b) CragMont

(c) Hi-C
(d) Ssips
(e) Capri Sun
(f) Welchade
(g) Sweet ripe
(h) Libby's

(2) Cherry
(a) CragMont
(b) Kool Aid
(c) Hi-C

(3) Apple
(a) Capri Sun
(b) Ssips
(c) Hi-C (Candy Apple Cooler)
(d) Mc Cain

(4) Sunshine Punch - Kool-Aid
(5) Mountain Berry Punch - Kool-Aid
(6) Tropical Punch - Kool-Aid
(7) Rainbow Punch - Kool-Aid
(8) Strawberry - Kool-Aid
(9) Black Cherry - Kool-Aid
(10) Wild Berry - Hi-C
(11) Double Fruit Cooler - Hi-C
(12) Cranberry Juice Cocktail - Ocean Spray
(13) Cranapple - Ocean Spray
(14) Cran-Grape - Ocean Spray
(15) Cran-Raspberry - Ocean Spray
(16) Cran-tastic - Ocean Spray
(17) Vegetable - V-8 (Spicy Hot, Regular)
(18) Mixed berry Grape - Boku (McCain)
(19) Black Cherry/White Grape - Boku
(20) Fruity Bubble Gum - Hi C
(21) Fruit Punch - Minute Maid
(22) Apple- Grape Raspberry - Welch's
(23) Apple/Cherry - McCain
(24) Great Bluedini - Kool-Aid
(25) Rock-A-Dile Red - Kool-Aid
(26) Raspberry - Kool-Aid

b. Plastic bottles

(1) General Mills (Squeezit - Silly billy, Strawberry, Chucklin'Cherry, Berry B. Wild, Mean Green Puncher, Grumpy Grape)

(2) Mondo (Fruit Squeezers - Global Grape, Chillin'Cherry, Legendary Berry)
(3) Kool-Aid (Kool Bursts - Grape, Great Bluedini, Rock-A-DileRed, Tropical Punch, Cherry)
(4) Little Hug (Fruit flavored Punch, Grape, Strawberry, Blue Raspberry)

53. Eggs

54. Fish and Seafood - Canned
a. Salmon
(1) Pillar Rock (Red)
(2) Libby's (Red, Pink)
(3) Bumble Bee (Red, Pink)
(4) Pink Beauty (Pink)
b. Sardines
(1) Empress (in Tomato Sauce)
(2) Spirit of Norway (in Water, Oil)
(3) Sea Trader (in Oil)
(4) King Oscar (in Oil)
(5) Underwood (in Oil, Mustard and Tomato Sauce)
(6) Fisherman's Net (in Oil, Mustard Sauce)
(7) Beach Cliff
c. Smoked Oysters - Empress
d. Shrimp- Orleans - Deveined- Tiny cocktail
e. Mackerel - Star-Kist
f. Kipper Snacks - King Oscar
g. Tuna Fish
(1) Star-Kist
(2) Bumble Bee
(3) Sea Trader
(4) Chicken of the Sea
(5) Deep Blue
h. Herring Steaks - Beach Cliff (Oil,Mustard/Hot Sauce)
i. Codfish Cakes - Gorton's
j. Clam Dip - Doxsee
k. Clams
(1) Doxsee (Chopped, Minced)
(2) American Original (Chopped)
(3) Sea Trader (Chopped, Minced)
(4) Crab Meat - Harris (Claw, White)

55. Flour
   a. Swans Down - Cake
   b. Betty Crocker - Softasilk- Cake
   c. Pillsbury- Shake and Blend (for Gravies), All Purpose, Bread
   d. Gold Medal - All Purpose, Wondra
   e. Mrs. Wright's (All Purpose, Whole Wheat, Old Fashioned)
   f. Washington
   g. Arrowhead Mills - Rye, Soy, Whole Wheat, Pastry, Buckwheat, Brown Rice
   h. Town House - All Purpose

56. Flour Tortillas - Pinata

57. Fruit- Canned
   a. Pears
      (1) Libby's (Lite)
      (2) Diet Delight
      (3) Town House
      (4) Del Monte
      (5) Country Pure (Lite)
   b. Peaches
      (1) Libby's (Lite)
      (2) Town House
      (3) Diet Delight
      (4) Del Monte
      (5) Country Pure (Lite)
   c. Pineapple
      (1) Dole (Sliced, Chunks, Crushed)
      (2) Del Monte (Sliced, Chunks, Crushed)
      (3) Town House (Crushed, Sliced -Juice Pack-, Chunks)
   d. Mixed Fruit - Libby's (Lite, Chunky)
   e. Fruit Cocktail
      (1) Town House (Regular)
      (2) Libby's (Lite)
      (3) Del Monte
      (4) Country Pure (Lite)
   f. Apricots- Country Pure

58. Fruits For Decorating Bakery Items
   a. Green Cherries - Liberty
   b. Red Pineapple Slices - Liberty
   c. Colored Pineapple Wedges - Liberty

d. Pineapple slices - Liberty
e. Red Cherries - Liberty
f. Red and Green Pineapple Slices - Liberty

59. Fruit- Dried
   a. Raisins
      (1) Town House
      (2) Sun Maid
      (3) Bonner
      (4) Sun Giant
   b. Prunes
      (1) Del Monte (Extra large)
      (2) Sunsweet (Large, Medium)
      (3) Town House (Large)
      (4) Scotch Buy
   c. Apricots
      (1) Sunsweet
      (2) Scotch Buy
   d. Spiced Apple Rings
      (1) White House
      (2) Musselman's
   e. Apples - Town House
   f. Mixed Fruit - Town House

60. Fruit Snacks
   a. Sunkist - Fun Fruits (Grape)
   b. Fruit Corners - Fruit Bar (Cherry, Grape), Fruit Roll-Ups- Cherry, Strawberry, Grape)
   c. Betty Crocker - Gushers, Fruit By The Foot(Grape, Strawberry), Incredibites

61. Granola Bars
   a. Nature Valley - Apple Cinnamon, Oats'N Honey
   b. Nature's Choice - Cinnamon and Raisin
   c. Kellogg's - Nutri-Grain- Raspberry, Apple

62. Gum
   a. Wrigley's - Freedent -Peppermint, Cinnamon, Spearmint-, Big Red - Cinnamon-, Spearmint, Juicy Fruit, Doublemint)
   b. Warner-Lambert - Clorets, Dentyne, Chewels
   c. Adams - Chiclets (Peppermint)
   d. Blammo - Fruit Flavor Bubble

e. Fleer - Doubble Bubble
f. Life Savers - Bubble Yum (Regular, Sugarless, Strawberry); Care-Free (Cinnamon, Peppermint, Bubble, Spearmint)
g. Trident (Cinnamon, Original, Spearmint, Bubble)
h. Topps - Bazooka Bubble Gum

63. Ham Glaze - Baked - Mrs. Schlorer's - Can't have the Nitrates

64. Honey
    a. Walker's (Clover)
    b. Sue Bee (Spun)
    c. Natural - Clover (Unfiltered)
    d. Smith Family's

65. Instant Breakfast Drink - Lucerne

66. International Foods
    a. Bean Sprouts- La Choy
    b. Chow Mein Noodles
        (1) Chun King
        (2) La Choy
    c. Tomatoes
        (1) With Jalapenos - Ole El Paso
        (2) In Chili Gravy - Gebhardt
    d. Green Chilies - Old El Paso
    e. Peppers
        (1) Jalapenos
            (a) Old El Paso - Pickled
            (b) Gebhardt (Whole, Sliced)
        (2) Salonika Peppers in Brine and Vinegar - Krinos
    f. Vegetables
        (1) Pinto - Gebhardt
        (2) Jalapeno Refried Beans - Gebhardt
        (3) Beans - Red Kidneys, Pink, White, Black, Roman, Pinto, Great Northern Lima, Frijoles Negros, Fideos - Goya
        (4) Lentils - Goya
        (5) Yellow Split Peas - Goya
        (6) Pickled Baby Corn - Castle Village
        (7) Grape Leaves - Krinos
        (8) Hearts of Palm - Rail
        (9) White Asparagus Spears - Bonavita
        (10) Whole Hearts of Artichokes - Cresca

g. Pickles- Crisp Hot Okra - Talko
h. Olives
    (1) Black- in Brine - Krinos
    (2) Calamata - in Oil and Vinegar - Krinos
i. Whole Mushrooms - Castle Village
j. Spice/Seasonings
    (1) Chili Powder - Gebhardt
    (2) Hot Sauce - Goya
    (3) Seasoning- for Vegetables, Gravies, soups - Maggi
    (4) Guava Paste - Ancel
    (5) Anchovy Paste - Giovannis
    (6) Hungarian Paprika - Szeged
    (7) Mild Curry Sauce - The Good Food People
k. Jellies - Robertson's (Blackberry, Red Currant, Black Currant, Strawberry)
l. Preserves
    (1) Damson Plum - Robertson's
    (2) Ginger - Robertson's
    (3) Jellied Mint Sauce - Reese
m. Mustard
    (1) Hot'n'Sweet - Chalif
    (2) English Hot Ready Mixed - Colman's
    (3) Prepared Old Style - Maille
    (4) Prepared Dijon - Maille
n. Cookies/Crackers
    (1) Fortune Cookies - Umeya
    (2) Wafers - Bremner
    (3) Sesame Crackers - Bremner
    (4) Cream Crackers - Jacob's
    (5) Biscuits for Cheese - Jacob's
    (6) Shortbread - Paterson's
    (7) Table Water Crackers - Carr's
    (8) Cocktail Toast - Jos Poell
    (9) Norwegiun Flatbread Thin - Kavli
    (10) Fiber Crisp Bread with Sesame Seeds - Ideal
    (11) Finn Crisp - Shafer, Clark, and Co.
    (12) Wasa Crisp Bread Fiber - Shafer, Clark, and Co.
    (13) Biscottes - Jaret
    (14) Stoned Wheat Thins - Red Oval Farms
    (15) Bread Sticks - Ferrara
    (16) Toasted Corn - Cornnuts
    (17) Unsalted Rice Crunch Crackers - Kitanihan

(18) Sesame Flavored Rice Crackers - Marukai
(19) Butter Cookies - Kjeldsens

o. Drinks/Mixes
   (1) Black Currant Drink Concentrate - Ribena
   (2) Cream of Coconut
      (a) Coco Lopez
      (b) Coco Casa
   (3) Pina Colada Mix - Coco Lopez
   (4) Non-Alcoholic Grape Juice - Meier's
   (5) Sparkling Catawba - Meier's
   (6) Pink Sparkling Catawba - Meier's
   (7) Clear Catawba - Meier's
   (8) Sparkling Cider - Non-Alcoholic- Martinelli's
   (9) Strawberry Colada Mix - Coco Lopez
p. Fish
   (1) Natural Snails - Helix
   (2) Caviar - Lumpfish, Whitefish - Romanoff
q. Swedish Pancake Mix - Lund's
r. Bavarian Potato Dumpling Mix - Panni
s. Irish Beef Steak and Mushroom Pie - Tipperard
t. Rice
   (1) Long Grain - Goya
   (2) Wild - Maille
u. Wheat- Bulgar - Old World
v. Caviar - Romanoff's - North American Salmon, Whitefish, Black Lumpfish, Red Lumpfish
w. Water Chestnuts
   (1) La Choy
   (2) Reese
x. Bamboo Shoots - Reese
y. Refried Beans
   (1) Ortega
   (2) Town House

67. Jelly
   a. Blackberry - Empress
   b. Apple - Empress
   c. Grape
      (1) Empress
      (2) Welch's (Concord)
   d. Strawberry - Empress
   e. Raspberry - Empress

f. Mint - Polaner
g. Grape Jam
  (1) Empress
  (2) Polaner
  (3) Welch's - Squeezable (Regular, Concord)
  (4) Polaner (Low-Sugar)
h. Guava - Polaner
i. Crab Apple - Empress

68. Juices- Can/Bottles
  a. Grape
    (1) Welch's (Red, White, Vineyard Juice Blend)
    (2) Town House
    (3) Minute Maid
    (4) Tree Ripe
    (5) Juice Works
    (6) Hi C
    (7) Gatorade
    (8) Very Fine
  b. Prune - Unsweetened
    (1) Sunsweet
    (2) Bennett's
    (3) Super Mott's
    (4) Town House
  c. Carrot - Hollywood Everady
  d. Cherry - Juice Works
  e. Pineapple
    (1) Dole
    (2) Del Monte
  f. Pure Purple - Juicy Juice
  g. Real Red - Juicy Juice
  h. Tomato Juice
    (1) Welch's
    (2) Town House
    (3) Libby's
    (4) Campbell's
    (5) Aunt Nellie's
    (6) Sacramento
    (7) Ritter
  i. Apple Juice
    (1) Town House (Country Style, Regular)
    (2) White House

(3) Red Cheek
(4) Tree Top
(5) Musselman's
(6) Mott's
(7) Very Fine
(8) Elliott's

j. Cranberry Juice Cocktail
   (1) Town House
   (2) Ocean Spray
   (3) Elliott's

k. Fruit Juice Punch
   (1) Tropicana (Chuggers)
   (2) Very Fine

l. Combinations
   (1) Ocean Spray (Cranberry-Raspberry, Cran-Strawberry, Cranapple, Cran Grape)
   (2) Town House - Cranberry-Raspberry
   (3) Apple and Eve - Raspberry Cranberry
   (4) R.W. Knudson (Black Cherry, Papaya Nectar, Cranberry Nectar)
   (5) Boku (McCain) - Mixed Berry Grape
   (6) After the Fall (Apple/apricot, Raspberries n' Cider, Oregon Berry, Apple Raspberry, Apple Cherry Juice, Apple Strawberry)
   (7) Tropicana (Cranberry-Raspberry, Strawberry)
   (8) Very Fine (Papaya Punch, Papaya Pineapple)

69. Juices- Chilled
   a. Grape Juice beverage - Welch's
   b. Apple/Papaya Juice - Daisy Fresh
   c. Apple Cider - Zeigler's
   d. Papaya Juice - Daisy Fresh

70. Ketchup - Del Monte

71. Kosher Food
   a. Borscht with Beets
      (1) Manischewitz
      (2) Mother's (Low Calorie, Old Fashioned)
   b. Soup Nuts - Horowitz Margareten
   c. Barley Shapes - Goodman's
   d. Alphabets (Barley) - Goodman's
   e. Egg Noodles - Goodman's
   f. Chow Mein Noodles - Horowitz Margareten

g. Roasted Buchwheat Kernels (Kasha) - Wolff's
h. Matzoh Meal
   (1) Seasoned, Unsalted - Horowitz Margareten
   (2) Unsalted- Manischewitz
i. Matzoh Crackers
   (1) Tam Tam-American Style, Miniatures - Manischewitz
   (2) Dietetic, Regular - Horowitz Margareten
j. Matzos
   (1) Dietetic Matzo Thins, Unsalted - Manischewitz
   (2) Whole Wheat, Unsalted - Horowitz Margareten
k. Tomatoes in Jar - Claussen
l. Horseradish
   (1) Kraft
   (2) Tulkoff
   (3) Herb's Double-H

72. Margarine - Liquid- Bottle
   a. Fleischmann's
   b. Parkay

73. Maraschino Cherries
   a. Town House
   b. Caspro

74. Margarine
   a. Lucerne
   b. Kitchen Queen
   c. Parkey
   d. Blue Bonnet
   e. Mrs. Filberts
   f. Promise
   g. Mazola
   h. Dew Fresh
   i. Imperial
   j. Land O' Lakes
   k Shedd's Spread- Country Crock

75. Mayonnaise
   a. Bright Day- Cholesterol Free
   b. Kraft (Light)

76. Meat- Canned
    a. Roast Beef Hash- Hormel
    b. Chili
        (1) Hormel (Beans- Hot, Regular)
        (2) Just-Rite (Hot Dog)
    c. Beef Stew- Hormel - Dinty Moore
    d. Beef with Barbeque Sauce
        (1) James River
        (2) Just-Rite
    e. Beef Tamales- Derby (With Sauce)
    f. Chicken in Broth- Swanson (Mixed, Premium Chunk White, Chunk White and Dark (Both in Water)

77. Fresh Meats - Ground Beef, Chicken, Chops, Steak, Roast, Brisket

78. Frozen Meats
    a. Turkey
        (1) Marval
        (2) Valley Star
        (3) Swift's Butterball
    b. Purdue's Oven Stuffer Roaster
    c. Calf Liver - Sweet'n Tender
    d. Cornish Game Hen - Tyson
    e. Diced Chicken Meat - Tyson
    f. Chick'n Chunks - Tyson
    g. Chicken Legs - Empire Kosher
    h. Turkey Roast - Empire Kosher
    i. Chicken Nuggets - Weaver
    j. Chicken Rondelets - Weaver
    k. Sandwich Steaks
        (1) Blue Diamond
        (2) Quaker Maid
        (3) Landis
        (4) Snow King

79. Milk in Cartons
    a. Regular, Low Fat - Farm Best
    b. Strawberry, Low Fat - Sips Ups

80. Milk - Canned and Dried
    a. Diet Milk Shakes - ALBA 77 (Vanilla, Strawberry)
    b. Instant Spiced Cider Mix - Alpine

c. Dairy Drink Mix - Alba 77
d. Malt Beverage
    (1) Ovaltine
    (2) Carnation
e. Diet Drink Mix - Nutrament - Vanilla
f. Creamers
    (1) Coffee Mate
    (2) Cremora
    (3) Lucerne
g. Milk in Box
    (1) Vanilla - Farm Best
    (2) Strawberry, Vanilla - Borden
h. Dried Milk
    (1) Sanalac
    (2) Lucerne
    (3) Carnation
i. Evaporated Milk
    (1) Lucerne
    (2) Pet
    (3) Carnation
j. Skimmed Milk - Carnation

81. Milk in Box - Borden (Strawberry, Vanilla)

82. Milk - Fresh (not Chocolate)

83. Molasses
    a. Mott's - Grandma's
    b. Brer Rabbit
    c. Plantation

84. Muffins
    a. Wheat's Honey - Mrs. Wright's
    b. Raisin Cinnamon - Mrs. Wright's
    c. Bran'nola - Arnold
    d. Hostess - Mini Muffins (Cinnamon Apple, Blueberry)
    e. Blueberry (box)
        (1) Duncan Hines
        (2) Betty Crocker
        (3) Martha White
        (4) Pillsbury

85. Muffins – Frozen - Pepperidge Farm (Blueberry, Corn)

86. Mustard
    a. Pure Prepared, Spicy - Town House
    b. Diable Hot, Spicy Brown - Gulden's
    c. Bold'n Spicy, Regular - French's
    d. Chinese Hot - La Choy
    e. Deli Horseradish - Tulkoff
    f. New York Deli Style - Herb's Double-H
    g. New York Deli Style - Ba-Tampte

87. Nach-Os - Safeway El Rio

88. Nectars
    a. Peach
        (1) Libby's
        (2) Heart's Delight
    b. Pear
        (1) Libby's
        (2) Heart's Delight
    c. Apricot
        (1) Town House
        (2) Libby's
        (3) Heart's Delight

89. Oil
    a. Olive
        (1) Progresso
        (2) Bertoilli Lucca
        (3) Pompeian
        (4) Lipi
        (5) Alessi Olio
        (6) Verdi
    b. Safflower - Hollywood
    c. Sesame - Kame
    d. Corn
        (1) Nu Made
        (2) Wesson
        (3) Town House
        (4) Crisco
        (5) Mazola
    e. Vegetable
        (1) Nu Made
        (2) Wesson

(3) Puritan
(4) Crisco
(5) Mazola
(6) Town House
(7) Piedmont
f. Sunflower Seed
(1) Wesson
(2) Nu Made
(3) Town House
g. Canola
(1) Town House
(2) Wesson

90. Olives
a. Chopped Ripe -Ehmann
b. Spanish Salad, Spanish Alcaparrodo, Super Colossal, Ripe, Jumbo Ripe , Extra Large Ripe, Chopped Ripe, Pitted, Spanish Manzanilla, Queen - All from Town House
c. Whole - Empress

91. Pancakes
a. Toaster Type - Downyflake
b. Microwave Type - Pillsbury
c. Blueberry, Butter, Buttermilk, Plain - Aunt Jemima

92. Pancake and Waffle Mix
a. Plain - Washington
b. Hungry Jack - Extra Light- Pillsbury
c. Buttermilk
(1) Pillsbury
(2) Mrs. Wright's
(3) Aunt Jemima
(4) Mrs. Butter-worth's
d. Complete Whole Wheat - Aunt Jemima
e. Buckwheat - Aunt Jemima
f. Shake'n Pour - Buttermilk, Blueberry - Bisquick
g, Bisquick (Original, Reduced Fat)

93. Pasta
a. Spaghetti - Thin and Regular
(1) San Giorgio
(2) Town House

(3) Mueller's
(4) Buitoni (#2,3)
(5) Casa de'Italia

b. Macaroni
(1) San Giorgio
(2) Town House
(3) Mueller's
(4) Casa de'Italia
(5) Light'n Fluffy (Macaroni Dumplings)

c. Fettuccini - San Giorgio

d. Shells
(1) San Giorgio
(2) Town House

e. Egg Noodles
(1) Mueller's (Old Fashioned, Regular)
(2) Pennsylvania Dutch
(3) Light 'n Fluffy (Spinach Egg)
(4) Prince (Spinach Egg)

f. Lasagna
(1) San Giorgio
(2) Town House

94. Peppers

a. Cherry
(1) Progresso
(2) Sun of Italy
(3) Town House

b. Tuscan - Progresso

c. Roasted - Progresso

d. Salad Chilli - Trappey's

e. Sweet - Ba Tampte

95. Pickles

a. Dill
(1) Town House (Baby Dill, Kosher Spears, Hamburger Dill)
(2) Heinz
(3) Vlasic (Kosher Spears)

b. Sweet Butter Chips - Vlasic (Half the Salt)

c. Bread and Butter - Best Foods

d. Gherkins
(1) Sweet Midget, Kosher Dill, Sweet - Heckman
(2) Sweet

(a) Town House
(b) Heinz
e. Sweet
(1) Slices
(a) Heckman
(b) Town House (Whole, Chips)
f. Sour- Heckman

96. Pie Crust Mix - in Box
a. Flako
b. Jiffy
c. Pillsbury
d. Betty Crocker
e. Keebler (Graham Cracker, Butter Flavored)
f. Nabisco (Graham Cracker Crumbs)

97. Pie Fillings
a. Cherry - Comstock (Lite, Regular)
b. Poppy - Solo
c. Peach - Comstock
d. Blueberry - Comstock
e. Mincemeat - Borden
f. Pumpkin - Libby's
g. Sliced Apples - White House

98. Pizza Kit - Tambellini

99. Popcorn - Jar and Bag
a. Jiffy Pop
b. Town House
c. TV Time
d. Orville Redenbacher's (Microwave- Natural/Butter, Natural Light)
e. Pops-Rite (in Popping Oil, Plain)
f. Jolly Time

100. Preserves
a. Black Raspberry- Empress
b. Apricot
(1) Empress
(2) Polaner (Low Sugar, Natural)
c. Raspberry
(1) Empress

(2) Polaner (Red)
d. Blackberry- Empress
e. Strawberry
(1) Empress
(2) Polaner (Regular, Low Sugar)
(3) Kraft
(4) Knott's
(5) Jam Lovers
f. Blackberry - Empress
g. Peach - Empress
h. Plum - Empress
i. Pineapple - Empress
j. Blueberry - Empress
k. Grape - Kraft
l. Boysenberry - Knott's
m. Plum - Sharon Valley

101. Pretzels
a. Old Fashioned Hard
(1) Synder's of Hanover (Salted, Unsalted)
(2) Utz (Salted, Unsalted)
(3) Synder's (Sour Dough)
(4) Synder's (Unsalted)
(5) Town House
(6) Rold Gold

102. Produce
a. Fruits - Kiwi, Apples, Melons, Grapes, Pears, Pineapple, Cantaloupe
b. Vegetables - Cabbage, Carrots, Tomatoes, Celery, Radish, Beets, Lettuce, Peppers, Brussels Sprouts, Cranberries, Escarole, Bok Choy, Eggplant, Spinach, String Beans, Squash, Bean Sprouts, Artichokes, Tomarillo, Corn, Asparagus, Okra, Cucumbers, Broccoli, Cauliflower, Turnips, Collard Greens, Kale, Potatoes, Alfalfa, Sprouts, Garlic, Mushrooms, Tofu, Parsley, Watercress

103. Relish
a. Sweet Pickle
(1) Heckman
(2) Town House
b. Hot Dog - Town House
c. India - Heinz

104. Rice
   a. Brown
      (1) Uncle Ben's
      (2) Mahatma
   b. Long Grain Enriched
      (1) Town House
      (2) Success Rice
      (3) Minute Rice

105. Rolls
   a. Dinner
      (1) Arnold
      (2) Mrs. Wright's (Party)
      (3) Home Pride
      (4) Pepperidge Farm
   b. Brown and Serve Party
      (1) Mrs. Wright's
      (2) Wonder (Regular, Gem Style)
   c. Sour Dough French - Colombo
   d. Parker House - Pepperidge Farm
   e. Club- Regular, Golden Twist - Pepperidge Farm
   f. Submarine - Mrs. Wright's
   g. Hard - Safeway.
   h. Hot Dog
      (1) Mrs. Wright's
      (2) European Bakers
   i. Hamburger
      (1) Mrs. Wright's
      (2) European Bakers
   j. Kaiser- Mrs. Wright's

106. Salad Bar
   a. Vegetables etc. - Bok Choy, Bean Sprouts, Noodles, Tofu, Garbanzo Beans, Lettuce, Kidney Beans, Beets, Red Cabbage, Broccoli, Cauliflower, Tomatoes, Celery, Squash, Green Peppers, Pickles, Cucumbers, Carrots, Olives, Hot Peppers, Tuna, Eggs, Artichoke, Mushrooms, Cantaloupe, Honeydew, Cottage Cheese, Jell-O
   b. Dressings - Walden Farms (Low Fat Thousand Island)
   c. Juices - Nice and Natural (Cranberry Plum, Very Cherry)

107. Salad Dressing
   a. French

(1) Nu Made
(2) Kraft (Regular, Reduced Calorie)
(3) Milami 1890
(4) Wishbone

b. Thousand Island - Nu Made
c. Italian
   (1) Seven Seas
   (2) Wishbone (Lite- Less Oil)
   (3) Henri's
d. Green Goddess
   (1) Nu Made
   (2) Seven Seas
e. Cole Slaw
   (1) Kraft
   (2) Marzettis
   (3) Eastern Foods
f. Poppy Seed - Eastern Foods
g. Chili con Queso - Eastern Foods
h. Cracked peppercorn - Marzettis

108. Salads in Jars
   a. Salad Cubes – Sweet - Town House
   b. Pepper - Progresso
   c. Olive - Progresso

109. Sandwich Steaks- Frozen
   a. Safeway
   b. Steak-umm

110. Sauces
   a. Barbecue
      (1) Heinz (100% Natural)
      (2) Bad News (All Purpose)
   b. Hot
      (1) Durkee (Red Hot, Cayenne Pepper)
      (2) Trappey's
      (3) Tabasco
      (4) Tulkoff (Tiger)
   c. Dip'Um (French, Creamy, Mustard, Char-broiled BBQ, Hot Mustard, Sweet n'Sour)
   d. Mint - Crosse and Blackwell
   e. Worcestershire

(1) Town House
(2) French's

f. Sandwich and Salad
(1) Durkee
(2) Aunt Nellie's (Old Style)

g. Oyster - China bowl

h. Sweet and Sour
(1) La Choy
(2) Ty Ling

i. Soy
(1) Kikkoman (Lite, Regular)
(2) La Choy
(3) Chung King
(4) Angostura
(5) Ty Ling
(6) Kame
(7) House of Tsang

j. Pizza - Progresso
k. Cocktail - Tulkoff
l. Tomato/Pasta - Classico
m. Chili Oil - Kame
n. Sesame Oil - Ty Ling
o. Duck - Ty Ling
p. Hoisin - Ty Ling
q. Chicken Wing (Hot) - Chelten House
r. Chicken Glaze - Chelten House

111. Sauces and Gravies - in Packages
a. Hollandaise - McCormick
b. Chicken - French's
c. Turkey - French's
d. Beef and Broccoli - Sun-Bird
e. Teriyaki Marinade - Sun-Bird

112. Seafood- Fresh-

a. Fish: Spots, Blue, Sea Trout, Orange Roughy, Sole, Perch, Whiting, Red Snapper, Monk, Salmon, Flounder, Sword, Hake, Rainbow Trout, Mackerel, others.
b. Shrimp
c. Crab
d. Lobster

113. Seafood- Frozen
   a. Shrimp
      (1) Carnation (Shrimp Crisps)
      (2) Sea Pak (Breaded Butterfly, Shrimp'n Batter)
      (3) Rik-Sha (Breaded Fantail- don't use Sauce Mix)
      (4) Bee Gee (Cooked Shrimp Ring, Cooked Shrimp Pieces)
      (5) El Dorado (Breaded Round)
      (6) Ocean Beauty
      (7) Sea Maid
      (8) Brilliant (Ready to Cook, Cooked)
      (9) Treasure Isle (Cooked)
   b. Turbot- Virginia Capes Seafood
   c. Ocean Perch
      (1) Van de Kamp
      (2) Taste O' Sea
   d. Flounder
      (1) Van de Kamp
      (2) Taste O' Sea
      (3) Mrs. Paul's (Light Breaded)
   e. Cod- Van de Kamp
   f. Haddock
      (1) Van de Kamp
      (2) Taste O' Sea
      (3) Mrs. Paul's (don't use Sauce Mix)
   g. Sole- Van de Kamp
   h. Fish Fillets
      (1) Van de Kamp
      (2) Mrs. Paul's (omit Sauce Mix: Supreme Crunchy Light, Buttered, All Natural Bread Crumbs)
   i. Crabmeat - Wakefield
   j. Crabmeat and Shrimp - Wakefield
   k. Salmon Steak - Wakefield (don't use seasoning mix)
   l. Halibut Steak - Wakefield (Alaska Style-don't use Seasoning Mix)
   m. Swordfish Steak - Wakefield (don't use Seasoning Mix)
   n. Crabs
      (1) Wakefield (Snow Crab Claws)
      (2) Jana's Ocean Magic (Imitation Crab Salad Meat)
   o. Lobster- Northern Light
   p. Squid- Sea Fresh USA (Calamari Style)
   q. Mixed Seafood- Delicaseas (Sea Tails- Whole, Sea Stix, Salad Style)
   r. Fish Sticks
      (1) Taste O' Sea

    (2) Mrs. Paul's (don't use Sauce Mix)
    (3) Cod- Taste O' Sea
s. Cod- Taste O' Sea
t. Fried Clams
    (1) Howard Johnson's
    (2) Mrs. Paul's (Light Batter-don't use Sauce Mix)
u. Crab Delights - Leg and Flake Style- Louis Kemp
v. Lobster Delights - Louis Kemp

114. Seasonings
a. McCormick/Schilling: Celery (Seed, Salt), Cardamon, Allspice, Anise Seed, Arrowroot, Basil Leaves, Bay Leaves, Nutmeg, Chili Powder, Chives, Cinnamon, Cloves, Curry Powder, Garlic Powder, Parsley Flakes, Coriander, Cream of Tartar, Marjoram, Italian, Powdered Horseradish, Ginger, Mustard, Mint Flakes, Paprika, Oregano, Dill Weed, Cumin, Fines Herbes, Fennel Seed, Thyme, Tarragon Leaves, Sesame Seed, Savory, Salad Herbs, Sage, Rosemary Leaves, Pumpkin, Pickling Spice, Apple Pie, Sour Salt, Imitation Butter Flavor Salt, Pepper, Old Bay
b. Crown Colony: Cloves, Leaf Sage, Pepper, Garlic Salt, Green Bell Peppers, Hot Chilies, Mint Flakes, Oregano, Sliced Mushroom, Allspice, Paprika, Cumin, Mustard, Marjoram, Cinnamon, Caraway Seed, Ginger, Nutmeg, Chili Powder, Poppy Seed, Dill Seed, Italian, Parsley Flakes, Imitation Butter Flavor, Basil, Ground Mace
c. Sugar
    (1) Domino (Regular, Brown, Confectionary)
    (2) Town House (Regular, Powdered, Brown)
d. Food Coloring
    (1) McCormick/Schilling
    (2) Crown Colony
e. Salt Substitute
    (1) McCormick/Schilling (Regular)
    (2) Adolph's
    (3) No Salt
f. Tenderizer- Adolph's (Seasoned, Unseasoned)
g. Salt
    (1) Morton (Lite, Regular, Coarse Kosher)
    (2) Crown Colony
h. Seafood
    (1) Old Bay
    (2) McCormick/Schilling
    (3) Crown Colony

115.Snacks in Containers

a. Currants - Fagus Ranch
b. Chopped Dates
    (1) Nabisco (Dromedary)
    (2) SunGiant
    (3) Dole
c. Pitted Dates
    (1) SunGiant
    (2) Nabisco (Dromedary)
    (3) Dole
d. Figs - Producer's (California Calimyran)
e. Apple Chunks - Sun-Maid
f. Peaches - Sun-Maid

116. Snack Spreads

a. Pineapple
b. Pimento
c. Olive and Pimento
d. Old English

117. Soft Drinks

a. Cola - Regular
    (1) RC
    (2) Pepsi
    (3) Coke (New Coke, Classic)
    (4) CragMont (Regular, Natural)
b. Cola- Cherry
    (1) RC
    (2) Coke
c. Diet Cola
    (1) RC (Diet RC 100, Diet Rite)
    (2) Pepsi (Diet, Diet Pepsi Free, Pepsi Light)
    (3) Coke
    (4) CragMont (No Caffeine)
    (5) Faygo
    (6) Tab (Regular, Caffeine Free)
d. Caffeine Free Cola
    (1) Pepsi (Pepsi Free)
    (2) Coke
e. Root Beer
    (1) Hires
    (2) A and W

(3) CragMont (Regular, Diet)
(4) Faygo (Diet - Western Style)
(5) Naturale 90

f. Ginger Ale
   (1) CragMont (Regular)
   (2) Canada Dry (Regular, Cherry)
   (3) Suburban (Golden, Pale Dry)
   (4) Faygo (Diet - English Style)
   (5) Seagram's
g. Black Cherry
   (1) CragMont
   (2) Suburban (Almond Smash)
   (3) Faygo (Diet - Red Pop, Cherry Berry)
   (4) Naturale 90
h. Grape - CragMont (Regular)
i. Strawberry - CragMont
j. Club
   (1) CragMont
   (2) Canada Dry
   (3) Suburban
k. Birch Beer - Pennsylvania Dutch (Caffeine Free)
l. Tonic Water
   (1) CragMont
   (2) Canada Dry
   (3) Schweppes
   (4) Seagram's
m. Seltzer Water - Vintage
n. Spring Water
   (1) Perrier (Natural - no twist of Lemon)
   (2) Safeway
   (3) Polar
   (4) Great Bear
   (5) Sundance (Raspberry, Cranberry, Black Currant, Sour Cherry)
   (6) Mistic (Raspberry, Boysenberry, Tropical Supreme)
   (7) Glacier Ridge (Raspberry Vanilla, Guava Berry)
o. Chocolate (Artifically Flavored)
   (1) Faygo - Diet (Chocolate Cream)
   (2) Canfield's - Diet Chocolate Fudge
p. Non-Alcoholic Malt Beverage
   (1) Heileman's Kingsbury
   (2) Birell
   (3) Moussy

(4) Kingsbury
(5) Black Label

q. Natural ginger Beer - Naturale 90
r. Raspberry - Naturale 90
s. Cream - Naturale 90
t. Non-Alcoholic Wines/Champagne
   (1) Meier's (Sparkling Burgundy, Catawba)
   (2) St. Regis (Red, Blanc, Rose, White Zinfandel, Chardonnay, Cabernet Sauvignon, Johannesburg Riesling Champagne)
   (3) Bauser - Champagne

118. Soft Margarine
   a. Lucerne (Light)
   b. Fleischmann's (Regular, Extra Light)
   c. Mrs. Filberts
   d. Land O' Lakes (Regular, Light)
   e. Chiffon
   f. Promise (Ultra, Extra Light)
   g. Shedd's Spread
   h. Parkay- Light
   i. Mazola
   j. Diet Imperial
   k. Soft Diet Parkay
   l. Weight Watchers
   m. Coldbrook - Safeway (Light)

119. Sour Beef Mix - Mrs. Minnick's

120. Sour Cream
   a. Lucerne
   b. Breakstone
   c. King (Cholesterol Free, Regular)

121. Soup - Campbell's (Healthy Request - Tomato, Chicken Broth, Split Pea)

122. Sparkling Cider - Martinelli's (Non-Alcoholic)

123. Specialty Items - Frozen
   a. Broccoli - Green Giant (Broccoli Fanfare, Broccoli-Cauliflower Medley)
   b. Corn Fritters - Mrs. Paul's
   c. Apples - Stouffer's - Escalloped
   d. Bellacicco - Safeway

e. Pretzels - Dutchie (Penn. Dutch Soft)
f. Microwave Popcorn
    (1) Orville Redenbacher (Butter Flavor)
    (2) Pillsbury (Butter Flavor, Regular)
g. Blintzes - Golden Brand (Blueberry)
h. Cavatelli - D'Orazio (Home Style)

124. Stuffing Mix - Safeway (Herb Seasoned)

125. Syrup
a. Karo (Dark, Light, Pancake)
b. King (Regular)
c. Cary's (Maple)
d. Polaner (Strawberry, Blueberry, Raspberry, Black Cherry)
e. Empress (Pancake) - (Regular, Lite)
f. Log Cabin (Regular, Lite)
g. Vermont Maid (Golden Griddle)
h. Aunt Jemima (Regular, Lite)
i. Mrs. Butterworth's (Regular, Lite)
j. Piedmont - Waffle and Pancake
k. Hungry Jack - Lite

126. Toaster Tarts (Pop Tarts)
a. Cherry
b. Blueberry
    (1) Town House
    (2) Kellogg's
    (3) Toast'em
c. Apple
d. Brown Sugar Cinnamon
    (1) Town House
    (2) Kellogg's
    (3) Toast'em
e. Strawberry
    (1) Kellogg's
    (2) Toast'em
f. Dutch Apple
g. Frosted Cherry - Kellogg's
h. Apple Cinnamon - Kellogg's

127. Toppings/Dressings for Vegetables
a. Imitation Bacon Bits

(1) Concord
(2) Libby's (Bacon Crumbles)
b. Potato Topping - Zebbies
c. Tempura Batter Mix - Zebbies
d. Mushroom Batter Mix - Zebbies
e. Vegetable Fry Coating

128. T.V. Dinners/Frozen Entrees
a. Swanson- Salisbury Steak Entree with Potato Nuggets
b. Tyson (Southern Fried - Breast Fillets, Chick'n Chunks, Breast Patties)
c. Shenandoah - Turkey Burgers
d. Weaver (Honey Batter Tenders - Chicken Breast, Regular Tenders)
e. Safeway (Fish Fillets, Fish Sticks - Valu Pack)

129. Vegetables
a. Frozen- in Bags
(1) Corn on the Cob
(a) Birds Eye (Little Ears, Regular)
(b) Green Giant (Niblet Ears, Nibblets)
(c) Bel-air
(2) Corn
(a) Green Giant (Sweet, Niblets in Butter Sauce)
(b) Garden Kiss (Golden Whole Kernel Sweet)
(c) Bel-air
(d) Hanover (White Shoepeg)
(3) Peas
(a) Hanover (Sweet)
(b) C + W (Petite Size)
(c) Bel-air
(d) Garden Kiss (Sweet)
(e) Birds Eye (Tender Tiny)
(f) Green Giant (Medley)
4) Green Beans
(a) Bel-air (Cut)
(b) Southland (French Cut)
(c) Hanover (Whole)
(d) Seabrook Farms (Whole) Vegetables
(5) Zucchini- Sliced - Southland
6) Cut Okra
(a) Southland
(b) Bel-air
(7) Squash- Sliced Yellow Crookneck - Southland

(8) Lima Beans - Baby- Hanover
(9) Summer Vegetables - Hanover
(10) Cut Carrots
  (a) Seabrook (Crinkle Cut)
  (b) Bel-air
(11) Green Peppers- Southland (Diced)
(12) Cauliflower Florets - Prime Frozen
(13) Speciality Combinations
  (a) Broccoli, Cauliflower, and Carrots
    (1) Birds Eye
    (2) Hanover
    (3) Prime Frozen (California Blend)
  (b) Macaroni, Broccoli, Carrots, Zucchini
    (1) Hanover (Pasta Primaveral)
    (2) Birds Eye (Broccoli, Carrots, Pasta Twists)
(14) Potatoes
  (a) French Fried
    (1) Heinz (Deep Fries -Regular, Shoestring)
    (2) Ore Ida (Lites - Shoestring, Regular, Shoestring, Country Style Dinner Fries, Potato Wedges, Golden Crinkles, Hash Browns, Golden Twirls)
    (3) Garden Kiss (Crinkle Cut)
    (4) Bel-air (Regular, Crinkle Cut, Shoestring, Criss Cross)
    (5) Scotch Buy (Shoestring)
    (6) Act II - Microwave
  (b) Stuffed
    (1) Belfast (Cheddar Cheese-Processed)
    (2) Penobscot (Sour Cream + Chives, Cheese)
(15) Candied Yams - Mrs. Paul's
(16) Eggplant Sticks - Mrs. Paul's
(17) Leaf Spinach - Bel-air

b. Frozen- in Boxes
  (1) Corn
    (a) Green Giant (Shoepeg White Corn in Butter Sauce, Niblets)
    (b) Bel-air
    (c) Garden Kiss (Sweet)
  (2) Mixed Vegetables
    (a) Green Giant (Butter Sauce)
    (b) Bel-air
  (3) Peas
    (a) Green Giant (Baby Early Peas- Butter Sauce)
    (b) Bel-air (Sweet)

(c) Birds Eye (Green)
(d) Garden Kiss (Sweet)

(4) Broccoli
(a) Green Giant (Cut)
(b) Bel-air (Chopped, Spears)
(c) Garden Kiss (Spears)
(d) Birds Eye (Spears, Chopped)

(5) Brussels Sprouts
(a) Bel-air
(b) Green Giant (Baby Sprouts - Butter Sauce)

(6) Cauliflower
(a) Bel-air
(b) Garden Kiss

(7) Green Beans
(a) Birds Eye (French Cut)
(b) Bel-air (French Style, Cut)
(c) C + W (Cut Italian)

(8) Lima Beans
(a) Garden Kiss
(b) Birds Eye
(c) Bel-air

(9) Okra - Bel-air

(10) Peas and Carrots - Bel-air

(11) Squash- Cooked - Bel-air

(12) Asparagus Spears
(a) Bel-air
(b) Birds Eye

(13) Leaf Spinach
(a) Green Giant (Butter Sauce)
(b) Bel-air (Chopped)
(c) Seabrook

(14) Succotash
(a) Quality Supreme
(b) Bel-air

(15) Turnip Greens Chopped - Bel-air

(16) Blackeye Peas - Bel-air

(17) Collard Greens - Bel-air

(18) Spinach
(a) Birds Eye
(b) Bel-air

c. Canned/Jar

(1) Tomatoes

(a) Italian Style
  (1) Hunt's
  (2) Progresso
  (3) Cento
(b) Del Monte (Wedges)
(c) Contadina (California Sliced)
(d) Whole
  (1) Hunt's (No-Salt Added)
  (2) Scotch Buy
  (3) Town House
(e) Puree - Pomi Contadina

(2) Chick Peas (Garbanzo Beans)
  (a) Hanover
  (b) Progresso
    (3) Peas
      (a) Sweet
        (1) Green Giant (Regular, Early June)
        (2) Town House
        (3) Del Monte (Regular, No Salt Added)
        (4) Le Sueur
        (5) Aunt Nellie's
        (6) Libby's (No Salt or Sugar Added)
      (b) Field Peas with Snaps (Kent's Pride)
      (c) Dried Peas - Benco (Yellow Split, Green Split)

(4) Whole Carrots
  (a) Recamier - Safeway
  (b) Reese - Safeway

(5) Mixed Vegetables
      (a) Del Monte
      (b) Town House

(6) Green Beans
  (a) Country Pure (No Salt, Whole, French Style, Regular)
  (b) Del Monte (Regular, French Style- both have no Salt)
  (c) Hanover

(7) Whole Kernel Yellow Corn
  (a) Del Monte (Regular, No Salt Added, Cream Style-Regular,No Salt Added)
  (b) Country Pure (Regular, No Salt)
  (c) Green Giant (Regular, Mexicorn)

(8) White Corn
  (a) Del Monte (Cream Style)
  (b) Green Giant (Regular, Cream Style)

(c) Mitchell's

(9) Sauerkraut

(a) Libby's

(b) Town House

(10) Beets

(a) Del Monte

(b) Town House

(11) Beans

(a) Del Monte (Italian, Lima)

(b) Town House (Lima, Light Red Kidney)

(c) Sea Side (Butter)

(d) Progresso (Fava, Roman, White Kidney)

e) Benco (Pinto, Lima, Navy, Great Northern)

(f) Campbell's (Barbecue Baked, Vegetarian)

(g) Green Giant - Something Special- Baked

(12) Italian Pasta Salad - Hanover

(13) Potatoes

(a) Town House (Sliced, Whole, Instant)

(b) Durkee (Shoestring Sticks)

(c) Betty Crocker (Potato Buds)

(d) French's (Idaho Mashed)

(e) Pillsbury (Hungry Jack- Mashed)

(14) Collard Greens - Allens Sunshine

(15) Mustard Greens – Chopped - Town House

(16) Okra

(a) Trappey's

(b) Superfine - Safeway

(17) White and Golden Hominy - Town House

(18) Succotash - Hanover

(19) Turnip Greens - Allens Sunshine

(20) Yams (Sweet Potatoes)

(a) Own House

(b) Taylor's (Safeway)

(c) Trappey's

(21) Mushrooms- in Jars and Cans

(a) B in B (Pieces and Stems)

(b) Town House (Sliced, Button, Minature Stems and Pieces)

(c) Progresso

(22) Tomato Paste

(a) Hunt's (All Natural-Regular, No Salt Added, Italian Style)

(b) Lucerne

(c) Contadina

(d) Progresso
(e) Town House
(23) Tomato Sauce - Hunts's (Mushrooms, All Natural- Regular, No Salt Added)

130. Vegetable Shortening
    a. Crisco (Regular, Butter Flavor)
    b. Nu Made
    c. Flair

131. Vinegar
    a. Heinz (White, Apple Cider)
    b. Town House (White, Apple Cider)
    c. White House (Apple Cider)

132. Waffles- Frozen
    a. Aunt Jemima (Blueberry, Original, Buttermilk)
    b. Downyflake (Plain, Blueberry, Buttermild)
    c. Roman Meal (Plain)
    d. Kellogg's Nutri (Grain Waffles with Whole Grain, Raisin and Bran, Oat Bran)
    e. Eggo (Fruit Top- Apple, Strawberries, Blueberries, Homestyle, Special K)

133. Watermelon Rind- Sweet Pickled - Old South

134. Whipped Cream - Hunt's (Reddi Whip)

135. Yeasts
    a. Red Star
    b. Fleischmann

Appendix B

Recipes

Breakfast Shake

1	cup	Skim Milk
4	cubes	Ice
5	medium	Strawberries, raw

- Blend all ingredients in a blender at high speed until smooth.
- Makes 1 serving.

Analysis per serving:

KCAL	CHO(GM)	PROT(GM)	FAT(GM)	CHOL(MG)	SOD(MG)	P/S
109	17	9	1	4	127	0.5

Appropriate for following diets: General, diabetic, low sodium, low cholesterol.

"Chocolate Milkshake"

1	tsp	Honey
1-1/4	cup	Milk
1	TBS	Carob Powder
1/2	tsp	Vanilla Extract

- Pour all ingredients into blender and beat well until smooth.
- Makes 1 serving.

Analysis per serving:

KCAL	CHO(GM)	PROT(GM)	FAT(GM)	CHOL(MG)	SOD(MG)	P/S
216	22	10	10	41	156	0.1

Appropriate for following diets: General, low sodium.

"Chocolate Milkshake" (Low Cholesterol)

1	tsp	Honey
1-1/4	cup	Skim Milk
1	TBS	Carob Powder
1/2	tsp	Vanilla Extract

- Pour all ingredients into blender and beat well until smooth.
- Makes 1 serving.

Analysis per serving:

KCAL	CHO(GM)	PROT(GM)	FAT(GM)	CHOL(MG)	SOD(MG)	P/S
136	22	11	0.6	5	163	0.1

Appropriate for following diets: General, low sodium, low cholesterol.

Creamiest Milkshake

4	cups	Milk
1		Apple, peeled, cored and diced
2	TBS	Honey
1	tsp	Vanilla Extract
1	tsp	Cinnamon

- Place all ingredients into blender and blend on low speed for 3 minutes. Serve immediately.
- Makes 4 servings.

Analysis per serving:

KCAL	CHO(GM)	PROT(GM)	FAT(GM)	CHOL(MG)	SOD(MG)	P/S
237	34	8	8	33	122	0.1

Appropriate for following diets: General, low sodium.

Creamiest Milkshake (Low Cholesterol)

4	cups	Skim Milk
1		Apple, peeled, cored and diced
2	TBS	Honey
1	tsp	Vanilla Extract
1	tsp	Cinnamon

- Place all ingredients into blender and blend on low speed for 3 minutes. Serve immediately.
- Makes 4 servings.

Analysis per serving:

KCAL	CHO(GM)	PROT(GM)	FAT(GM)	CHOL(MG)	SOD(MG)	P/S
140	26	8	0.6	4	127	0.2

Appropriate for following diets: General, low sodium, low cholesterol.

Frosty Shake

1	cup	Skim Milk
1	tsp	Vanilla Extract
1	medium	Peach, peeled and pitted, or
2	halves	Peach, canned
1	TBS	Sugar
4		Ice Cubes, crushed

- Blend all ingredients together until smooth.
- Makes 1 serving.

Analysis per serving:

KCAL	CHO(GM)	PROT(GM)	FAT(GM)	CHOL(MG)	SOD(MG)	P/S
168	34	9	1	4	126	0.2

Appropriate for following diets: General, diabetic, low sodium, low cholesterol.

Frosty Fiber Shake

1	cup	Skim Milk
2	TBS	Oat Bran Cereal, uncooked
1	tsp	Vanilla Extract
1	medium	Peach, peeled and pitted, or
2	halves	Peach, canned
1	TBS	Sugar
4		Ice Cubes, crushed

- Blend all ingredients together until smooth.
- Makes 1 serving.

Analysis per serving:

KCAL	CHO(GM)	PROT(GM)	FAT(GM)	CHOL(MG)	SOD(MG)	P/S
222	43	11	1	4	127	0.9

Appropriate for following diets: General, low sodium, low cholesterol.

Hot Spiced Cider

1	qt	Apple Cider
2	whole	Cloves
1	stick	Cinnamon

- Heat all ingredients together in saucepan until about to boil.
- Remove from heat; skim out cloves and cinnamon stick.
- Makes 4 servings.

Analysis per serving:

KCAL	CHO(GM)	PROT(GM)	FAT(GM)	CHOL(MG)	SOD(MG)	P/S
116	29	0	0	0	7	1.6

Appropriate for following diets: General, diabetic, low sodium, low cholesterol.

Spicy Cranberry-Apple Cider

2	qt	Apple Cider
1	qt	Cranberry Juice Cocktail
1/4	cup	Brown Sugar, packed
4		Cinnamon Sticks
1-1/4	tsp	Whole Cloves

- Mix all ingredients in 5 qt saucepan.
- Bring mixture to boiling, reduce to simmer for 20 minutes.
- Skim out cinnamon sticks, and cloves.
- Makes 20 servings.

Analysis per serving:

KCAL	CHO(GM)	PROT(GM)	FAT(GM)	CHOL(MG)	SOD(MG)	P/S
86	22	0	0	0	6	1.8

Appropriate for following diets: General, diabetic, low sodium, low cholesterol.

Vanilla Milkshake

1/2	cup	Evaporated Skim Milk
1/2	cup	Water, cold
2	TSB	Whipped Dessert Topping, frozen
1	tsp	Vanilla Extract
6		Ice Cubes, crushed

- Put all ingredients into blender and whip until smooth and thick.
- Makes 2 servings.

Analysis per serving:

KCAL	CHO(GM)	PROT(GM)	FAT(GM)	CHOL(MG)	SOD(MG)	P/S
99	7	4	6	18	68	0.1

Appropriate for following diets: General, diabetic, low sodium, low cholesterol.

Recipes - Bread, Cereals And Starches

Applesauce Oatmeal

1	cup	Skim Milk
1-1/2	oz	Oatmeal, uncooked
1/2	cup	Applesauce
1	TBS	Sugar
1/8	tsp	Vanilla Extract
1/4	tsp	Cinnamon

- Heat milk on top of double boiler over boiling water.
- Add oats and stir.
- When cereal starts to thicken, stir in the rest of the ingredients.
- Continue cooking until cereal is desired consistency.
- Makes 2 servings.

Analysis per serving:

KCAL	CHO(GM)	PROT(GM)	FAT(GM)	CHOL(MG)	SOD(MG)	P/S
187	38	7	2	2	68	1.4

Appropriate for following diets: General, low sodium, low cholesterol.

Basic Biscuits

2	cup	Flour
1	TBS	Baking Powder
1/4	cup	Vegetable Shortening
3/4	cup	Skim Milk or Buttermilk

- Stir flour, and baking powder together in a bowl; cut shortening into flour mixture.
- Pour milk onto flour mixture and stir in quickly with a fork until dough thickens.
- Knead dough lightly on a floured board with floured hands about 10 turns.
- Roll dough out with floured rolling pin to a thickness of 1/2".
- Cut biscuits with floured biscuit cutter.
- Place biscuits on ungreased baking sheet; cover with waxed paper and let set for 10 minutes.
- Preheat oven to 450 degrees F.
- Bake biscuits 10-12 minutes or until lightly browned.
- Makes about 12 biscuits.

Analysis per biscuit:

KCAL	CHO(GM)	PROT(GM)	FAT(GM)	CHOL(MG)	SOD(MG)	P/S
124	17	3	5	2	183	0.8

Appropriate for following diets: General, diabetic, low sodium.

Basic Biscuits (Low Cholesterol)

2	cup	Flour
1	TBS	Baking Powder
1/2	tsp	Salt
1/4	cup	Vegetable Shortening
3/4	cup	Skim Milk or Buttermilk

- Stir flour, baking powder, and salt together in a bowl.
- Pour oil and milk onto flour mixture and stir in quickly with a fork until dough thickens.
- Knead dough lightly on a floured board with floured hands about 10 turns.
- Roll dough out with floured rolling pin to a thickness of 1/2".
- Cut biscuits with floured biscuit cutter.
- Place biscuits on ungreased baking sheet; cover with waxed paper and let set for 10 minutes.
- Preheat oven to 450 degrees F.
- Bake biscuits 10-12 minutes or until lightly browned.
- Makes about 12 biscuits.

Analysis per biscuit:

KCAL	CHO(GM)	PROT(GM)	FAT(GM)	CHOL(MG)	SOD(MG)	P/S
123	17	3	5	0.5	181	2.2

Appropriate for following diets: General, diabetic, low cholesterol.

Basic Biscuits (Low Sodium)

2	cup	Flour
1	TBS	Baking Powder, low sodium type
1/4	cup	Vegetable Shortening
3/4	cup	Skim Milk or Buttermilk

- Stir flour, and baking powder together in a bowl; cut shortening into flour mixture.
- Pour milk onto flour mixture and stir in quickly with a fork until dough thickens.
- Knead dough lightly on a floured board with floured hands about 10 turns.
- Roll dough out with floured rolling pin to a thickness of 1/2".
- Cut biscuits with floured biscuit cutter.
- Place biscuits on ungreased baking sheet; cover with waxed paper and let set for 10 minutes.
- Preheat oven to 450 degrees F.
- Bake biscuits 10-12 minutes or until lightly browned.
- Makes about 12 biscuits.

Analysis per biscuit:

KCAL	CHO(GM)	PROT(GM)	FAT(GM)	CHOL(MG)	SOD(MG)	P/S
124	17	3	5	2	8	0.8

Appropriate for following diets: General, diabetic, low sodium.

Basic Pancakes

2		Eggs
1/2	cup	Skim Milk
1/2	cup	Water, cold
1-1/4	cup	Flour
1-1/2	tsp	Baking Powder
2	TBS	Vegetable Oil
1/2	tsp	Sugar
1/8	tsp	Salt

- Lightly beat eggs, milk and water.
- Whip in remaining ingredients until smooth.
- Lightly grease heavy skillet and heat to medium heat.
- Makes about 8 pancakes.

Analysis per pancake:

KCAL	CHO(GM)	PROT(GM)	FAT(GM)	CHOL(MG)	SOD(MG)	P/S
132	16	4	5	71	120	1.2

Appropriate for following diets: General, diabetic.

Basic Pancakes (Low Cholesterol)

1/2	cup	Egg Substitute
1/2	cup	Skim Milk
1/2	cup	Water, cold
1-1/4	cup	Flour
1-1/2	tsp	Baking Powder
2	TBS	Vegetable Oil
1/2	tsp	Sugar
1/8	tsp	Salt

- Lightly beat egg substitute, milk, and water.
- Whip in remaining ingredients until smooth.
- Lightly grease heavy skillet and heat to medium heat.
- Makes about 8 pancakes.

Analysis per pancake:

KCAL	CHO(GM)	PROT(GM)	FAT(GM)	CHOL(MG)	SOD(MG)	P/S
122	16	4	4	0.4	131	2.4

Appropriate for following diets: General, diabetic, low cholesterol.

Basic Pancakes (Low Sodium)

2		Eggs
1/2	cup	Milk
1/2	cup	Water, cold
1-1/4	cup	Flour
1-1/2	tsp	Baking Powder, low sodium type
2	TBS	Vegetable Oil
1/2	tsp	Sugar

- Lightly beat eggs, milk, and water.
- Whip in remaining ingredients until smooth.
- Lightly grease heavy skillet and heat to medium heat.
- Makes about 8 pancakes.

Analysis per pancake:

KCAL	CHO(GM)	PROT(GM)	FAT(GM)	CHOL(MG)	SOD(MG)	P/S
132	16	4	5	71	25	1.2

Appropriate for following diets: General, diabetic, low sodium.

Bran Muffins

3/4	cup	Skim Milk
1-1/2	cup	Bran Cereal
2		Egg Whites
1/2	cup	Vegetable Oil
1-1/4	cup	Flour
1/4	cup	Brown Sugar
3	tsp	Baking Powder
1	tsp	Salt

- Preheat oven to 400 degrees.
- Pour milk onto bran cereal, let stand 2 minutes.
- Stir in oil and egg whites.
- Stir in brown sugar and salt.
- Stir in flour and baking powder just until flour is moistened.
- Grease bottoms only of about 12 medium muffin cups.
- Fill muffin cups about 3/4 full.
- Bake at 400 degrees for about 20 minutes (until tops are brown).
- Remove from pan immediately after removing them from the oven.
- Makes about 12 muffins.

Analysis per muffin:

KCAL	CHO(GM)	PROT(GM)	FAT(GM)	CHOL(MG)	SOD(MG)	P/S
132	16	4	5	71	25	1.2

Appropriate for following diets: General, diabetic, low cholesterol.

Bran Muffins (Low Sodium)

3/4	cup	Skim Milk
1-1/2	cup	Bran Cereal
2		Egg Whites
1/2	cup	Vegetable Oil
1-1/4	cup	Flour
1/4	cup	Brown Sugar
3	tsp	Baking Powder, low sodium type

- Preheat oven to 400 degrees.
- Pour milk onto bran cereal, let stand 2 minutes.
- Stir in oil and egg whites
- Stir in brown sugar and salt.
- Stir in flour and baking powder just until flour is moistened.
- Grease bottoms only of about 12 medium muffin cups.
- Fill muffin cups about 3/4 full.
- Bake at 400 degrees for about 20 minutes (until tops are brown).
- Remove from pan immediately after removing them from the oven.
- Makes about 12 muffins.

Analysis per muffin:

KCAL	CHO(GM)	PROT(GM)	FAT(GM)	CHOL(MG)	SOD(MG)	P/S
181	24	4	9	0.3	138	2.5

Appropriate for following diets: General, diabetic, low sodium, low cholesterol.

Cinnamon Pancakes

1		Egg
1	cup	All-purpose Flour
3/4-1	cup	Skim Milk
2	TBS	Vegetable Oil
1	TBS	Sugar
1	TBS	Baking Powder
1	tsp	Cinnamon
1/2	tsp	Salt

- Beat egg until foamy with wire whisk.
- Beat in rest of ingredients, just until batter is smooth.
- Pour about 3 TBS of the batter onto heated greased griddle or skillet.
- Turn pancakes when edges have set.
- Makes about nine 4-inch pancakes.

Analysis per pancake:

KCAL	CHO(GM)	PROT(GM)	FAT(GM)	CHOL(MG)	SOD(MG)	P/S
101	14	3	4	31	240	1.8

Appropriate for following diets: General, diabetic, low cholesterol.

Cinnamon Pancakes (Low Sodium)

1		Egg
1	cup	All-purpose Flour
3/4-1	cup	Skim Milk
2	TBS	Vegetable Oil
1	TBS	Sugar
1	TBS	Baking Powder, low sodium type
1	tsp	Cinnamon

- Beat egg until foamy with wire whisk.
- Beat in rest of ingredients, just until batter is smooth.
- Pour about 3 TBS of the batter onto heated greased griddle or skillet.
- Turn pancakes when edges have set.
- Makes about nine 4-inch pancakes.

Analysis per pancake:

KCAL	CHO(GM)	PROT(GM)	FAT(GM)	CHOL(MG)	SOD(MG)	P/S
101	14	3	4	31	19	1.9

Appropriate for following diets: General, diabetic, low sodium.

Corn Bread

1-1/2	cup	Cornmeal
1/2	cup	Flour
2	tsp	Baking Powder
2	tsp	Sugar
1	tsp	Salt
1/2	tsp	Baking Soda
1/4	cup	Shortening
1-1/2	cup	Buttermilk
2		Eggs, slightly beaten

- Preheat oven to 450 degree F.
- Beat all ingredients together with an electric mixer at slow speed for 30 seconds and then at high for 30 seconds.
- Pour into greased 8x8 inch baking pan.
- Bake for 25-30 minutes.
- Makes 8 servings- 2"x4" size.

Analysis per serving:

KCAL	CHO(GM)	PROT(GM)	FAT(GM)	CHOL(MG)	SOD(MG)	P/S
222	30	6	9	70	446	0.8

Appropriate for following diets: General, diabetic.

Corn Bread (Low Cholesterol)

1-1/2	cup	Cornmeal
1/2	cup	Flour
2	tsp	Baking Powder
2	tsp	Sugar
1	tsp	Salt
1/2	tsp	Baking Soda
1/4	cup	Vegetable Oil
1-1/2	cup	Buttermilk
3		Egg Whites

- Preheat oven to 450 degree F.
- Beat all ingredients together with an electric mixer at slow speed for 30 seconds and then at high for 30 seconds.
- Pour into greased 8x8 inch baking pan.
- Bake for 25-30 minutes.
- Makes 8 servings- 2"x4" piece each.

Analysis per serving:

KCAL	CHO(GM)	PROT(GM)	FAT(GM)	CHOL(MG)	SOD(MG)	P/S
208	30	6	7	2	448	1.2

Appropriate for following diets: General, diabetic, low cholesterol.

Corn Bread (Low Sodium)

1-1/2	cup	Cornmeal
1/2	cup	Flour
2	tsp	Baking Powder, low sodium type
2	tsp	Sugar
1/2	tsp	Baking Soda
1/4	cup	Shortening
1-1/2	cup	Buttermilk
2		Eggs, slightly beaten

- Preheat oven to 450 degree F.
- Beat all ingredients together with an electric mixer at slow speed for 30 seconds and then at high for 30 seconds.
- Pour into greased 8x8 inch baking pan.
- Bake for 25-30 minutes.
- Makes 8 servings- 2"x4" each piece.

Analysis per serving:

KCAL	CHO(GM)	PROT(GM)	FAT(GM)	CHOL(MG)	SOD(MG)	P/S
222	30	6	9	70	117	0.8

Appropriate for following diets: General, diabetic, low sodium.

Crepes

2		Eggs
1/2	cup	Milk
1/2	cup	Water, cold
1	cup	Flour
2	TB S	Vegetable Oil
1/2	tsp	Sugar
1/8	tsp	Salt

- Lightly beat eggs, milk, and water.
- Whip in remaining ingredients. Spray non-stick vegetable spray onto bottom of small skillet.
- Heat skillet at medium heat.
- Pour about 2 TBS of batter to coat bottom of pan; tilt pan to spread batter.
- Cook 1 minute or just until set; turn; cook 30 seconds longer until browned.
- Makes 8 crepes.
- May be filled with sliced, sweetened fresh or canned fruits.

Analysis per crepe:

KCAL	CHO(GM)	PROT(GM)	FAT(GM)	CHOL(MG)	SOD(MG)	P/S
117	13	4	5	71	57	1.2

Appropriate for following diets: General, diabetic, low sodium.

Crepes (Low Cholesterol)

1/2	cup	Egg Substitute
1/2	cup	Milk
1/2	cup	Water, cold
1	cup	Flour
2	TBS	Vegetable Oil
1/2	tsp	Sugar
1/8	tsp	Salt

- Lightly beat egg substitute, milk, and water.
- Whip in remaining ingredients.
- Spray non-stick vegetable spray onto bottom of small skillet.
- Heat skillet at medium heat.
- Pour about 2 TBS of batter to coat bottom of pan; tilt pan to spread batter.
- Cook 1 minutes or just until set; turn; cook 30 seconds longer until browned.
- Makes 8 crepes.
- May be filled with sliced, sweetened fresh or canned fruits.

Analysis per crepe:

KCAL	CHO(GM)	PROT(GM)	FAT(GM)	CHOL(MG)	SOD(MG)	P/S
107	13	4	4	0.4	68	2.4

Appropriate for following diets: General, diabetic, low sodium, low cholesterol.

Crunchy Breadsticks

1/2	pkg	Active Dry Yeast
1/3	cup plus 2 TBS	Warm Water
1	cup	Warm Skim Milk (scalded then cooled)
1-1/2	TBS	Brown Sugar
1-1/2	TBS	Vegetable Oil
1/2	TBS	Salt
4	cups	Flour
3	TBS	Sesame Seeds

- Dissolve yeast in warm water.
- Stir in milk, brown sugar, oil, salt, and 2 cups of the flour.
- Beat mixture until smooth.
- Stir in only enough of the remaining flour to make a stiff but workable dough.
- Knead dough on a floured board with floured hands for about 10 minutes.
- Put dough back into bowl and cover bowl with a damp cloth.
- Let dough rise in a warm place for 45-60 minutes.
- Turn dough onto floured board and divide dough into 18 even sized balls.
- Roll each ball against the board into a stick about 4 inches in length.
- Roll each stick in sesame seeds and place on a greased baking sheet.
- Cover filled baking sheet with waxed paper and let set 30 minutes.
- Preheat oven to 425 degrees F. during the last 5 minutes of the sticks last rising.
- Bake for 10-12 minutes until lightly brown and done inside.
- Makes 18 sticks.

Analysis per breadstick:

KCAL	CHO(GM)	PROT(GM)	FAT(GM)	CHOL(MG)	SOD(MG)	P/S
129	23	4	2	0.2	171	1.9

Appropriate for following diets: General, diabetic, low cholesterol.

Crunchy Oat Sticks

1	pkg	Active Dry Yeast
1/3	cup plus 2 TBS	Warm Water
1	cup	Warm Skim Milk (scalded then cooled)
1-1/2	TBS	Brown Sugar
1-1/2	TBS	Vegetable Oil
1/2	TBS	Salt
3-1/2	cups	Flour
1/2	cup	Oatmeal, uncooked
3	TBS	Sesame Seeds
1	TBS	Oat Bran Cereal, uncooked

- Mix together sesame seeds and oat bran cereal and set aside.
- Dissolve yeast in warm water.
- Stir in milk, brown sugar, oil, salt, 2 cups of flour, and the oatmeal.
- Beat mixture until smooth.
- Stir in only enough of the remaining flour to form a stiff but workable dough.
- Knead dough on floured board with floured hands for about 10 minutes.
- Put dough back in bowl and cover with a damp cloth. Let dough rise in a warm place for 45-60 minutes.
- Turn dough onto a floured board and divide into 18 even sized balls.
- Roll each ball against the board into a stick about 4 inches in length.
- Roll each stick in sesame seed/oat bran mixture and place on a greased baking sheet.
- Cover filled baking sheet with waxed paper and let set 30 minutes.
- Preheat oven to 425 degrees F. during lst 5 minutes of oat sticks last rising.
- Bake for 10-12 minutes until lightly brown and done inside.
- Makes 18 sticks.

Analysis per breadstick:

KCAL	CHO(GM)	PROT(GM)	FAT(GM)	CHOL(MG)	SOD(MG)	P/S
130	23	4	2	0.2	171	2.0

Appropriate for following diets: General, diabetic, low cholesterol.

Hearth Bread

3	pkg	Active Dry Yeast
1/2	cup	Warm Water
1-1/2	cups	Oatmeal, uncooked
3/4	cup	Cracked Wheat
2	cups	Wheat Germ
3/4	tsp	Salt
3	TBS	Vegetable Oil
3-1/2	cups	Hot Water
3/4	cup	Molasses
3	cups	Whole Wheat Flour
3	cups	Bread Flour
3	TBS	Margarine, melted

- Dissolve yeast in 1/2 cup warm water.
- In large bowl, mix oatmeal, cracked wheat, wheat germ, salt, oil, and hot water.
- Cool to room temperature.
- Stir in honey, molasses, yeast mixture, and flours.
- Beat with spoon to form a soft elastic dough.
- Knead with floured hands on floured board for 5 minutes; add more flour if necessary to control stickiness.
- Return dough to bowl; spray with non-stick vegetable spray.
- Cover bowl with damp towel and let dough rise in a warm place until it doubles in size, about 1 hour.
- Divide dough into three loaves and place into greased loaf pans.
- Brush with melted margarine and cover with waxed paper until each loaf has doubled in size.
- Preheat oven to 350 degrees F. Bake for 50-60 minutes.
- Makes 3 loaves, 12 slices per loaf.

Analysis per slice:

KCAL	CHO(GM)	PROT(GM)	FAT(GM)	CHOL(MG)	SOD(MG)	P/S
162	29	6	3	0	83	2.5

Appropriate for following diets: General, diabetic, low sodium, low cholesterol.

Herb Biscuits

1/3	cup	Shortening
1-3/4	cup	Flour
2-1/2	tsp	Baking Powder
3/4	tsp	Salt
1/2	tsp	Dill Weed
1/4	tsp	Thyme
3/4	cup	Skim Milk

- Cut shortening into flour, baking powder, salt, and herbs with fork or pastry blender until mixture resembles bread crumbs.
- Stir in milk.
- Knead dough on floured board, about 10 turns.
- Roll dough out with floured rolling pin to a 1/2 inch thickness.
- Cut out biscuits with 2 inch biscuit cutter.
- Place on ungreased baking sheet, sides of biscuits not touching.
- Preheat oven to 450 degrees F.
- Allow biscuits to set 10 minutes.
- Bake biscuits 10-12 minutes.
- Remove immediately from pan after removing from oven.
- Makes about 12 biscuits.

Analysis per biscuit:

KCAL	CHO(GM)	PROT(GM)	FAT(GM)	CHOL(MG)	SOD(MG)	P/S
123	15	2	6	0.3	201	1.0

Appropriate for following diets: General, diabetic.

Herb Biscuits (Low Sodium)

1/3	cup	Shortening
1-3/4	cups	Flour
2-1/2	tsp	Baking Powder, low sodium type
1/2	tsp	Dill Weed
1/4	tsp	Thyme
3/4	cup	Skim Milk

- Cut shortening into flour, baking powder, and herbs with a fork or pastry blender until mixture resembles bread crumbs.
- Stir in milk.
- Turn dough out onto a floured board and knead about 10 turns.
- Roll out dough with floured rolling pin to 1/2" thickness.
- Cut out biscuits with 2 inch biscuit cutter.
- Place on ungreased baking sheet, sides of biscuits not touching.
- Preheat oven to 450 degrees F.
- Allow biscuits to set 10 minutes.
- Bake biscuits 10-12 minutes.
- Remove immediately from pan after removing from oven.
- Makes about 12 biscuits.

Analysis per biscuit:

KCAL	CHO(GM)	PROT(GM)	FAT(GM)	CHOL(MG)	SOD(MG)	P/S
123	15	2	6	0.3	8	1.0

Appropriate for following diets: General, diabetic, low sodium.

Low Cholesterol Cinnamon Pancakes

2		Egg Whites
1	cup	Flour
3/4-1	cup	Skim Milk
2	TBS	Vegetable Oil
1	TBS	Brown Sugar
2	TBS	Oat Bran Cereal, uncooked
1	TBS	Baking Powder
1	tsp	Cinnamon
1/2	tsp	Salt

- Beat all ingredients together with wire whisk just until batter is smooth.
- Pour about 3 TBS of batter onto heated, greased griddle or skillet.
- Turn pancakes when edges have set.
- Makes about nine 4-inch pancakes.

Analysis per pancake:

KCAL	CHO(GM)	PROT(GM)	FAT(GM)	CHOL(MG)	SOD(MG)	P/S
102	15	3	3	0.3	244	2.3

Appropriate for following diets: General, diabetic, low cholesterol.

Low Saturated Fat Herb Biscuits

1/3	cup	Vegetable Oil
1-3/4	cups	Flour
2-1/2	tsp	Baking Powder
3/4	tsp	Salt
1/2	tsp	Dill Weed
1/4	tsp	Thyme
3/4	cup	Skim Milk

- Mix all ingredients together in a large mixing bowl until the dough starts to thicken.
- Turn dough out onto a floured board and knead about 10 turns.
- Roll out dough with floured rolling pin to 1/2" thickness.
- Cut out biscuits with 2 inch biscuit cutter.
- Place on ungreased baking sheet, sides of biscuits not touching.
- Preheat oven to 450 degrees F.
- Allow biscuits to set 10 minutes.
- Bake biscuits 10-12 minutes.
- Remove immediately from pan after removing from oven.
- Makes about 12 biscuits.

Analysis per biscuit:

KCAL	CHO(GM)	PROT(GM)	FAT(GM)	CHOL(MG)	SOD(MG)	P/S
126	15	2	6	0.3	201	2.5

Appropriate for following diets: General, diabetic, low cholesterol.

Oat Bran Muffin

2		Egg Whites
3/4	cup	Skim Milk
1/2	cup	Vegetable Oil
1	cup	Flour
1/2	cup	Oatmeal, quick cooking type, uncooked
1/2	cup	Oat Bran Cereal, uncooked
1	cup	Raisins
1/3	cup	Brown Sugar
1	TBS	Baking Powder
1	tsp	Salt

- Preheat oven to 400 degrees F.
- Grease 12 muffin cups.
- Beat together egg whites, milk, and oil.
- Stir in remaining ingredients just until flour is moistened.
- Fill muffin cups 3/4 full.
- Bake about 20 minutes.
- Makes 12 muffins.

Analysis per muffin:

KCAL	CHO(GM)	PROT(GM)	FAT(GM)	CHOL(MG)	SOD(MG)	P/S
223	31	4	10	0.2	268	2.5

Appropriate for following diets: General, diabetic, low cholesterol.

Oat Bread

1	pkg	Active Dry Yeast
1-1/2	cups	Warm Water
3	TBS	Brown Sugar
1/2	cup	Nonfat Dried Milk Powder
1	tsp	Salt
3-1/4	cups	Flour
1/4	cup	Vegetable Oil
1-1/2	cups	Oatmeal, uncooked

- Dissolve yeast in warm water.
- Stir in sugar, milk powder, and salt.
- Stir in 2 cups of the flour and 1 cup of oatmeal; beat for 3 minutes.
- Stir in oil and rest of flour and oats.
- Turn dough onto a floured board and knead with floured hands for about 10 minutes.
- Return dough to bowl, cover with damp cloth and allow to rise in a warm place for 1 hour.
- Punch down dough and allow to rise an additional 30 minutes.
- Shape dough into a loaf and place into greased loaf pan.
- Let set and rise for 30 minutes.
- Preheat oven during the last 5 minutes of the last dough rising time to 350 degrees F.
- Bake for about 1 hour.
- Makes 1 loaf or 20 slices.

Analysis per slice:

KCAL	CHO(GM)	PROT(GM)	FAT(GM)	CHOL(MG)	SOD(MG)	P/S
145	24	4	3	0.3	108	2.3

Appropriate for following diets: General, diabetic, low cholesterol.

Potato Pancakes

1	TBS	Margarine
1/4	cup	Celery, diced
1	cup	Potatoes, peeled, boiled, and mashed
1		Egg, slightly beaten
1 TBS plus 1 tsp		Flour
1/4	tsp	Salt
1/4	tsp	Black Pepper
2	tsp	Vegetable Oil

- Sautee celery in margarine until celery in soft.
- Stir celery into potatoes, egg, flour, salt, and pepper until well blended.
- Heat oil into bottom of a heavy skillet.
- Form 4 patties from the potato mixture and fry in skillet until bottom is lightly browned; turn patties and brown other side.
- Makes 4 pancakes.

Analysis per pancake:

KCAL	CHO(GM)	PROT(GM)	FAT(GM)	CHOL(MG)	SOD(MG)	P/S
105	9	2	7	69	181	1.8

Appropriate for following diets: General, diabetic.

Potato Pancakes (Low Cholesterol)

1	TBS	Margarine
1/4	cup	Celery, diced
1	cup	Potatoes, peeled, boiled, and mashed
1/4	cup	Egg Substitute
1 TBS plus 1 tsp		Flour
1/4	tsp	Salt
1/4	tsp	Black Pepper
2	tsp	Vegetable Oil

- Sautee celery in margarine until celery in soft.
- Stir celery into potatoes, egg substitute, flour, salt, and pepper until well blended.
- Heat oil into bottom of a heavy skillet.
- Form 4 patties from the potato mixture and fry in skillet until bottom is lightly browned; turn patties and brown other side.
- Makes 4 pancakes.

Analysis per pancake:

KCAL	CHO(GM)	PROT(GM)	FAT(GM)	CHOL(MG)	SOD(MG)	P/S
99	9	3	6	0.2	192	2.5

Appropriate for following diets: General, diabetic, low cholesterol.

Potato Pancakes (Low Sodium)

1	TBS	Margarine
1/4	cup	Celery, diced
1	cup	Potatoes, peeled, boiled, and mashed
1		Egg, slightly beaten
1 TBS plus 1 tsp		Flour
1/4	tsp	Black Pepper
2	tsp	Vegetable Oil

- Sautee celery in margarine until celery in soft.
- Stir celery into potatoes, egg, flour, salt, and pepper until well blended.
- Heat oil into bottom of a heavy skillet.
- Form 4 patties from the potato mixture and fry in skillet until bottom is lightly browned; turn patties and brown other side.
- Makes 4 pancakes.

Analysis per pancake:

KCAL	CHO(GM)	PROT(GM)	FAT(GM)	CHOL(MG)	SOD(MG)	P/S
105	9	2	7	69	59	1.8

Appropriate for following diets: General, diabetic, low sodium.

Soft Dutch Pretzels

1	pkg	Active Dry Yeast
1-1/2	cups	Warm Water
1	tsp	Salt
3	tsp	Sugar
4	cups	Flour
1		Egg, beaten

- Preheat oven to 425 degrees F.
- Dissolve yeast in water.
- Stir in salt, sugar, and flour.
- Knead with floured hands on floured board for 5-10 minutes; add more flour if necessary to control stickiness.
- Pinch off tablespoon sized lumps of dough and shape into sticks, pretzels, or circles.
- Place on lightly greased baking sheet.
- Brush with beaten egg.
- Bake for about 15 minutes or until lightly browned.
- Makes 5 dozen pretzels.

Analysis per pretzel:

KCAL	CHO(GM)	PROT(GM)	FAT(GM)	CHOL(MG)	SOD(MG)	P/S
33	7	1	0.1	5	34	0.3

Appropriate for following diets: General, diabetic.

Soft Dutch Pretzels (Low Cholesterol)

1	pkg	Active Dry Yeast
1-1/2	cups	Warm Water
1	tsp	Salt
3	tsp	Sugar
4	cups	Flour
1		Egg Substitute

- Preheat oven to 425 degrees F.
- Dissolve yeast in water.
- Stir in salt, sugar, and flour.
- Knead with floured hands on floured board for 5-10 minutes; add more flour if necessary to control stickiness.
- Pinch off tablespoon sized lumps of dough and shape into sticks, pretzels, or circles.
- Place on lightly greased baking sheet.
- Brush with egg substitute.
- Bake for about 15 minutes or until lightly browned.
- Makes 5 dozen pretzels.

Analysis per pretzel:

KCAL	CHO(GM)	PROT(GM)	FAT(GM)	CHOL(MG)	SOD(MG)	P/S
32	7	1	0.1	0	35	0.9

Appropriate for following diets: General, diabetic, low cholesterol.

Soft Dutch Pretzels (Low Sodium)

1	pkg	Active Dry Yeast
1-1/2	cups	Warm Water
1/4	tsp	Salt
3	tsp	Sugar
4	cups	Flour
1		Egg, beaten

- Preheat oven to 425 degrees F.
- Dissolve yeast in water.
- Stir in salt, sugar, and flour.
- Knead with floured hands on floured board for 5-10 minutes; add more flour if necessary to control stickiness.
- Pinch off tablespoon sized lumps of dough and shape into sticks, pretzels, or circles.
- Place on lightly greased baking sheet.
- Brush with beaten egg.
- Bake for about 15 minutes or until lightly browned.
- Makes 5 dozen pretzels.

Analysis per pretzel:

KCAL	CHO(GM)	PROT(GM)	FAT(GM)	CHOL(MG)	SOD(MG)	P/S
26	5	1	0.2	5	9	0.3

Appropriate for following diets: General, diabetic, low sodium.

Tropical Oatbran Cereal

1	cup	Skim Milk
1-1/2	oz	Oat Bran Cereal, uncooked
1	cup	Fruit Cocktail, drained
2	tsp	Sugar
1/8	tsp	Ginger
1/8	tsp	Cinnamon
2	tsp	Coconut, dried, shredded

- Heat milk on low heat until hot; stir in oat bran cereal.
- Cook 3 minutes or until cereal starts to thicken.
- Stir in rest of ingredients and continue to cook cereal for 30 seconds.
- Makes 2 servings.

Analysis per serving:

KCAL	CHO(GM)	PROT(GM)	FAT(GM)	CHOL(MG)	SOD(MG)	P/S
227	38	8	6	17	66	0.2

Appropriate for following diets: General, diabetic, low sodium.

Tropical Oatbran Cereal (Low Cholesterol)

1	cup	Skim Milk
1-1/2	oz	Oat Bran Cereal, uncooked
1	cup	Fruit Cocktail, drained
2	tsp	Sugar
1/8	tsp	Ginger
1/8	tsp	Cinnamon

- Heat milk on low heat until hot; stir in oat bran cereal.
- Cook 3 minutes or until cereal starts to thicken.
- Stir in rest of ingredients and continue to cook cereal for 30 seconds.
- Makes 2 servings.

Analysis per serving:

KCAL	CHO(GM)	PROT(GM)	FAT(GM)	CHOL(MG)	SOD(MG)	P/S
188	38	8	1	2	68	1.4

Appropriate for following diets: General, diabetic, low sodium, low cholesterol.

Waffles

3		Eggs
1-1/2	cups	Skim Milk
1/3	cup	Vegetable Oil
2	cups	Flour
2	tsp	Baking Powder
2	tsp	Sugar
1/2	tsp	Salt

- Whip eggs, milk, and oil in blender for 2 minutes.
- Blend in dry ingredients until smooth.
- Bake in preheated waffle iron.
- Makes 4 large waffles.

Analysis per waffle:

KCAL	CHO(GM)	PROT(GM)	FAT(GM)	CHOL(MG)	SOD(MG)	P/S
512	55	14	26	218	512	1.3

Appropriate for following diets: General, diabetic.

Waffles (Low Cholesterol)

3/4	cup	Egg Substitute
1-1/2	cups	Skim Milk
1/3	cup	Vegetable Oil
2	cups	Flour
2	tsp	Baking Powder
2	tsp	Sugar
1/2	tsp	Salt

- Whip egg substitute, milk, and oil in blender for 2 minutes.
- Blend in dry ingredients until smooth.
- Bake in preheated waffle iron.
- Makes 4 large waffles.

Analysis per waffle:

KCAL	CHO(GM)	PROT(GM)	FAT(GM)	CHOL(MG)	SOD(MG)	P/S
468	55	15	20	2	545	2.4

Appropriate for following diets: General, diabetic, low cholesterol.

Waffles (Low Sodium)

3		Eggs
1-1/2	cups	Skim Milk
1/3	cup	Vegetable Oil
2	cups	Flour
2	tsp	Baking Powder, low sodium type
2	tsp	Sugar

- Whip eggs, milk, and oil in blender for 2 minutes.
- Blend in dry ingredients until smooth.
- Bake in preheated waffle iron.
- Makes 4 large waffles.

Analysis per waffle:

KCAL	CHO(GM)	PROT(GM)	FAT(GM)	CHOL(MG)	SOD(MG)	P/S
512	55	14	26	218	98	1.3

Appropriate for following diets: General, diabetic, low sodium.

Whole Wheat Quick Bread

4	cups	Whole Wheat Flour
1	tsp	Salt
1/2	tsp	Cream of Tartar
1	tsp	Baking Soda
1 cup plus 2 TBS		Buttermilk

- Preheat oven to 425 degree F.
- Grease 2 loaf pans.
- Mix all dry ingredients together; stir in buttermilk.
- Beat dough into sticky, elastic mass.
- Divide the mixture between the pans and bake for 40 minutes.
- Makes 12 slices per loaf.

Analysis per slice:

KCAL	CHO(GM)	PROT(GM)	FAT(GM)	CHOL(MG)	SOD(MG)	P/S
71	15	3	0.4	0.4	128	0.1

Appropriate for following diets: General, diabetic, low cholesterol.

Baked Pork Chops

4	1/2" thick	Lean Pork Loin Chops
1/2	tsp	Garlic Powder
1/2	tsp	Black Pepper
1/4	cup	Apple Juice
1/4	cup	Water

- Preheat oven to 350 degrees F.
- Place chops in 9x13 baking pan.
- Sprinkle chops with garlic powder and pepper.
- Pour apple juice and water onto bottom of pan (do not rinse spices off of tops of the chops).
- Baked for about 45-60 minutes until done through.
- Makes 4 servings.

Analysis per serving:

KCAL	CHO(GM)	PROT(GM)	FAT(GM)	CHOL(MG)	SOD(MG)	P/S
223	2	24	14	83	127	0.4

Appropriate for following diets: General, diabetic, low sodium, low cholesterol.

Baked Veal Chops

4	1/2" thick	Lean Veal Chops or Cutlets
1/2	tsp	Garlic Powder
1/2	tsp	Black Pepper
1/4	cup	Apple Juice
1/4	cup	Water

- Preheat oven to 350 degrees F.
- Place chops in 9x13 baking pan.
- Sprinkle chops with garlic powder and pepper.
- Pour apple juice and water onto bottom of the pan (do not rinse the spices off the tops of the chops).
- Bake for about 40-45 minutes or until done through.
- Makes 4 servings.

Analysis per serving:

KCAL	CHO(GM)	PROT(GM)	FAT(GM)	CHOL(MG)	SOD(MG)	P/S
191	1	23	9	87	69	0.1

Appropriate for following diets: General, diabetic, low sodium, low cholesterol.

BBQ Scallops (Low Sodium)

1/3	cup	Margarine
1/2	tsp	Curry Powder
1	clove	Garlic, minced
1/8	tsp	Black Pepper
2	TBS	Parsley
2	lb	Scallops

- Cream margarine with remaining ingredients except scallops.
- Divide scallops evenly between 6 pieces of aluminum foil.
- Top each pile of scallops with margarine mixture.
- Fold top and sides of foil tightly over scallops; place packets directly on hot coals in the barbeque.
- Cook for 5-7 minutes.
- Makes 6 servings.

Analysis per serving:

KCAL	CHO(GM)	PROT(GM)	FAT(GM)	CHOL(MG)	SOD(MG)	P/S
260	3	35	12	80	518	2.5

Appropriate for following diets: General, diabetic, low sodium, low cholesterol.

BBQ Seafood (Low Cholesterol)

1/4	cup	Margarine
1/2	tsp	Curry Powder
1	clove	Garlic, minced
1/2	tsp	Salt
1/8	tsp	Black Pepper
2	TBS	Parsley
1	lb	Shrimp, raw, peeled
1	lb	Scallops

- Cream margarine with remaining ingredients except seafood.
- Divide seafood evenly between 6 pieces of aluminum foil.
- Top each pile of seafood with margarine mixture.
- Fold top and sides of foil tightly over seafood; place packets directly on hot coals in the barbeque.
- Cook for 5-7 minutes.
- Makes 6 servings.

Analysis per serving:

KCAL	CHO(GM)	PROT(GM)	FAT(GM)	CHOL(MG)	SOD(MG)	P/S
265	3	36	10	154	1220	2.5

Appropriate for following diets: General, diabetic, low cholesterol.

BBQ Shrimp

1/3	cup	Margarine
1/2	tsp	Curry Powder
1	clove	Garlic, minced
1/2	tsp	Salt
1/8	tsp	Black Pepper
2	TBS	Parsley
1	lb	Shrimp, raw, peeled

- Cream margarine with remaining ingredients except shrimp.
- Divide shrimp evenly between 6 pieces of aluminum foil.
- Top each pile of shrimp with margarine mixture.
- Fold top and sides of foil tightly over shrimp; place packets directly on hot coals in the barbeque.
- Cook for 5-7 minutes.
- Makes 6 servings.

Analysis per serving:

KCAL	CHO(GM)	PROT(GM)	FAT(GM)	CHOL(MG)	SOD(MG)	P/S
268	2	38	12	228	1759	2.1

Appropriate for following diets: General, diabetic.

Cheese Souffle

1/4	cup	Margarine
1/4	cup	Flour
1/2	tsp	Salt
1	dash	Cayenne Pepper
1	cup	Milk
8	oz	American Cheese, sharp processed-type, thinly sliced
4		Eggs, separated

- Preheat oven to 300 degrees F.
- Melt margarine in small saucepan, and then blend in flour, salt, and cayenne.
- Stir in milk over medium heat until mixture starts to thicken and bubble.
- Remove from heat and stir in cheese until it melts.
- In bowl, whip egg yolks until thick and lemon yellow.
- Slowly beat in cheese mixture.
- In separate bowl, whip egg whites until stiff.
- Fold yolk mixture into egg whites.
- Pour into ungreased 1-1/2 qt casserole dish.
- Bake for 1 hour 15 minutes.
- Makes 4 servings.

Analysis per serving:

KCAL	CHO(GM)	PROT(GM)	FAT(GM)	CHOL(MG)	SOD(MG)	P/S
461	10	22	37	337	1299	0.4

Appropriate for following diets: General.

Cheese Souffle (Low Cholesterol)

1/4	cup	Margarine
1/4	cup	Flour
1/2	tsp	Salt
1	dash	Cayenne Pepper
1	cup	Skim Milk
8	oz	American Cheese, low-fat type, thinly sliced
1/4	cup	Egg Substitute
4		Egg Whites

- Preheat oven to 300 degrees F.
- Melt margarine in small saucepan, and then blend in flour, sal, and cayenne.
- Stir in milk over medium heat until mixture starts to thicken and bubble.
- Remove from heat and stir in cheese until it melts.
- Beat egg substitute until very foamy.
- Fold in cheese mixture.
- In bowl, whip egg whites until stiff.
- Fold egg substitute/cheese mixture into egg whites.
- Pour into ungreased 1-1/2 qt casserole dish.
- Bake for 1 hour 15 minutes.
- Makes 4 servings.

Analysis per serving:

KCAL	CHO(GM)	PROT(GM)	FAT(GM)	CHOL(MG)	SOD(MG)	P/S
201	10	9	14	6	563	1.6

Appropriate for following diets: General, diabetic, low cholesterol.

Cheese Souffle (Low Sodium)

1/4	cup	Margarine
1/4	cup	Flour
1	dash	Cayenne Pepper
1	cup	Milk
8	oz	American Cheese, low sodium type, thinly sliced
4		Eggs, Separated

- Preheat oven to 300 degrees F.
- Melt margarine in small saucepan, and then blend in flour, salt, and cayenne.
- Stir in milk over medium heat until mixture starts to thicken and bubble.
- Remove from heat and stir in cheese until it melts.
- In bowl, whip egg yolks until thick and lemon yellow.
- Slowly beat in cheese mixture.
- In separate bowl, whip egg whites until stiff.
- Fold yolk mixture into egg whites.
- Pour into ungreased 1-1/2 qt casserole dish.
- Bake for 1 hour 15 minutes.
- Makes 4 servings.

Analysis per serving:

KCAL	CHO(GM)	PROT(GM)	FAT(GM)	CHOL(MG)	SOD(MG)	P/S
262	10	12	19	284	234	1.1

Appropriate for following diets: General, diabetic, low sodium.

Chicken Lo-Mein

1	lb	Chicken Breast, boneless
1	tsp	Cornstarch
1-1/2	TBS	Soy Sauce
3	TBS	Vegetable Oil
1/4	lb	Spaghetti
1/4	tsp	Salt
2	cups	Cabbage, thinly shredded
1/2	cup	Chicken Broth, homemade
1/4	tsp	Black Pepper
1/2	lb	Mushrooms, thinly sliced

- Cut chicken into thin strips about 2" long.
- Mix together chicken, cornstarch, 1/2 TBS soy sauce, and 1/2 TBS oil.
- Cook spaghetti according to pkg. directions, drain.
- Heat 1/2 TBS oil in wok or large heavy fry pan on high.
- Add 1/8 tsp salt and cabbage; stir-fry for 2 minutes; remove from pan.
- Pour remaining oil into pan and let heat until very hot.
- Add chicken and stir-fry until cooked through.
- Add mushrooms, soy sauce, salt, chicken broth, and noodles; toss gently.
- Sprinkle with pepper and then fold in cabbage.
- Makes 4 servings.

Analysis per serving:

KCAL	CHO(GM)	PROT(GM)	FAT(GM)	CHOL(MG)	SOD(MG)	P/S
363	26	33	14	72	581	1.9

Appropriate for following diets: General, diabetic, low cholesterol.

Chicken Lo-Mein (Low Sodium)

1	lb	Chicken Breast, boneless
1	tsp	Cornstarch
1-1/2	TBS	Soy Sauce, low sodium type
3	TBS	Vegetable Oil
1/4	lb	Spaghetti
2	cup	Cabbage, thinly shredded
1/2	cup	Chicken Broth, homemade
1/4	tsp	Black Pepper
1/2	lb	Mushrooms, thinly sliced

- Cut chicken into thin strips about 2" long.
- Mix together chicken, cornstarch, 1/2 TBS soy sauce, and 1/2 TBS oil.
- Cook spaghetti according to pkg. directions, drain.
- Heat 1/2 TBS oil in wok or large heavy fry pan on high.
- Add cabbage; stir-fry for 2 minutes then remove from pan.
- Pour remaining oil into pan and let heat until very hot.
- Add chicken and stir-fry until cooked through.
- Add mushrooms, soy sauce, chicken broth, and noodles; toss gently.
- Sprinkle with pepper and then fold in cabbage.
- Makes 4 servings.

Analysis per serving:

KCAL	CHO(GM)	PROT(GM)	FAT(GM)	CHOL(MG)	SOD(MG)	P/S
361	26	33	14	72	266	1.9

Appropriate for following diets: General, diabetic, low sodium, low cholesterol.

Chicken Salad

1-1/2	cups	Cut-up Cooked Chicken
2	TBS	Diced Celery
2	TBS	Shredded Carrot
1	tsp	Parsley
1/4	tsp	Black Pepper
1/2	tsp	Vinegar
1/2	cup	Mayonnaise or Salad Dressing
3/4	tsp	Curry Powder

- Stir together all ingredients except chicken.
- Stir mayonnaise mixture and chicken together.
- Makes 1-3/4 cup chicken salad.

Analysis per 1/4 cup serving:

KCAL	CHO(GM)	PROT(GM)	FAT(GM)	CHOL(MG)	SOD(MG)	P/S
180	1	11	15	42	123	2.9

Appropriate for following diets: General, diabetic, low sodium, low cholesterol.

Crispy Oven-fried Chicken

4		Chicken breast halves, raw
1	TBS	Vegetable Oil
1/4	cup	Plain Bread Crumbs
1	tsp	Garlic Powder
1	tsp	Black Pepper

- Preheat oven to 350 degrees.
- Mix together bread crumbs and spices; set aside.
- Wash chicken pieces, removing and discarding the skin.
- Pat chicken dry with paper towels.
- Rub oil onto chicken with hands, discarding any unused oil.
- Toss oil coated chicken pieces in bread crumbs and arrange in baking pan so that pieces do not touch.
- Bake for 1 hour or until done.
- Makes 4 servings.

Analysis per serving:

KCAL	CHO(GM)	PROT(GM)	FAT(GM)	CHOL(MG)	SOD(MG)	P/S
200	5	29	8	8	11-	1/4

Appropriate for following diets: General, diabetic, low sodium, low cholesterol.

Crispy Oven-fried Oat Chicken

4		Chicken breast halves, raw
1	TBS	Vegetable Oil
2	TBS	Oat Bran Cereal, uncooked
2	TBS	Plain Bread Crumbs
1	tsp	Garlic Powder
1	tsp	Black Pepper

- Preheat oven to 350 degrees F.
- Mix together oat cereal, bread crumbs, and spices; set aside.
- Wash chicken pieces, removing and discarding the skin.
- Pat chicken dry with paper towels.
- Rub oil onto chicken with hands, discarding any unused oil.
- Toss oil coated chicken pieces in crumb mixture and arrange in baking pan so that pieces do not touch.
- Bake for 1 hour or until done.
- Makes 4 servings.

Analysis per serving:

KCAL	CHO(GM)	PROT(GM)	FAT(GM)	CHOL(MG)	SOD(MG)	P/S
201	5	28	7	73	87	1.4

Appropriate for following diets: General, diabetic, low sodium, low cholesterol.

Flounder Florentine

1	lb	Flounder Fillets
1/2	tsp	Salt
1/2	tsp	Black Pepper
1/2	tsp	Garlic Powder
1/4	cup	Low-fat Cottage Cheese
1	cup	Spinach, thawed frozen-type
1	TBS	Margarine, melted

- Preheat oven to 400 degrees F.
- Lay fillets across greased baking pan.
- Toss together salt, pepper, garlic, cheese, and spinach.
- Spread spinach mixture over fillets, and roll up fillets.
- Secure fillets with a toothpick if necessary.
- Drizzle margarine over rolls.
- Bake 20-25 minutes.
- Makes 4 servings.

Analysis per serving:

KCAL	CHO(GM)	PROT(GM)	FAT(GM)	CHOL(MG)	SOD(MG)	P/S
199	3	26	9	70	439	1.7

Appropriate for following diets: General, diabetic, low cholesterol.

Flounder Florentine (Low Sodium)

1	lb	Flounder Fillets
1/2	tsp	Black Pepper
1/2	tsp	Garlic Powder
1/4	cup	Low-fat , Low-sodium Cottage Cheese
1	cup	Broccoli, thawed frozen-type
1	TBS	Margarine, melted

- Preheat oven to 400 degrees F.
- Lay fillets across greased baking pan.
- Toss together pepper, garlic, cheese, and broccoli.
- Spread broccoli mixture over fillets, and roll up fillets.
- Secure fillets with a toothpick if necessary.
- Drizzle margarine over rolls.
- Bake 20-25 minutes.
- Makes 4 servings.

Analysis per serving:

KCAL	CHO(GM)	PROT(GM)	FAT(GM)	CHOL(MG)	SOD(MG)	P/S
202	4	26	10	72	174	1.7

Appropriate for following diets: General, diabetic, low sodium, low cholesterol.

Ginger Chicken

1	TBS	Soy Sauce
1	tsp	Ginger
1	clove	Garlic, minced
1	tsp	Sugar
1/4	tsp	Mustard Powder
6	oz	Chicken Breast, boneless

- Combine first 5 ingredients; add chicken and refrigerate for 2-3 hours.
- Broil chicken pieces 8 minutes per side or until cooked through.
- Makes 2 servings.

Analysis per serving:

KCAL	CHO(GM)	PROT(GM)	FAT(GM)	CHOL(MG)	SOD(MG)	P/S
136	4	23	3	60	568	0.8

Appropriate for following diets: General, diabetic, low cholesterol.

Ginger Chicken (Low Sodium)

1	TBS	Soy Sauce, low sodium type
1	tsp	Ginger
1	clove	Garlic, minced
1	tsp	Sugar
1/4	tsp	Mustard Powder
6	oz	Chicken Breast, boneless

- Combine first 5 ingredients; add chicken and refrigerate for 2-3 hours.
- Broil chicken pieces 8 minutes per side or until cooked through.
- Makes 2 servings.

Analysis per serving:

KCAL	CHO(GM)	PROT(GM)	FAT(GM)	CHOL(MG)	SOD(MG)	P/S
133	4	23	3	60	310	0.8

Appropriate for following diets: General, diabetic, low sodium, low cholesterol.

Hawaiian Lamb Chops

4		Lamb Chop- lean, 1" thick
1	13.5 oz can	Pineapple Chunks, reserve juice
1/4	cup	Soy Sauce
1/4	cup	Vinegar
1/2	tsp	Mustard, dry
1/2	tsp	Cloves
1/4	cup	Brown Sugar

- Place chops in shallow baking dish.
- Stir together rest of ingredients and pour over chops; cover and refrigerate for at least 4 hours.
- Preheat oven to 350 degrees F.
- Bake uncovered for 45-50 minutes or until chops are cooked through.
- Makes 4 servings.

Analysis per serving:

KCAL	CHO(GM)	PROT(GM)	FAT(GM)	CHOL(MG)	SOD(MG)	P/S
360	31	34	12	112	1113	0.1

Appropriate for following diets: General, low cholesterol.

Hawaiian Lamb Chops (Low Sodium)

4		Lamb Chop- lean, 1" thick
1	13.5 oz can	Pineapple Chunks, reserve juice
1/4	cup	Soy Sauce, low sodium type
1/4	cup	Vinegar
1/2	tsp	Mustard, dry
1/2	tsp	Cloves
1/4	cup	Brown Sugar

- Place chops in shallow baking dish.
- Stir together rest of ingredients and pour over chops; cover and refrigerate for at least 4 hours.
- Preheat oven to 350 degrees F.
- Bake uncovered for 45-50 minutes or until chops are cooked through.
- Makes 4 servings.

Analysis per serving:

KCAL	CHO(GM)	PROT(GM)	FAT(GM)	CHOL(MG)	SOD(MG)	P/S
535	30	33	12	112	620	0.1

Appropriate for following diets: General, low sodium, low cholesterol.

Marinated Fish Fillets

1	lb	Fish Fillets (eg., haddock, flounder, cod)
3	TBS	Olive Oil
2	cloves	Garlic, minced
1	TBS	Parsley
1	dash	Paprika

- Mix oil, garlic, and parsley; add fish fillets.
- Refrigerate together for 1-2 hours.
- Drain oil off of fish fillets; sprinkle with paprika.
- Broil 5-10 minutes or until fish flakes, turning only once.
- Makes 4 servings.

Analysis per serving:

KCAL	CHO(GM)	PROT(GM)	FAT(GM)	CHOL(MG)	SOD(MG)	P/S
142	0.9	20	7	55	72	0.6

Appropriate for following diets: General, diabetic, low sodium, low cholesterol.

Meatballs

1	lb	Lean Ground Beef
1/2	cup	Plain Bread Crumbs
1/4	cup	Milk
1/4	tsp	Garlic Powder
1	tsp	Salt
1	tsp	Basil
1	tsp	Oregano
1		Egg White

- Stir together all ingredients except ground beef.
- Knead mixture into ground beef.
- Gently form into 16 even sized balls.
- Brown in skillet, turning occasionally, for about 20 minutes or until cooked through.
- Makes 16- 1 oz. meatballs.

Analysis per meatball:

KCAL	CHO(GM)	PROT(GM)	FAT(GM)	CHOL(MG)	SOD(MG)	P/S
88	3	8	5	24	170	0.1

Appropriate for following diets: General, diabetic, low cholesterol.

Meatless Chili

2	cloves	Garlic, finely minced
1	8oz can	Whole Cooking Tomatoes
1	8oz can	Tomato Sauce
1	stalk	Celery, diced
2-3	TBS	Chili Powder
1/2	tsp	Cumin
1	tsp	Oregano
1	tsp	Salt
1	tsp	Sugar
1/4	tsp	Crushed Red Pepper
1	15oz can	Kidney Beans
1	15oz can	Pinto Beans
1	8oz can	Corn, drained

- Mix together all ingredients except beans and corn.
- Simmer mixture in large sauce pan for 1 hour.
- Stir in beans and corn; simmer mixture 20 minutes or until desired consistency.
- Makes 5-6 servings, 1 cup each.

Analysis per serving:

KCAL	CHO(GM)	PROT(GM)	FAT(GM)	CHOL(MG)	SOD(MG)	P/S
248	49	14	2	0	1026	3.4

Appropriate for following diets: General, diabetic, low cholesterol.

Meatless Chili (Low Sodium)

2	cloves	Garlic, finely minced
1	8oz can	Whole Cooking Tomatoes, no salt added type
1	8oz can	Tomato Sauce, no salt added type
1	stalk	Celery, diced
2-3	TBS	Chili Powder
1/2	tsp	Cumin
1	tsp	Oregano
1	tsp	Sugar
1/4	tsp	Crushed Red Pepper
1	15oz can	Kidney Beans
1	15oz can	Pinto Beans
1	8oz can	Corn, drained

- Mix together all ingredients except beans and corn.
- Simmer mixture in large sauce pan for 1 hour.
- Stir in beans and corn; simmer mixture 20 minutes or until desired consistency.
- Makes 5-6 servings, 1 cup each.

Analysis per serving:

KCAL	CHO(GM)	PROT(GM)	FAT(GM)	CHOL(MG)	SOD(MG)	P/S
255	50	14	2	0	328	3.6

Appropriate for following diets: General, diabetic, low sodium, low cholesterol.

Moo-Goo Gai Pan

1	lb	Chicken Breast, boneless
1	dash	Black Pepper
1/2	tsp	Salt
1/2	TBS	Cornstarch
1		Egg White
1	cup	Celery, sliced 1/4"
1/2	lb	Mushrooms, sliced 1/4"
3	TBS	Vegetable Oil
1	tsp	Ginger
1	tsp	Garlic, minced
1/4	tsp	Sugar
1	TBS	Oyster Sauce
1	tsp	Cornstarch
1	TBS	Water

- Slice chicken into thin slices and mix with pepper, 1/4 tsp salt, cornstarch, and egg white; set aside.
- Heat oil in wok on moderately high, add chicken and cook until it is white in color; remove from wok.
- Empty all but 1 TBS of oil from pan and reserve.
- On high, stir-fry celery for 30 seconds then remove from pan.
- Add mushrooms, and 1/4 tsp salt; cook for 1 minute; remove from pan.
- Add 1 TBS reserved oil and drop in ginger and garlic; stir in chicken, vegetables, and sugar.
- Dissolve cornstarch in water, add to pan; cook until thick.
- Makes 4 servings.

Analysis per serving:

KCAL	CHO(GM)	PROT(GM)	FAT(GM)	CHOL(MG)	SOD(MG)	P/S
252	6	29	12	72	675	2.1

Appropriate for following diets: General, diabetic, low cholesterol.

Omelet and Cottage Cheese

1	TB S	Margarine
4		Eggs
1/8	tsp	Salt
1/8	tsp	Black Pepper
1/2	cup	Cottage Cheese, smoothed in blender

- Melt margarine in heavy skillet on low-medium heat.
- Whip rest of ingredients until smooth.
- Pour mixture into pan.
- At first, as edges set, scrape to center of pan and let liquefy top flow to edges to cook.
- Cover to let steam set top of omelet for about 20 seconds.
- When top is set, fold omelet in half and slide onto plate.
- Makes 2 servings.

Analysis per serving:

KCAL	CHO(GM)	PROT(GM)	FAT(GM)	CHOL(MG)	SOD(MG)	P/S
251	3	19	18	556	611	0.9

Appropriate for following diets: General, diabetic.

Omelet and Cottage Cheese (Low Cholesterol)

1	TB S	Margarine
1	cup	Egg Substitute
1/8	tsp	Salt
1/8	tsp	Black Pepper
1/2	cup	Low-fat Cottage Cheese, smoothed in blender

- Melt margarine in heavy skillet on low-medium heat.
- Whip rest of ingredients until smooth.
- Pour mixture into pan.
- At first, as edges set, scrape to center of pan and let liquid top flow to edges to cook.
- Cover to let steam set top of omelet for about 20 seconds.
- When top is set, fold omelet in half and slide onto plate.
- Makes 2 servings.

Analysis per serving:

KCAL	CHO(GM)	PROT(GM)	FAT(GM)	CHOL(MG)	SOD(MG)	P/S
185	2	22	9	4	712	2.2

Appropriate for following diets: General, diabetic, low cholesterol.

Omelet and Cottage Cheese (Low Sodium)

1	TBS	Margarine
4		Eggs
1/8	tsp	Black Pepper
1/2	cup	Cottage Cheese, unsalted, smoothed in blender

- Melt margarine in heavy skillet on low-medium heat.
- Whip rest of ingredients until smooth.
- Pour mixture into pan.
- At first, as edges set, scrape to center of pan and let liquid top flow to edges to cook.
- Cover to let steam set top of omelet for about 20 seconds.
- When top is set, fold omelet in half and slide onto plate.
- Makes 2 servings.

Analysis per serving:

KCAL	CHO(GM)	PROT(GM)	FAT(GM)	CHOL(MG)	SOD(MG)	P/S
228	2	18	16	551	276	1.1

Appropriate for following diets: General, diabetic, low sodium.

Savory Chicken Stew

1		Chicken, cutup, skinned
2-1/2	cups	Water
1	cup	Chicken Broth, homemade
1	16 oz can	Tomatoes, cooking type
1	medium	Carrot, peeled and sliced
1	medium	Potato, cut into chunks
4	stalks	Celery, sliced
1/2	tsp	Black Pepper
1/4	tsp	Thyme
1		Bay Leaf
2	TBS	Cornstarch

- The day before serving dish, simmer chicken, 2-1/4 cup water, chicken broth, tomatoes, carrots, celery, pepper, thyme, and bay leaf in 4 quart sauce pan for 2 hours.
- Add potato in during last 30 minutes of simmer.
- Remove from heat and chill overnight.
- Skim any fat from the surface and bone the chicken, returning the meat to the stew and discarding bones.
- Mix 1/4 cup water and cornstarch and add to stew.
- Reheat stew to boiling, stirring occasionally.
- Reduce the heat to simmer for 15 minutes.
- Makes 6, 1 cup servings.

Analysis per serving:

KCAL	CHO(GM)	PROT(GM)	FAT(GM)	CHOL(MG)	SOD(MG)	P/S
156	13	18	4	51	109	0.9

Appropriate for following diets: General, diabetic, low cholesterol.

Savory Chicken Stew (Low Sodium)

1		Chicken, cutup, skinned
2-1/2	cup	Water
1	cup	Chicken Broth, homemade, no salt
1	16 oz can	Tomatoes, cooking type, no salt added
1	medium	Carrot, peeled and sliced
1	medium	Potato, cut into chunks
4	stalks	Celery, sliced
1/2	tsp	Black Pepper
1/4	tsp	Thyme
1		Bay Leaf
2	TBS	Cornstarch

- The day before serving dish, simmer chicken, 2-1/4 cup water, chicken broth, tomatoes, carrots, celery, pepper, thyme, and bay leaf in 4 quart sauce pan for 2 hours.
- Add potato in during last 30 minutes of simmer.
- Remove from heat and chill overnight.
- Skim any fat from the surface and bone the chicken, returning the meat to the stew and discarding bones.
- Mix 1/4 cup water and cornstarch and add to stew.
- Reheat stew to boiling, stirring occasionally.
- Reduce the heat to simmer for 15 minutes.
- Makes 6, 1 cup servings.

Analysis per serving:

KCAL	CHO(GM)	PROT(GM)	FAT(GM)	CHOL(MG)	SOD(MG)	P/S
158	13	18	4	51	86	0.9

Appropriate for following diets: General, diabetic, low sodium, low cholesterol.

Scalloped Oysters

1	pint	Oysters
1/2	cup	Half-n-Half
3	cups	Soft Bread Crumbs
1/2	cup	Margarine, melted
1	tsp	Salt
2	tsp	Celery Seed
1/4	tsp	Black Pepper

- Preheat oven to 375 degrees F.
- Grease glass baking dish (11-1/2"x7-1/2"); arrange oysters in baking dish.
- Pour half of cream over oysters.
- Mix bread crumbs, margarine, and seasonings together; sprinkle over oysters.
- Pour remaining cream over crumb mixture.
- Bake uncovered for 35-40 minutes.
- Makes 4 servings.

Analysis per serving:

KCAL	CHO(GM)	PROT(GM)	FAT(GM)	CHOL(MG)	SOD(MG)	P/S
619	61	21	32	70	1480	1.4

Appropriate for following diets: General.

Scalloped Oysters (Low Cholesterol)

1	pint	Oysters
1/2	cup	Evaporated Skimmed Milk
3	cups	Soft Bread Crumbs
1/4	cup	Margarine, melted
1	tsp	Salt
2	tsp	Celery Seed
1/4	tsp	Black Pepper

- Preheat oven to 375 degrees F.
- Grease glass baking dish (11-1/2"x7-1/2"); arrange oysters in baking dish.
- Pour half of milk over oysters.
- Mix bread crumbs, margarine, and seasonings together; sprinkle over oysters.
- Pour remaining milk over crumb mixture.
- Bake uncovered for 35-40 minutes.
- Makes 4 servings.

Analysis per serving:

KCAL	CHO(GM)	PROT(GM)	FAT(GM)	CHOL(MG)	SOD(MG)	P/S
479	63	22	15	60	1504	1.9

Appropriate for following diets: General, diabetic, low cholesterol.

Scallops and Rice (Low Sodium)

2	cups	Tomatoes, canned, cooking, no salt added
1/2	6 oz can	Tomato Paste, no salt added
2	TBS	Parsley, dried
2	cups	Celery, diced
1/4	tsp	Basil
1/2	tsp	Oregano
1/8	tsp	Black Pepper
14	oz	Scallops
2	cups	Rice, cooked without salt

- Stir all ingredients except scallops and rice in large heavy skillet.
- Bring to a boil and then reduce to a simmer for about 30 minutes; stir occasionally.
- Add scallops and simmer an additional 7-10 minutes.
- Serve scallops and sauce over rice.
- Makes 4 servings.

Analysis per serving:

KCAL	CHO(GM)	PROT(GM)	FAT(GM)	CHOL(MG)	SOD(MG)	P/S
306	47	29	2	53	361	1.5

Appropriate for following diets: General, diabetic, low sodium, low cholesterol.

Seafood and Rice

2	cups	Tomatoes, canned, cooking type
1/2	6 oz can	Tomato Paste, no salt added
2	TBS	Parsley, dried
2	cups	Celery, diced
1/4	tsp	Basil
1/2	tsp	Oregano
1	tsp	Salt
1/8	tsp	Black Pepper
1	7 oz pkg	Shrimp, frozen, peeled
1/2	lb	Scallops
2	cups	Rice, cooked

- Stir all ingredients except shrimp, scallops, and rice in large heavy skillet.
- Bring to a boil; reduce to a simmer for about 30 minutes; stir occasionally.
- Add seafood and simmer an additional 7-10 minutes.
- Serve seafood and sauce over rice.
- Makes 4 servings.

Analysis per serving:

KCAL	CHO(GM)	PROT(GM)	FAT(GM)	CHOL(MG)	SOD(MG)	P/S
298	39	32	2	116	1212	1.8

Appropriate for following diets: General, diabetic, low cholesterol.

Sesame Chicken With Green Beans

2	tsp	Olive Oil
1/2	tsp	Sesame Seeds
1/2	lb	Chicken Breast, boneless, cubed (3/4")
2	tsp	Coconut, dried, shredded
1/2	tsp	Salt
1/8	tsp	Black Pepper
1/2	tsp	Soy Sauce
2	cups	Green Beans, frozen, French cut, cooked

- Cook sesame seeds in oil until light brown.
- Add chicken and sauté until cooked through.
- Stir in coconut, salt, pepper, and soy sauce.
- Serve over hot green beans.
- Makes 2 servings.

Analysis per serving:

KCAL	CHO(GM)	PROT(GM)	FAT(GM)	CHOL(MG)	SOD(MG)	P/S
237	11	29	9	72	641	0.6

Appropriate for following diets: General, diabetic, low cholesterol.

Sesame Chicken With Green Beans (Low Sodium)

2	tsp	Olive Oil
1/2	tsp	Sesame Seeds
1/2	lb	Chicken Breast, boneless, cubed (3/4")
2	tsp	Coconut, dried, shredded
1/8	tsp	Black Pepper
1/2	tsp	Soy Sauce, low sodium type
2	cups	Green Beans, frozen, French cut, cooked without salt

- Cook sesame seeds in oil until light brown.
- Add chicken and sauté until cooked through.
- Stir in coconut, pepper, and soy sauce.
- Serve over hot green beans.
- Makes 2 servings.

Analysis per serving:

KCAL	CHO(GM)	PROT(GM)	FAT(GM)	CHOL(MG)	SOD(MG)	P/S
236	11	29	9	72	110	0.6

Appropriate for following diets: General, diabetic, low sodium, low cholesterol.

Shrimp and Rice

2	cups	Tomatoes, canned, cooking type
1/2	6 oz can	Tomato Paste, no salt added
2	TBS	Parsley, dried
2	cups	Celery, diced
1/4	tsp	Basil
1/2	tsp	Oregano
1	tsp	Salt
1/8	tsp	Black Pepper
2	7 oz pkg	Shrimp, frozen, peeled
2	cups	Rice, cooked

- Stir all ingredient except shrimp and rice in large heavy skillet.
- Bring to a boil; reduce to a simmer for about 30 minutes; stir occasionally.
- Add shrimp and simmer an additional 7-10 minutes.
- Serve shrimp and sauce over rice.
- Makes 4 servings.

Analysis per serving:

KCAL	CHO(GM)	PROT(GM)	FAT(GM)	CHOL(MG)	SOD(MG)	P/S
285	39	29	2	150	1218	1.9

Appropriate for following diets: General, diabetic.

Spinach Frittata

4		Eggs, well beaten
3/4	cup	Spinach, cooked, drained
2	TBS	Parsley
1/4	tsp	Salt
1/8	tsp	Black Pepper
1/2	clove	Garlic, minced
1/4	tsp	Nutmeg
1	TBS	Margarine
1	tsp	Sesame Seeds, lightly toasted

- Combine first 7 ingredients in large bowl.
- Melt margarine in bottom of heavy skillet on low-medium heat.
- Pour in egg/spinach mixture; shaking occasionally to prevent sticking.
- Cover pan to steam cook the top of frittata.
- Makes 2 servings.

Analysis per serving:

KCAL	CHO(GM)	PROT(GM)	FAT(GM)	CHOL(MG)	SOD(MG)	P/S
242	6	15	18	548	517	0.9

Appropriate for following diets: General, diabetic.

Spinach Frittata (Low Cholesterol)

1	Cup	Egg Substitute
3/4	cup	Spinach, cooked, drained
2	TBS	Parsley
1/4	tsp	Salt
1/8	tsp	Black Pepper
1/2	clove	Garlic, minced
1/4	tsp	Nutmeg
1	TBS	Margarine
1	tsp	Sesame Seeds, lightly toasted

- Combine first 7 ingredients in large bowl.
- Melt margarine in bottom of heavy skillet on low-medium heat.
- Pour in egg substitute/spinach mixture; shaking occasionally to prevent sticking.
- Cover pan to steam cook the top of frittata.
- Makes 2 servings.

Analysis per serving:

KCAL	CHO(GM)	PROT(GM)	FAT(GM)	CHOL(MG)	SOD(MG)	P/S
190	6	18	11	2	601	2.4

Appropriate for following diets: General, diabetic, low cholesterol.

Spinach Frittata (Low Sodium)

4		Eggs, well beaten
3/4	cup	Spinach, cooked, drained
2	TBS	Parsley
1/8	tsp	Black Pepper
1/2	clove	Garlic, minced
1/4	tsp	Nutmeg
1	TBS	Margarine
1	tsp	Sesame Seeds, lightly toasted

- Combine first 7 ingredients in large bowl.
- Melt margarine in bottom of heavy skillet on low-medium heat.
- Pour in egg/spinach mixture; shaking occasionally to prevent sticking.
- Cover pan to steam cook the top of frittata.
- Makes 2 servings.

Analysis per serving:

KCAL	CHO(GM)	PROT(GM)	FAT(GM)	CHOL(MG)	SOD(MG)	P/S
242	6	15	18	548	273	0.9

Appropriate for following diets: General, diabetic, low sodium.

Spinach Lasagna

4	cups	Tomato Sauce*
1	8 oz. pkg	Lasagna Noodles, uncooked
1	cup	Low-fat Cottage Cheese
1	TBS	Parsley
1/2	tsp	Garlic Powder
1	cup	Spinach, thawed frozen-type
1		Egg White

* see recipe elsewhere in this book

- Cook Lasagna noodles according to package directions.
- Preheat oven to 350 degrees F.
- Mix cottage cheese, parsley, garlic, spinach, and egg white together.
- Spoon small amount of sauce on bottom of 9x13 baking pan.
- Layer noodles then spinach mixture then tomato sauce; repeat layers a second time.
- Finish top with a layer of sauce.
- Bake uncovered for 45 minutes; let stand 15 minutes after baking to set before serving.
- Makes 8 servings.

Analysis per serving:

KCAL	CHO(GM)	PROT(GM)	FAT(GM)	CHOL(MG)	SOD(MG)	P/S
144	27	9	1	1.3	883	0.5

Appropriate for following diets: General, diabetic, low cholesterol.

Spinach Lasagna (Low Sodium)

4	cups	Tomato Sauce, low sodium*
1	8 oz. pkg	Lasagna Noodles, uncooked
1	cup	Low-fat Cottage Cheese, unsalted type
1	TBS	Parsley
1/2	tsp	Garlic Powder
1	cup	Spinach, thawed frozen-type
1		Egg White

* see recipe elsewhere in this book

- Cook Lasagna noodles according to package directions.
- Preheat oven to 350 degrees F.
- Mix cottage cheese, parsley, garlic, spinach, and egg white together.
- Spoon small amount of sauce on bottom of 9x13 baking pan.
- Layer noodles then spinach mixture then tomato sauce; repeat layers a second time.
- Finish top with a layer of sauce.
- Bake uncovered for 45 minutes; let stand 15 minutes after baking to set before serving.
- Makes 8 servings.

Analysis per serving:

KCAL	CHO(GM)	PROT(GM)	FAT(GM)	CHOL(MG)	SOD(MG)	P/S
153	27	9	1	1.3	175	0.2

Appropriate for following diets: General, diabetic, low sodium, low cholesterol.

Split Pea Soup

6	cups	Chicken Broth, homemade
1	lb	Split Peas, dried type
3	medium	Carrots, sliced
1	medium	Potato, cut into chunks
1-1/2	tsp	Salt
1/2	tsp	Garlic Powder
1/2	tsp	Black Pepper

- About 1-1/2 hours before serving, stir all ingredients into pot.
- Bring to a boil.
- Reduce the heat and simmer, covered, for an hour.
- Makes 8 servings of 1 cup each.

Analysis per serving:

KCAL	CHO(GM)	PROT(GM)	FAT(GM)	CHOL(MG)	SOD(MG)	P/S
154	27	11	1	0	380	0.2

Appropriate for following diets: General, diabetic, low cholesterol.

Split Pea Soup (Low Sodium)

6	cups	Chicken Broth, homemade
1	lb	Split Peas, dried type
3	medium	Carrots, sliced
1	medium	Potato, cut into chunks
1	tsp	Salt
1/2	tsp	Garlic Powder
1/2	tsp	Black Pepper

- Stir all of the ingredients together in a 3 quart saucepan and bring to a boil.
- Reduce the heat and simmer, covered, for an hour.
- Makes 8 servings of 1 cup each.

Analysis per serving:

KCAL	CHO(GM)	PROT(GM)	FAT(GM)	CHOL(MG)	SOD(MG)	P/S
142	27	9	1	0	259	2.0

Appropriate for following diets: General, diabetic, low sodium, low cholesterol.

Tuna Casserole

1-1/2	cups	Stuffing Mix
1	cup	Milk
2		Eggs
2	5.25 oz cans	Tuna
1/2	tsp	Salt

- Preheat oven to 350 degrees F.
- Grease a 1 quart casserole dish.
- In large bowl, combine stuffing mix and milk, let stand 5 minutes.
- Stir in remaining ingredients; spread into casserole dish.
- Bake for 30 minutes.
- Makes 4 servings.

Analysis per serving:

KCAL	CHO(GM)	PROT(GM)	FAT(GM)	CHOL(MG)	SOD(MG)	P/S
213	14	26	6	303	805	0.3

Appropriate for following diets: General, diabetic.

Tuna Casserole (Low Cholesterol)

1-1/2	cups	Stuffing Mix
1	cup	Skim Milk
1/2	cup	Egg Substitute
2	5.25 oz cans	Tuna
1/2	tsp	Salt

- Preheat oven to 350 degrees F.
- Grease a 1 quart casserole dish.
- In large bowl, combine stuffing mix and milk, let stand 5 minutes.
- Stir in remaining ingredients; spread into casserole dish.
- Bake for 30 minutes.
- Makes 4 servings.

Analysis per serving:

KCAL	CHO(GM)	PROT(GM)	FAT(GM)	CHOL(MG)	SOD(MG)	P/S
184	14	27	2	159	827	2.7

Appropriate for following diets: General, diabetic, low cholesterol.

Turkey Meatballs

1	lb	Ground Turkey
1/2	cup	Plain Bread Crumbs
1/4	cup	Milk
2	tsp	Vegetable Oil
1/4	tsp	Garlic Powder
1	tsp	Salt
1	tsp	Basil
1	tsp	Oregano
1		Egg White

- Stir together all ingredients except ground turkey.
- Knead mixture into ground turkey.
- Gently form into 16 even sized balls.
- Brown in skillet, turning occasionally, for about 20 minutes or until cooked through.
- Makes 12- 1 oz. meatballs.

Analysis per meatball:

KCAL	CHO(GM)	PROT(GM)	FAT(GM)	CHOL(MG)	SOD(MG)	P/S
73	3	9	3	24	173	1.0

Appropriate for following diets: General, diabetic, low cholesterol.

Chickpeas (Garbanzos) Italiano

1	TBS	Olive Oil
2	cloves	Garlic, minced
1	12 oz can	Garbanzo Beans (Chickpeas)
1/2	cup	Tomato Sauce, plain
1/4	cup	Water
1/4	tsp	Oregano
1/4	tsp	Basil
1/8	tsp	Salt
1/8	tsp	Pepper
2	tsp	Parsley

- Sautee garlic in oil.
- Stir in rest of ingredients and cook 20 minutes.
- Makes 2 servings.

Analysis per serving:

KCAL	CHO(GM)	PROT(GM)	FAT(GM)	CHOL(MG)	SOD(MG)	P/S
251	34	9	10	0	1176	0.6

Appropriate for following diets: General, diabetic, low cholesterol.

Chickpeas (Garbanzos) Italiano (Low Sodium)

1	TBS	Olive Oil
2	cloves	Garlic, minced
1	12 oz can	Garbanzo Beans (Chickpeas), no salt added
1/2	cup	Tomato Sauce, plain, no salt added
1/4	cup	Water
1/4	tsp	Oregano
1/4	tsp	Basil
1/8	tsp	Pepper
2	tsp	Parsley

- Sautee garlic in oil.
- Stir in rest of ingredients and cook 20 minutes.
- Makes 2 servings.

Analysis per serving:

KCAL	CHO(GM)	PROT(GM)	FAT(GM)	CHOL(MG)	SOD(MG)	P/S
216	30	9	7	0	86	0.7

Appropriate for following diets: General, diabetic, low sodium, low cholesterol.

Corn Casserole

2	TBS	Margarine, melted
1	tsp	Flour
2	TBS	Chicken Broth, homemade
1/4	tsp	Mustard, powder
2	tsp	Chives, chopped
1	tsp	Parsley
2	cups	Corn, frozen, thawed
1	cup	Cottage Cheese, whipped smooth in blender

- Preheat oven to 325 degrees F.
- Blend margarine with flour until smooth.
- Stir in rest of ingredients until well mixed.
- Pour into greased 1-1/2 qt casserole dish.
- Bake for 30 minutes.
- Makes 6 servings.

Analysis per serving:

KCAL	CHO(GM)	PROT(GM)	FAT(GM)	CHOL(MG)	SOD(MG)	P/S
123	13	7	6	5	188	1.0

Appropriate for following diets: General, diabetic, low cholesterol.

Corn Casserole (Low Sodium)

2	TBS	Margarine, melted
1	tsp	Flour
2	TBS	Chicken Broth, homemade, no salt
1/4	tsp	Mustard, powder
2	tsp	Chives, chopped
1	tsp	Parsley
2	cups	Corn, frozen, thawed
1	cup	Cottage Cheese, unsalted, type, whipped smooth in blender

- Preheat oven to 325 degrees F.
- Blend margarine with flour until smooth.
- Stir in rest of ingredients until well mixed.
- Pour into greased 1-1/2 qt casserole dish.
- Bake for 30 minutes.
- Makes 6 servings.

Analysis per serving:

KCAL	CHO(GM)	PROT(GM)	FAT(GM)	CHOL(MG)	SOD(MG)	P/S
101	12	6	4	2	50	2.3

Appropriate for following diets: General, diabetic, low sodium, low cholesterol.

Parsley Potatoes

2	medium	All-purpose Potatoes
1	TBS	Margarine
1/2	TBS	Parsley
1/8	tsp	Black Pepper

- Peel, quarter, and boil potatoes until tender - about 20 minutes.
- Drain potatoes and set aside in a medium sized mixing bowl.
- Melt margarine and stir in parsley and pepper.
- Pour margarine mixture over potatoes, toss gently, and serve immediately.
- Makes 4 servings, 1/2 cup each.

Analysis per serving:

KCAL	CHO(GM)	PROT(GM)	FAT(GM)	CHOL(MG)	SOD(MG)	P/S
84	14	1	3	0	42	2.1

Appropriate for following diets: General, diabetic, low sodium, low cholesterol.

Pineapple Sweet Potatoes

1-1/2	lb	Sweet Potatoes, peeled, boiled until tender
1-1/2	tsp	Salt
1/8	tsp	Black Pepper
2	cups	Pineapple Tidbits (do NOT drain)
2	TBS	Margarine

- Preheat oven to 350 degrees F.
- Lightly grease 1 quart casserole dish.
- Mash sweet potatoes until smooth.
- Stir in remaining ingredients.
- Bake for 20 minutes.
- Makes 8 servings.

Analysis per serving:

KCAL	CHO(GM)	PROT(GM)	FAT(GM)	CHOL(MG)	SOD(MG)	P/S
136	27	2	3	0	446	2.5

Appropriate for following diets: General, low cholesterol.

Pineapple Sweet Potatoes (Low Sodium)

1-1/2	lbs	Sweet Potatoes, peeled, boiled until tender
1/8	tsp	Black Pepper
2	cups	Pineapple Tidbits (do NOT drain)
2	TBS	Margarine

- Preheat oven to 350 degrees F.
- Lightly grease 1 quart casserole dish.
- Mash sweet potatoes until smooth.
- Stir in remaining ingredients.
- Bake for 20 minutes.
- Makes 8 servings.

Analysis per serving:

KCAL	CHO(GM)	PROT(GM)	FAT(GM)	CHOL(MG)	SOD(MG)	P/S
136	27	2	3	0	80	2.5

Appropriate for following diets: General, low sodium, low cholesterol.

Rice Pilaf

1	clove	Garlic, minced
2	TBS	Diced Green Pepper
2	TBS	Margarine
1	cup	Uncooked Rice
2	cups	Chicken Broth, homemade

- Cook garlic, green pepper, margarine, and rice in 1 quart saucepan.
- Stir in chicken broth and bring to a boil.
- Reduce heat so that the mixture is simmering; cover.
- Allow to simmer for 15 minutes.
- Without removing lid, remove the pan from the heat and allow the rice to sit for 10 minutes.
- Remove lid, fluff rice with a fork and serve.
- Makes 3 cups of rice.

Analysis per 1/2 cup serving:

KCAL	CHO(GM)	PROT(GM)	FAT(GM)	CHOL(MG)	SOD(MG)	P/S
161	26	4	4	0.3	163	1.8

Appropriate for following diets: General, diabetic, low cholesterol.

Rice Pilaf (Low Sodium)

1	clove	Garlic, minced
2	TBS	Diced Green Pepper
2	TBS	Margarine
1	cup	Uncooked Rice
2	cups	Chicken Broth, homemade, no salt

- Cook garlic, green pepper, margarine, and rice in 1 quart saucepan.
- Stir in chicken broth and bring to a boil.
- Reduce heat so that the mixture is simmering, cover.
- Allow to simmer for 15 minutes.
- Without removing lid, remove the pan from the heat and allow the rice to sit for 10 minutes.
- Remove lid, fluff rice with a fork and serve.
- Makes 3 cups of rice.

Analysis per 1/2 cup serving:

KCAL	CHO(GM)	PROT(GM)	FAT(GM)	CHOL(MG)	SOD(MG)	P/S
144	23	3	4	0	59	2.0

Appropriate for following diets: General, diabetic, low sodium, low cholesterol.

Spanish Potatoes

1/2	cup	Celery, diced
1	clove	Garlic, minced
2	TBS	Olive Oil
3/4	cup	Parsley, fresh, chopped
1/4	cup	Pimiento, chopped
1/8	tsp	Black Pepper
1	cup	Chicken Broth, homemade
6	medium	Potatoes, thinly sliced

- Sauté celery and garlic in oil until soft in a heavy skillet.
- Stir in parsley, pimiento, pepper, and broth; remove from heat.
- Layer potato slices in broth in skillet.
- Bring to a boil, reduce heat and simmer, covered, until potatoes are tender (about 20 minutes).
- Lift potatoes out of pan with a slotted spoon into serving dish and then pour cooking liquid over top.
- Makes 8 servings.

Analysis per serving:

KCAL	CHO(GM)	PROT(GM)	FAT(GM)	CHOL(MG)	SOD(MG)	P/S
126	21	3	4	0	22	0.7

Appropriate for following diets: General, diabetic, low cholesterol.

Spanish Potatoes (Low Sodium)

1/2	cup	Celery, diced
1	clove	Garlic, minced
2	TBS	Olive Oil
3/4	cup	Parsley, fresh, chopped
1/4	cup	Pimiento, chopped
1/8	tsp	Black Pepper
1	cup	Chicken Broth, homemade, no salt
6	medium	Potatoes, thinly sliced

- Sauté celery and garlic in oil until soft in a heavy skillet.
- Stir in parsley, pimiento, pepper, and broth; remove from heat.
- Layer potato slices in broth in skillet.
- Bring to a boil, reduce heat and simmer, covered, until potatoes are tender (about 20 minutes).
- Lift potatoes out of pan with a slotted spoon into serving dish and then pour cooking liquid over top.
- Makes 8 servings.

Analysis per serving:

KCAL	CHO(GM)	PROT(GM)	FAT(GM)	CHOL(MG)	SOD(MG)	P/S
123	21	2	4	0	15	0.7

Appropriate for following diets: General, diabetic, low sodium, low cholesterol.

Succotash

2	cup	Lima Beans, cooked
1	TBS	Vegetable Oil
1	clove	Garlic, minced
2-1/2	cups	Corn, frozen or canned
1	small	Red, Sweet Pepper, diced
1/4	cup	Celery, diced

- Sauté garlic, celery, and red pepper in oil for about 5 minutes.
- Stir in lima beans and corn.
- Simmer covered for 12-15 minutes, stirring occasionally.
- Makes 4 servings.

Analysis per serving:

KCAL	CHO(GM)	PROT(GM)	FAT(GM)	CHOL(MG)	SOD(MG)	P/S
206	39	9	4	0	71	2.5

Appropriate for following diets: General, diabetic, low cholesterol.

Succotash (Low Sodium)

2	cup	Lima Beans, cooked, unsalted
1	TBS	Vegetable Oil
1	clove	Garlic, minced
2-1/2	cups	Corn, frozen or canned, no salt type
1	small	Red, Sweet Pepper, diced
1/4	cup	Celery, diced

- Sauté garlic, celery, and red pepper in oil for about 5 minutes.
- Stir in lima beans and corn.
- Simmer covered for 12-15 minutes, stirring occasionally.
- Makes 4 servings.

Analysis per serving:

KCAL	CHO(GM)	PROT(GM)	FAT(GM)	CHOL(MG)	SOD(MG)	P/S
204	28	8	4	0	57	2.5

Appropriate for following diets: General, diabetic, low sodium, low cholesterol.

Sweet and Sour Red Cabbage

1	small	Head Red Cabbage, shredded
1/2	cup	Water
2	tsp	Cornstarch
1/2	cup	Vinegar
3	TBS	Sugar
1/4	tsp	Salt
1/2	tsp	Caraway Seeds

- Steam cabbage for 10 minutes; drain thoroughly.
- Mix water and cornstarch, then add vinegar, sugar, salt, and caraway seeds.
- Simmer cornstarch mixture until it starts to thicken.
- Toss sauce with hot cabbage, serve immediately.
- Makes 8 servings.

Analysis per serving:

KCAL	CHO(GM)	PROT(GM)	FAT(GM)	CHOL(MG)	SOD(MG)	P/S
31	0	0.6	0.1	0	69	3.0

Appropriate for following diets: General, diabetic, low sodium, low cholesterol.

Tomato Sauce

1	clove	Garlic, minced
1	TBS	Olive Oil, or any vegetable oil
1	16 oz can	Whole Cooking Tomatoes
1	16 oz can	Tomato Sauce
1	tsp	Salt
1/2	tsp	Sugar
1	tsp	Basil
1	tsp	Oregano
1/8	tsp	Crushed Red Pepper
1/2	tsp	Crushed Fennel Seed
1/2	tsp	Parsley
1	medium	Bay Leaf

- Heat oil in 3 quart sauce pan.
- Sauté garlic.
- Stir in all other ingredients and bring to a boil.
- Reduce heat and simmer (covered loosely) for 1 hour.
- Stir in cooked meatballs, if desired, 20 minutes before serving.
- Makes 4 cups sauce.

Analysis per 1/2 cup serving:

KCAL	CHO(GM)	PROT(GM)	FAT(GM)	CHOL(MG)	SOD(MG)	P/S
48	8	2	2	0	713	0.9

Appropriate for following diets: General, diabetic, low cholesterol.

Tomato Sauce (Low Sodium)

1	clove	Garlic, minced
1	TBS	Olive Oil, or any vegetable oil
1	16 oz can	Whole Cooking Tomatoes, no salt added
1	16 oz can	Tomato Sauce, no salt added
1/2	tsp	Sugar
1	tsp	Basil
1	tsp	Oregano
1/8	tsp	Crushed Red Pepper
1/2	tsp	Crushed Fennel Seed
1/2	tsp	Parsley
1	medium	Bay Leaf

- Heat oil in 3 quart sauce pan.
- Sauté garlic.
- Stir in all other ingredients and bring to a boil.
- Reduce heat and simmer (covered loosely) for 1 hour.
- Stir in cooked meatballs, if desired, 20 minutes before serving.
- Makes 4 cups sauce.

Analysis per 1/2 cup serving:

KCAL	CHO(GM)	PROT(GM)	FAT(GM)	CHOL(MG)	SOD(MG)	P/S
52	8	2	2	0	24	0.8

Appropriate for following diets: General, diabetic, low sodium, low cholesterol.

Apple Salad

1/2	cup	Apples, thinly sliced
1/2	cup	Cottage Cheese, low-fat
2	TBS	Mayonnaise
1/2	cup	Carrot, raw, shredded
1/2	cup	Celery, raw, diced
1/8	tsp	Salt

- Mix all ingredients together.
- Serve immediately.
- Makes 4 servings, 1/2 cup each.

Analysis per serving:

KCAL	CHO(GM)	PROT(GM)	FAT(GM)	CHOL(MG)	SOD(MG)	P/S
105	8	4	7	8	227	1.9

Appropriate for following diets: General, diabetic, low cholesterol.

Apple Salad (Low Sodium)

1/2	cup	Apples, thinly sliced
1/2	cup	Cottage Cheese, unsalted type, low-fat
2	TBS	Mayonnaise
1/2	cup	Carrot, raw, shredded
1/2	cup	Celery, raw, diced

- Mix all ingredients together.
- Serve immediately.
- Makes 4 servings, 1/2 cup each.

Analysis per serving:

KCAL	CHO(GM)	PROT(GM)	FAT(GM)	CHOL(MG)	SOD(MG)	P/S
93	8	4	6	5	60	2.5

Appropriate for following diets: General, diabetic, low sodium, low cholesterol.

Carrot/Raisin Salad

2	cups	Carrot, shredded
1/3	cup	Raisins
1/3	cup	Mayonnaise or Salad Dressing
1/4	tsp	Salt

- Toss all ingredients together and serve.
- Makes 5 servings, 1/2 cup each.

Analysis per serving:

KCAL	CHO(GM)	PROT(GM)	FAT(GM)	CHOL(MG)	SOD(MG)	P/S
54	12	1	1	0.5	119	3.2

Appropriate for following diets: General, diabetic, low cholesterol.

Coleslaw

1/4	cup	Vinegar
1	TBS	Vegetable Oil
1	tsp	Celery Seed
1/4	tsp	Mustard, dried
1/8	tsp	Garlic Powder
2	cups	Cabbage, shredded
1/2	cup	Carrot, shredded
1/4	cup	Green Sweet Pepper, diced

- Mix first 5 ingredients.
- Toss in vegetables, cover, and refrigerate at least 2 hours.
- Toss before serving; makes 3 servings.

Analysis per serving:

KCAL	CHO(GM)	PROT(GM)	FAT(GM)	CHOL(MG)	SOD(MG)	P/S
67	7	1	5	0	19	2.6

Appropriate for following diets: General, diabetic, low sodium, low cholesterol.

Cucumber/Tomato Salad

1	TBS	Vegetable Oil
1	TBS	Vinegar
1/4	tsp	Sugar
1/2	clove	Garlic, minced
1/4	tsp	Black Pepper
1/2	tsp	Salt
1	medium	Tomato, raw, cut into chunks
3/4	medium	Cucumber, raw, peeled, sliced

- Mix first six ingredients together.
- Add tomato and cucumber and toss gently.
- Refrigerate mixture for 1 hour, tossing mixture once during that time and again before serving.
- Makes 4 servings, 1/2 cup each.

Analysis per serving:

KCAL	CHO(GM)	PROT(GM)	FAT(GM)	CHOL(MG)	SOD(MG)	P/S
46	4	1	4	0	248	2.5

Appropriate for following diets: General, diabetic, low cholesterol.

Marinated Tomatoes

1/2	TBS	Vegetable Oil
1	TBS	Vinegar
1/2	tsp	Basil
1/2	tsp	Oregano
1/4	tsp	Black Pepper
1/4	tsp	Sugar
1/2	clove	Garlic, minced
3	medium	Tomatoes- raw, ripe, cut into chunks

- Mix first seven ingredients; add tomato chunks and toss gently.
- Refrigerate mixture at least 2 hours, tossing mixture occasionally.
- Makes 4 servings, 1/2 cup each

Analysis per serving:

KCAL	CHO(GM)	PROT(GM)	FAT(GM)	CHOL(MG)	SOD(MG)	P/S
38	5	1	2	0	8	2.6

Appropriate for following diets: General, diabetic, low sodium, low cholesterol.

Marinated Zucchini Sticks

1/2	TBS	Vegetable Oil
1	TBS	Vinegar
1/2	tsp	Basil
1/2	tsp	Oregano
1/4	tsp	Black Pepper
1/4	tsp	Sugar
1/2	clove	Garlic, minced
2		Zucchini, raw, cut into 2"x1/4"x1/4" sticks

- Mix first seven ingredients; add zucchini sticks and toss gently.
- Refrigerate mixture at least 4 hours, tossing mixture occasionally.
- Makes 4 servings, 1/2 cup each.

Analysis per serving:

KCAL	CHO(GM)	PROT(GM)	FAT(GM)	CHOL(MG)	SOD(MG)	P/S
27	3	1	2	0	1.8	2.5

Appropriate for following diets: General, diabetic, low sodium, low cholesterol.

Apple Ring Cake

3	cups	Flour
2-1/2	cups	Sugar
4		Eggs
1	cup	Vegetable Oil
1/3	cup	Pineapple Juice
1	TBS	Baking Powder
1/2	tsp	Salt
2-1/2	tsp	Vanilla Extract
6		Apples, raw, peeled, cored, thinly sliced
2	tsp	Cinnamon
3	TBS	Sugar

- Preheat oven to 350 degrees F.
- Grease and flour tube pan or bundt pan.
- Mix first 8 ingredients; blend until smooth.
- In a small bowl, mix apples, cinnamon, and 3 TBS sugar together.
- Pour 1/2 of cake batter into pan; top with 1/2 of apple mixture.
- Put remainder of batter and then apples into pan.
- Bake for about 1-1/2 hours.
- Makes 12 servings.

Analysis per serving:

KCAL	CHO(GM)	PROT(GM)	FAT(GM)	CHOL(MG)	SOD(MG)	P/S
509	79	5	21	91	191	2.2

Appropriate for following diets: General.

Apple Ring Cake (Low Cholesterol)

3	cups	Flour
2-1/2	cups	Sugar
1	cup	Egg Substitute
1	cup	Vegetable Oil
1/3	cup	Pineapple Juice
1	TBS	Baking Powder
1/2	tsp	Salt
2-1/2	tsp	Vanilla Extract
6		Apples, raw, peeled, cored, thinly sliced
2	tsp	Cinnamon
3	TBS	Sugar

- Preheat oven to 350 degrees F.
- Grease and flour tube pan or bundt pan.
- Mix first 8 ingredients; blend until smooth.
- In a small bowl, mix apples, cinnamon, and 3 TBS sugar together.
- Pour 1/2 of cake batter into pan; top with 1/2 of apple mixture.
- Put remainder of batter and then apples into pan.
- Bake for about 1-1/2 hours.
- Makes 12 servings.

Analysis per serving:

KCAL	CHO(GM)	PROT(GM)	FAT(GM)	CHOL(MG)	SOD(MG)	P/S
500	79	6	19	0.3	205	2.5

Appropriate for following diets: General, low cholesterol.

Apple Ring Cake (Low Sodium)

3	cups	Flour
2-1/2	cups	Sugar
4		Eggs
1	cup	Vegetable Oil
1/3	cup	Pineapple Juice
1	TBS	Baking Powder, low sodium type
1/2	tsp	Salt
2-1/2	tsp	Vanilla Extract
6		Apples, raw, peeled, cored, thinly sliced
2	tsp	Cinnamon
3	TBS	Sugar

- Preheat oven to 350 degrees F.
- Grease and flour tube pan or bundt pan.
- Mix first 7 ingredients; blend until smooth.
- In a small bowl, mix apples, cinnamon, and 3 TBS sugar together.
- Pour 1/2 of cake batter into pan; top with 1/2 of apple mixture.
- Put remainder of batter and then apples into pan.
- Bake for about 1-1/2 hours.
- Makes 12 servings.

Analysis per serving:

KCAL	CHO(GM)	PROT(GM)	FAT(GM)	CHOL(MG)	SOD(MG)	P/S
509	80	5	21	01	25	2.2

Appropriate for following diets: General, low sodium.

Aunt Eudice's Noodle Kugel

12	oz	Cream cheese, softened
1	lb	Wide Egg Noodles, cooked, drained
6		Eggs
1 cup minus 1 TBS		Sugar
2	tsp	Salt
4	cups	Milk
1/2	cup	Margarine
1/2	cup	Cornflake Cereal Crumbs

- Preheat oven to 350 degrees F.
- Grease 9x13 baking pan.
- Beat cream cheese; stir in warm noodles.
- In separate bowl, beat eggs, sugar, and salt; stir into noodle mixture.
- Bring milk and margarine to a boil; add to noodle mixture.
- Spread noodle mixture in baking pan; sprinkle with cornflake crumbs.
- Bake for 1 hour.
- Makes 15 servings.

Analysis per serving:

KCAL	CHO(GM)	PROT(GM)	FAT(GM)	CHOL(MG)	SOD(MG)	P/S
420	49	12	20	183	490	0.4

Appropriate for following diets: General.

Baked Apple

4	medium	Apples, cored, unpeeled
4	sq	Graham Crackers, crushed to crumbs
2	TBS	Brown Sugar
2	tsp	Cinnamon
1	TBS	Margarine, melted
1/2	cup	Water

- Preheat oven to 375 degrees F.
- Mix graham cracker crumbs, sugar, cinnamon, and margarine together.
- Place apples in 8x8 baking pan; fill center of each apple with one fourth of cracker mixture.
- Pour water onto bottom of baking dish.
- Bake for 30-40 minutes, uncovered, or until apple is tender.
- Makes 4 servings.

Analysis per serving:

KCAL	CHO(GM)	PROT(GM)	FAT(GM)	CHOL(MG)	SOD(MG)	P/S
162	34	1	4	0	75	1.9

Appropriate for following diets: General, low sodium, low cholesterol.

Blueberry Kugel

1	8 oz pkg	Egg Noodles, cooked to pkg directions and drained
2		Eggs, well beaten
1/3	cup	Sugar
1	14 oz can	Blueberries, drained
1	cup	Sour Cream
1/2	cup	Cottage Cheese
2	TBS	Margarine, melted

- Preheat oven to 375 degrees F. for glass pan, 350 degrees F for metal baking pan.
- Grease 9x13 baking pan.
- In large bowl, beat eggs and sugar.
- Stir in sour cream, cottage cheese, and margarine.
- Fold in noodles and blueberries.
- Spread into prepared baking pan and bake for about 45 minutes or until brown and crisp.
- Makes 12 servings.

Analysis per serving:

KCAL	CHO(GM)	PROT(GM)	FAT(GM)	CHOL(MG)	SOD(MG)	P/S
238	34	6	8	81	84	0.3

Appropriate for following diets: General.

Blueberry Kugel (Low Cholesterol)

1	8 oz pkg	Egg Noodles, cooked to pkg directions and drained
1/2	cup	Egg Substitute, lightly beaten
1/3	cup	Sugar
1	14 oz can	Blueberries, drained
1	cup	Low Cholesterol Sour Cream*
1/2	cup	Low Fat Cottage Cheese
2	TBS	Margarine, melted

*Recipe elsewhere in this book

- Preheat oven to 375 degrees F. for glass pan, 350 degrees F for metal baking pan.
- Grease 9x13 baking pan.
- In large bowl, beat egg substitute and sugar.
- Stir in sour cream, cottage cheese, and margarine.
- Fold in noodles and blueberries.
- Spread into prepared baking pan and bake for about 45 minutes or until brown and crisp.
- Makes 12 servings.

Analysis per serving:

KCAL	CHO(GM)	PROT(GM)	FAT(GM)	CHOL(MG)	SOD(MG)	P/S
204	34	9	4	26	109	1.7

Appropriate for following diets: General, low cholesterol.

Blueberry Kugel (Low Sodium)

1	8 oz pkg	Egg Noodles, cooked to pkg directions and drained
2		Eggs, well beaten
1/3	cup	Sugar
1	14 oz can	Blueberries, drained
1	cup	Sour Cream
1/2	cup	Cottage Cheese, unsalted
2	TBS	Margarine, melted

- Preheat oven to 375 degrees F. for glass pan, 350 degrees F for metal baking pan.
- Grease 9x13 baking pan.
- In large bowl, beat eggs and sugar.
- Stir in sour cream, cottage cheese, and margarine.
- Fold in noodles and blueberries.
- Spread into prepared baking pan and bake for about 45 minutes or until brown and crisp.
- Makes 12 servings.

Analysis per serving:

KCAL	CHO(GM)	PROT(GM)	FAT(GM)	CHOL(MG)	SOD(MG)	P/S
290	36	18	8	84	57	0.3

Appropriate for following diets: General, low sodium.

Cheese Cake

1-1/2	cups	Graham Cracker Crumbs
3	TBS	Sugar
1/3	cup	Margarine, melted
3	8 oz pkg	Cream Cheese, softened
5		Eggs
1	cup	Sugar
1	cup	Sour Cream
2	TBS	Sugar

- Preheat oven to 350 degrees F.
- Mix together graham cracker crumbs, 3 TBS sugar, and margarine.
- Press all but 3 TBS of mixture into bottom and sides of 9" springform pan, set extra crumb mixture aside.
- Beat cream cheese, eggs, and 1 cup sugar until smooth, pour into pan.
- Bake for 45-55 minutes or until top cracks.
- Remove cake from oven and cool for 20 minutes.
- Blend sour cream and 2 TBS sugar together and spread over top of cake.
- Sprinkle leftover crumb mixture over top.
- Return cake to oven for 5 minutes.
- Allow to cool completely.
- Makes 12 slices.

Analysis per slice:

KCAL	CHO(GM)	PROT(GM)	FAT(GM)	CHOL(MG)	SOD(MG)	P/S
467	36	9	33	185	350	0.2

Appropriate for following diets: General.

Cranberry-Peach Cobbler

1/2	cup	Flour
2	tsp	Sugar
1-1/4	tsp	Baking Powder
1/4	tsp	Salt
1/4	cup	Oatmeal, uncooked
1/4	cup	Skim Milk
1		Egg, slightly beaten
1	tsp	Margarine
1	TBS	Cornstarch
1/4	cup	Sugar
1	cup	Cranberry Juice Cocktail
2	cups	Peaches, fresh sliced or canned sliced
1/2	cup	Cranberries

- Stir together first 8 ingredients just until flour is moistened; set aside as topping.
- In saucepan, combine cornstarch, 1/4 cup sugar, and cranberry juice and cook over medium heat until thick and bubbly.
- Stir in peaches and cranberries.
- Continue cooking mixture until the cranberry skins pop (about 5 minutes).
- Pour peaches into a greased 1 qt casserole dish.
- Spoon topping in blobs over top and bake for 20-25 minutes.
- Makes 8 servings.

Analysis per serving:

KCAL	CHO(GM)	PROT(GM)	FAT(GM)	CHOL(MG)	SOD(MG)	P/S
129	26	3	2	35	134	0.8

Appropriate for following diets: General.

Cranberry-Peach Cobbler (Low Cholesterol)

1/2	cup	Flour
2	tsp	Sugar
1-1/4	tsp	Baking Powder
1/4	tsp	Salt
1/4	cup	Oatmeal, uncooked
1/4	cup	Skim Milk
1/4	cup	Egg Substitute
1	tsp	Margarine
1	TBS	Cornstarch
1/4	cup	Sugar
1	cup	Cranberry Juice Cocktail
2	cups	Peaches, fresh sliced or canned sliced
1/2	cup	Cranberries

- Stir together first 8 ingredients just until flour is moistened; set aside as topping.
- In saucepan, combine cornstarch, 1/4 cup sugar, and cranberry juice and cook over medium heat until thick and bubbly.
- Stir in peaches and cranberries.
- Continue cooking mixture until the cranberry skins pop (about 5 minutes).
- Pour peaches into a greased 1 qt casserole dish.
- Spoon topping in blobs over top and bake for 20-25 minutes.
- Makes 8 servings.

Analysis per serving:

KCAL	CHO(GM)	PROT(GM)	FAT(GM)	CHOL(MG)	SOD(MG)	P/S
123	26	3	1	0.2	139	2.2

Appropriate for following diets: General, low cholesterol.

Cranberry-Peach Cobbler (Low Sodium)

1/2	cup	Flour
2	tsp	Sugar
1-1/4	tsp	Baking Powder, low sodium type
1/4	cup	Oatmeal, uncooked
1/4	cup	Skim Milk
1		Egg, slightly beaten
1	tsp	Margarine
1	TBS	Cornstarch
1/4	cup	Sugar
1	cup	Cranberry Juice Cocktail
2	cups	Peaches, fresh sliced or canned sliced
1/2	cup	Cranberries

- Stir together first 7 ingredients just until flour is moistened; set aside as topping.
- In saucepan, combine cornstarch, 1/4 cup sugar, and cranberry juice and cook over medium heat until thick and bubbly.
- Stir in peaches and cranberries.
- Continue cooking mixture until the cranberry skins pop (about 5 minutes).
- Pour peaches into a greased 1 qt casserole dish.
- Spoon topping in blobs over top and bake for 20-25 minutes.
- Makes 8 servings.

Analysis per serving:

KCAL	CHO(GM)	PROT(GM)	FAT(GM)	CHOL(MG)	SOD(MG)	P/S
129	27	3	2	35	20	0.8

Appropriate for following diets: General, low sodium.

Fruit Cocktail Cake

2	cups	Flour
1	15 oz can	Fruit Cocktail (do NOT drain off liquid)
1	tsp	Salt
2	tsp	Baking Soda
1-1/2	cups	Sugar
2		Eggs
1/4	cup	Brown Sugar
3/4	cup	Sugar
1/2	cup	Evaporated Milk
1/2	cup	Margarine
1	cup	Coconut, dried, shredded

- Mix first 6 ingredients together; beat for 1 minute.
- Pour batter into ungreased 9x13 baking pan.
- Sprinkle brown sugar over top of batter.
- Bake cake for 30-35 minutes.
- Simmer last 4 ingredients in saucepan over medium heat until slightly thickened.
- Spread over hot cake.
- Makes 15 servings.

Analysis per serving:

KCAL	CHO(GM)	PROT(GM)	FAT(GM)	CHOL(MG)	SOD(MG)	P/S
306	55	3	9	39	333	0.8

Appropriate for following diets: General.

Fruit Cocktail Cake (Low Cholesterol)

2	cups	Flour
1	15 oz can	Fruit Cocktail (do NOT drain off liquid)
1	tsp	Salt
2	tsp	Baking Soda
1-1/2	cups	Sugar
1/2	cup	Egg Substitute
1/4	cup	Brown Sugar
3/4	cup	Sugar
1/2	cup	Evaporated Skim Milk
1/2	cup	Margarine
1	cup	Pineapple, drained, crushed

- Preheat oven to 350 degrees F.
- Mix first 6 ingredients together; beat for 1 minute.
- Pour batter into ungreased 9x13 baking pan.
- Sprinkle brown sugar over top of batter.
- Bake cake for 30-35 minutes.
- Simmer last 4 ingredients in saucepan over medium heat until slightly thickened.
- Spread over hot cake.
- Makes 15 servings.

Analysis per serving:

KCAL	CHO(GM)	PROT(GM)	FAT(GM)	CHOL(MG)	SOD(MG)	P/S
244	44	4	7	0.4	339	2.4

Appropriate for following diets: General, low cholesterol.

Fruit Cocktail Cake (Low Sodium)

2	cups	Flour
1	15 oz can	Fruit Cocktail (do NOT drain off liquid)
1-1/2	TBS	Baking Powder, low sodium type
1-1/2	cups	Sugar
2		Eggs
1/4	cup	Brown Sugar
3/4	cup	Sugar
1/2	cup	Evaporated Milk
1/2	cup	Margarine
1	cup	Coconut, dried, shredded

- Preheat oven to 350 degrees F.
- Mix first 6 ingredients together; beat for 1 minute.
- Pour batter into ungreased 9x13 baking pan.
- Sprinkle brown sugar over top of batter.
- Bake cake for 30-35 minutes.
- Simmer last 4 ingredients in saucepan over medium heat until slightly thickened.
- Spread over hot cake.
- Makes 15 servings.

Analysis per serving:

KCAL	CHO(GM)	PROT(GM)	FAT(GM)	CHOL(MG)	SOD(MG)	P/S
307	55	3	9	39	94	0.8

Appropriate for following diets: General, low sodium.

Gingerbread

2-1/2	cups	Flour
1/3	cup	Sugar
1	cup	Molasses
3/4	cup	Hot Water
1/2	cup	Margarine
1		Egg
1	tsp	Baking Soda
1	tsp	Ginger
1	tsp	Cinnamon
3/4	tsp	Salt

- Preheat oven to 325 degrees F.
- Grease and flour 9x9 baking pan.
- Beat all ingredient together in large bowl until smooth, about 3 minutes.
- Pour mixture into pan and bake for about 50 minutes.
- Makes 9, 3x3 servings.

Analysis per serving:

KCAL	CHO(GM)	PROT(GM)	FAT(GM)	CHOL(MG)	SOD(MG)	P/S
330	55	4	11	3-	400	1.9

Appropriate for following diets: General.

Gingerbread (Low Cholesterol)

2-1/2	cups	Flour
1/3	cup	Sugar
1	cup	Molasses
3/4	cup	Hot Water
1/2	cup	Margarine
2		Egg Whites
1	tsp	Baking Soda
1	tsp	Ginger
1	tsp	Cinnamon
3/4	tsp	Salt

- Preheat oven to 325 degrees F.
- Grease and flour 9x9 baking pan.
- Beat all ingredient together in large bowl until smooth, about 3 minutes.
- Pour mixture into pan and bake for about 50 minutes.
- Makes 9, 3x3 servings.

Analysis per serving:

KCAL	CHO(GM)	PROT(GM)	FAT(GM)	CHOL(MG)	SOD(MG)	P/S
329	533	4	10	0	301	0.9

Appropriate for following diets: General, low cholesterol.

Gingerbread (Low Sodium)

2-1/2	cups	Flour
1/3	cup	Sugar
1	cup	Molasses
3/4	cup	Hot Water
1/2	cup	Margarine
2		Egg Whites
2	tsp	Baking Powder, low sodium type
1	tsp	Ginger
1	tsp	Cinnamon

- Preheat oven to 325 degrees F.
- Grease and flour 9x9 baking pan.
- Beat all ingredient together in large bowl until smooth, about 3 minutes.
- Pour mixture into pan and bake for about 50 minutes.
- Makes 9, 3x3 servings.

Analysis per serving:

KCAL	CHO(GM)	PROT(GM)	FAT(GM)	CHOL(MG)	SOD(MG)	P/S
329	54	4	10	0	179	2.1

Appropriate for following diets: General, low sodium, low cholesterol.

Oat 'n Berry Cookies

2	cups	Flour
1	cup	Sugar
1/2	tsp	Baking Soda
1	tsp	Salt
1/4	tsp	Nutmeg
3/4	tsp	Cinnamon
3/4	cup	Margarine
2		Egg Whites
3/4	cup	Applesauce
1-3/4	cups	Oatmeal, uncooked
1-1/2	cups	Blackberries, canned or frozen (thawed), drained

- Preheat oven to 400 degrees F.
- Mix flour, sugar, baking soda, salt, nutmeg, and cinnamon in a large mixing bowl.
- Beat in thoroughly: margarine, egg white, and applesauce.
- Gently fold in oats, and berries.
- Drop by teaspoonful onto ungreased baking sheet.
- Bake for 12-15 minutes.
- Remove from pan immediately to cooling rack.
- Makes 60 cookies.

Analysis per cookie:

KCAL	CHO(GM)	PROT(GM)	FAT(GM)	CHOL(MG)	SOD(MG)	P/S
60	9	1	2	0	72	2.5

Appropriate for following diets: General, low cholesterol.

Oat 'n Berry Cookies (Low Sodium)

2	cups	Flour
1	cup	Sugar
1/2	tsp	Baking Powder, low sodium type
1	tsp	Salt
1/4	tsp	Nutmeg
3/4	tsp	Cinnamon
3/4	cup	Margarine
2		Egg Whites
3/4	cup	Applesauce
1-3/4	cups	Oatmeal, uncooked
1-1/2	cups	Blackberries, canned or frozen (thawed), drained

- Preheat oven to 400 degrees F.
- Mix flour, sugar, baking soda, nutmeg, and cinnamon in a large mixing bowl.
- Beat in thoroughly: margarine, egg white, and applesauce.
- Gently fold in oats, and berries.
- Drop by teaspoonful onto ungreased baking sheet.
- Bake for 12-15 minutes.
- Remove from pan immediately to cooling rack.
- Makes 60 cookies.

Analysis per cookie:

KCAL	CHO(GM)	PROT(GM)	FAT(GM)	CHOL(MG)	SOD(MG)	P/S
61	9	1	2	0	32	2.1

Appropriate for following diets: General, low sodium, low cholesterol.

Pineapple-Coconut Tidbits

1		Pineapple, raw, pared, and cubed (1" cubes)
1/2	cup	Honey
2/3	cup	Coconut, dried, shredded

- Dip pineapple cubes in honey.
- Roll honeyed cubes in coconut; spear with toothpicks and serve.
- Makes about 36 cubes.

Analysis per cube:

KCAL	CHO(GM)	PROT(GM)	FAT(GM)	CHOL(MG)	SOD(MG)	P/S
35	9	0.2	1	0	1	0.1

Appropriate for following diets: General, low sodium, low cholesterol.

Pumpkin Bread

3-1/3	cups	Flour
2	tsp	Baking Soda
3	cups	Sugar
1-1/2	tsp	Salt
2	tsp	Cinnamon
1/2	tsp	Nutmeg
1/2	tsp	Cloves
1	cup	Vegetable Oil
4		Eggs
2/3	cup	Water
2	cups	Pumpkin, mashed fresh or canned

- Preheat oven to 350 degrees F.
- Grease and flour 3 loaf pans.
- Sift together first 7 ingredients in large bowl; make a well in the center of the dry ingredients.
- Pour into the well the rest of the ingredients.
- Beat until smooth and then pour equally into the loaf pans.
- Bake for about 1 hour.
- Makes 12 slices per loaf.

Analysis per slice:

KCAL	CHO(GM)	PROT(GM)	FAT(GM)	CHOL(MG)	SOD(MG)	P/S
170	26	2	7	30	136	2.1

Appropriate for following diets: General.

Pumpkin Bread (Low Cholesterol)

3-1/3	cups	Flour
2	tsp	Baking Soda
3	cups	Sugar
1-1/2	tsp	Salt
2	tsp	Cinnamon
1/2	tsp	Nutmeg
1/2	tsp	Cloves
1	cup	Vegetable Oil
1	cup	Egg Substitute
2/3	cup	Water
2	cups	Pumpkin, mashed fresh or canned

- Preheat oven to 350 degrees F.
- Grease and flour 3 loaf pans.
- Sift together first 7 ingredients in large bowl; make a well in the center of the dry ingredients.
- Pour into the well the rest of the ingredients.
- Beat until smooth and then pour equally into the loaf pans.
- Bake for about 1 hour.
- Makes 12 slices per loaf.

Analysis per slice:

KCAL	CHO(GM)	PROT(GM)	FAT(GM)	CHOL(MG)	SOD(MG)	P/S
167	26	2	6	0	141	2.4

Appropriate for following diets: General, low cholesterol.

Pumpkin Bread (Low Sodium)

3-1/3	cups	Flour
4	tsp	Baking Powder, low sodium type
3	cups	Sugar
2	tsp	Cinnamon
1/2	tsp	Nutmeg
1/2	tsp	Cloves
1	cup	Vegetable Oil
4		Eggs
2/3	cup	Water
2	cups	Pumpkin, mashed fresh or canned

- Preheat oven to 350 degrees F.
- Grease and flour 3 loaf pans.
- Sift together first 7 ingredients in large bowl; make a well in the center of the dry ingredients.
- Pour into the well the rest of the ingredients.
- Beat until smooth and then pour equally into the loaf pans.
- Bake for about 1 hour.
- Makes 12 slices per loaf.

Analysis per slice:

KCAL	CHO(GM)	PROT(GM)	FAT(GM)	CHOL(MG)	SOD(MG)	P/S
170	26	2	7	30	9	2.1

Appropriate for following diets: General, low sodium.

Pumpkin Pie

1	lb	Pumpkin, canned
3/4	cup	Brown Sugar, firmly packed
3		Eggs
1/4	tsp	Salt
1	tsp	Cinnamon
1/2	tsp	Ginger
1/2	tsp	Nutmeg
1/4	tsp	Cloves
1/4	tsp	Allspice
1	13 oz can	Evaporated Milk
1	9"	Pie crust

- Preheat oven to 400 degrees F.
- Beat pumpkin, brown sugar, eggs, salt, and spices.
- Blend in milk until smooth.
- Pour mixture into pie shell and bake for 50 minutes or until center is set.
- Makes 8 servings.

Analysis per serving:

KCAL	CHO(GM)	PROT(GM)	FAT(GM)	CHOL(MG)	SOD(MG)	P/S
309	40	8	14	118	288	0.1

Appropriate for following diets: General.

Pumpkin Pie (Low Cholesterol)

1	lb	Pumpkin, canned
3/4	cup	Brown Sugar, firmly packed
3/4	cup	Egg Substitute
1/4	tsp	Salt
1	tsp	Cinnamon
1/2	tsp	Ginger
1/2	tsp	Nutmeg
1/4	tsp	Cloves
1/4	tsp	Allspice
1	13 oz can	Evaporated Skimmed Milk
1	9"	Pie crust

- Preheat oven to 400 degrees F.
- Beat pumpkin, brown sugar, egg substitute, salt, and spices.
- Blend in milk until smooth.
- Pour mixture into pie shell and bake for 50 minutes or until center is set.
- Makes 8 servings.

Analysis per serving:

KCAL	CHO(GM)	PROT(GM)	FAT(GM)	CHOL(MG)	SOD(MG)	P/S
271	41	9	9	2	309	0.2

Appropriate for following diets: General, low cholesterol.

Raisin-Oatmeal Cookies

3/4	cup	Apple Juice
6	TBS	Vegetable Oil
3/4	cup	Honey
½ cup plus 1 TBS		Milk
1	TBS	Vanilla Extract
1/2	cup	Flour
1/2	cup	Whole Wheat Pastry Flour
1-3/4	cups	Oatmeal, uncooked
1/2	tsp	Baking Soda
1/2	tsp	Salt
1/2	tsp	Baking Powder
1	tsp	Cinnamon
1	tsp	Nutmeg
1-1/2	cup	Raisins

- Preheat oven to 300 degrees F.
- Mix apple juice, oil, honey, milk, and vanilla.
- In separate bowl, combine rest of ingredients and stir into liquid mixture.
- Mix until well blended.
- Drop by heaping teaspoonful on lightly greased baking sheets.
- Bake for 20 minutes.
- Makes 3-1/2 dozen cookies.

Analysis per cookie:

KCAL	CHO(GM)	PROT(GM)	FAT(GM)	CHOL(MG)	SOD(MG)	P/S
83	15	1	3	0.4	40	2.0

Appropriate for following diets: General.

Raisin-Oatmeal Cookies (Low Cholesterol)

3/4	cup	Apple Juice
6	TBS	Vegetable Oil
3/4	cup	Honey
1/2 cup plus 1 TBS		Skim Milk
1	TBS	Vanilla Extract
1/2	cup	Flour
1/2	cup	Whole Wheat Pastry Flour
1-3/4	cups	Oatmeal, uncooked
1/2	tsp	Baking Soda
1/2	tsp	Salt
1/2	tsp	Baking Powder
1	tsp	Cinnamon
1	tsp	Nutmeg
1-1/2	cup	Raisins

- Preheat oven to 300 degrees F.
- Mix apple juice, oil, honey, milk, and vanilla.
- In separate bowl, combine rest of ingredients and stir into liquid mixture.
- Mix until well blended.
- Drop by heaping teaspoonful on lightly greased baking sheets.
- Bake for 20 minutes.
- Makes 3-1/2 dozen cookies.

Analysis per cookie:

KCAL	CHO(GM)	PROT(GM)	FAT(GM)	CHOL(MG)	SOD(MG)	P/S
82	15	1	2	0	40	2.3

Appropriate for following diets: General, low cholesterol.

Raisin-Oatmeal Cookies (Low Sodium)

3/4	cup	Apple Juice
6	TBS	Vegetable Oil
3/4	cup	Honey
½ cup plus 1 TBS		Skim Milk
1	TBS	Vanilla Extract
1/2	cup	Flour
1/2	cup	Whole Wheat Pastry Flour
1-3/4	cups	Oatmeal, uncooked
1	tsp	Baking Powder, low sodium type
1	tsp	Cinnamon
1	tsp	Nutmeg
1-1/2	cup	Raisins

- Preheat oven to 300 degrees F.
- Mix apple juice, oil, honey, milk, and vanilla.
- In separate bowl, combine rest of ingredients and stir into liquid mixture.
- Mix until well blended.
- Drop by heaping teaspoonful on lightly greased baking sheets.
- Bake for 20 minutes.
- Makes 3-1/2 dozen cookies.

Analysis per cookie:

KCAL	CHO(GM)	PROT(GM)	FAT(GM)	CHOL(MG)	SOD(MG)	P/S
83	15	1	2	0.4	3	2.0

Appropriate for following diets: General, low sodium, low cholesterol.

Spice Cookies

1-1/2	cups	Sugar
1	cup	Shortening
1/4	cup	Skim Milk
1	tsp	Vanilla Extract
1/2	tsp	Artificial Almond Extract
1	tsp	Ginger
1/2	tsp	Nutmeg
1/4	tsp	Cloves
1/4	tsp	Allspice
2-1/2	cups	Flour
1		Egg
1	tsp	Baking Soda

- Cream sugar and shortening together.
- Mix in milk, extracts, and spices.
- Stir in remaining ingredients and mix well.
- Refrigerate dough for 2 hours.
- Preheat oven to 350 degree F.
- Roll out half of the dough on a lightly floured board to about 1/4 inch thickness.
- Cut dough into shapes with cookie cutters.
- Place cookies on greased baking sheet.
- Bake for about 8 minutes.
- Let cool on baking sheet for 2-3 minutes before removing cookies to cooling racks.
- Makes 40 cookies.

Analysis per cookie:

KCAL	CHO(GM)	PROT(GM)	FAT(GM)	CHOL(MG)	SOD(MG)	P/S
104	13	1	5	7	23	1.0

Appropriate for following diets: General.

Spice Cookies (Low Sodium)

1-1/2	cups	Sugar
1	cup	Shortening
1/4	cup	Skim Milk
1	tsp	Vanilla Extract
1/2	tsp	Artificial Almond Extract
1	tsp	Ginger
1/2	tsp	Nutmeg
1/4	tsp	Cloves
1/4	tsp	Allspice
2-1/2	cups	Flour
1		Egg
2	tsp	Baking Powder, low sodium type

- Cream sugar and shortening together.
- Mix in milk, extracts, and spices.
- Stir in remaining ingredients and mix well.
- Refrigerate dough for 2 hours.
- Preheat oven to 350 degree F.
- Roll out half of the dough on a lightly floured board to about 1/4 inch thickness.
- Cut dough into shapes with cookie cutters.
- Place cookies on greased baking sheet.
- Bake for about 8 minutes.
- Let cool on baking sheet for 2-3 minutes before removing cookies to cooling racks.
- Makes 40 cookies.

Analysis per cookie:

KCAL	CHO(GM)	PROT(GM)	FAT(GM)	CHOL(MG)	SOD(MG)	P/S
104	13	1	5	7	3	1.0

Appropriate for following diets: General.

Zucchini Bread

3		Eggs
3/4	cup	Vegetable Oil
2	cups	Sugar
2	tsp	Vanilla Extract
2	cups	Zucchini, raw, grated
1	tsp	Baking Soda
3	tsp	Cinnamon
1/2	tsp	Baking Powder
1	tsp	Salt
3-1/2	cups	Flour

- Preheat oven to 350 degrees F.
- Grease 2 loaf pans.
- Thoroughly beat all ingredients together in large bowl.
- Pour batter into pans and bake for about 1 hour.
- Makes 12 slices per loaf

Analysis per slice:

KCAL	CHO(GM)	PROT(GM)	FAT(GM)	CHOL(MG)	SOD(MG)	P/S
199	31	3	8	34	132	2.2

Appropriate for following diets: General.

Zucchini Bread (Low Cholesterol)

3/4	cup	Egg Substitute
3/4	cup	Vegetable Oil
2	cups	Sugar
2	tsp	Vanilla Extract
2	cups	Zucchini, raw, grated
1	tsp	Baking Soda
3	tsp	Cinnamon
1/2	tsp	Baking Powder
1	tsp	Salt
3-1/2	cups	Flour

- Preheat oven to 350 degrees F.
- Grease 2 loaf pans.
- Thoroughly beat all ingredients together in large bowl.
- Pour batter into pans and bake for about 1 hour.
- Makes 12 slices per loaf

Analysis per slice:

KCAL	CHO(GM)	PROT(GM)	FAT(GM)	CHOL(MG)	SOD(MG)	P/S
191	30	3	7	0	137	2.5

Appropriate for following diets: General, low cholesterol.

Zucchini Bread (Low Sodium)

3		Eggs
3/4	cup	Vegetable Oil
2	cups	Sugar
2	tsp	Vanilla Extract
2	cups	Zucchini, raw, grated
1	tsp	Baking Soda
3	tsp	Cinnamon
1	tsp	Baking Powder, low sodium type
3-1/2	cups	Flour

- Preheat oven to 350 degrees F.
- Grease 2 loaf pans.
- Thoroughly beat all ingredients together in large bowl.
- Pour batter into pans and bake for about 1 hour.
- Makes 12 slices per loaf

Analysis per slice:

KCAL	CHO(GM)	PROT(GM)	FAT(GM)	CHOL(MG)	SOD(MG)	P/S
194	30	3	8	34	9	2.2

Appropriate for following diets: General, low sodium.

Cottage Cheese Spread

1	cup	Low-fat Cottage Cheese
1/4	cup	Margarine

- Rinse cottage cheese under cold water; drain well, and press out any excess water still present.
- Blend cottage cheese and margarine in blender or food processor until smooth.
- Makes about 1 cup.

Analysis per 1 tablespoon serving:

KCAL	CHO(GM)	PROT(GM)	FAT(GM)	CHOL(MG)	SOD(MG)	P/S
11	0.4	2	0.2	0.6	58	0.3

Appropriate for following diets: General, diabetic, low sodium, low cholesterol.

Dill Dip

8	oz	Cream Cheese, softened
2	TBS	Green Olives, chopped
1	TBS	Dill Weed
1/4	tsp	Garlic Salt
3	TBS	Mayonnaise
3	TBS	Skim Milk

- Blend all ingredient together until smooth.
- Refrigerate for at least 3 hours before serving for flavor to develop.
- Makes 1 cup.

Analysis per 1 TBS serving:

KCAL	CHO(GM)	PROT(GM)	FAT(GM)	CHOL(MG)	SOD(MG)	P/S
73	0.8	1	7	18	127	0.4

Appropriate for following diets: General, diabetic.

Dill Dip (Low Cholesterol)

8	oz	Cottage Cheese Spread*
2	TBS	Green Olives, chopped
1	TBS	Dill Weed
1/4	tsp	Garlic Salt
3	TBS	Mayonnaise
3	TBS	Skim Milk

* Receipe elsewhere in this book

- Blend all ingredient together until smooth.
- Refrigerate for at least 3 hours before serving for flavor to develop.
- Makes 1 cup.

Analysis per 1 TBS serving:

KCAL	CHO(GM)	PROT(GM)	FAT(GM)	CHOL(MG)	SOD(MG)	P/S
38	0.7	2	3	2	150	2.6

Appropriate for following diets: General, diabetic, low cholesterol.

Garlic Topping

1/2	cup	Margarine
1/2	tsp	Garlic Powder
1/8	tsp	Crushed Red Pepper
1	tsp	Oregano
1/2	tsp	Basil

- Melt margarine; stir in the rest of ingredients.
- Heat mixture 1 minute more.
- Drizzle mixture over slices of Italian bread.
- Wrap bread slices in foil and heat in 400 degree oven for 10 minutes.
- Makes 24 servings, 1 tsp. each.

Analysis per serving:

KCAL	CHO(GM)	PROT(GM)	FAT(GM)	CHOL(MG)	SOD(MG)	P/S
34	0.1	0	4	0	51	2.1

Appropriate for following diets: General, diabetic, low sodium, low cholesterol.

Low Cholesterol Sour Cream

1	cup	Low-fat Cottage Cheese
1	tsp	Vinegar

- Wrap cottage cheese in cheese cloth and suspend over a bowl for 12-24 hours in the refrigerator; squeeze any remaining fluid out gently.
- Blend resultant cheese and vinegar in blender or food processor until smooth.
- Makes 1 cup.

Analysis per 1 tablespoon serving:

KCAL	CHO(GM)	PROT(GM)	FAT(GM)	CHOL(MG)	SOD(MG)	P/S
10	0.4	2	0.1	0.6	57	0.1

Appropriate for following diets: General, diabetic, low sodium, low cholesterol.

Appendix C

RELAXATION TAPES

BMA AUDIO CASSETTES
200 Park Avenue South
New York, NY 10003
1-800-221-3966 or (212) 674-1900

1. **RELAXATION TRAINING PROGRAM**

   Dr. Budzynski narration, Cat. No. MV3-B;
   Judith Proctor narration, Cat. No. MV3-P — $35.00

   INDIVIDUAL TAPES:

   a. Tense-Slo Relax/Differential Relaxation (1 tape)
      Cat. No. MV3-B1/2 (Budzynski narration)
      Cat. No. MV3-P1/2 (Proctor narration) — $11.50

   b. Limb/Heaviness/Arms and Legs Heavy and Warm (1 tape)
      Cat. No. MV3-B3/4 (Budzynski narration)
      Cat. No. MV3-P3/4 (Proctor narration) — $11.50

   c. Forehead and Facial Relaxation/Stress Management (1 tape)
      Cat. No. MV3-B5/6 (Budzynski narration)
      Cat. No. MV3-P5/6 (Proctor narration) — $11.50

2. **BIOFEEDBACK TECHNIQUES IN CLINICAL PRACTICE, VOL. 2**

   Per Cassette

   a. On Stress: Johann Stoyva, Ph. D., Cat. No. T14 — $19.95

   b. On Biofeedback Procedures: Thomas H. Budzynski, Ph. D., Cat. No. T18 — $ 9.95

3. **RELAXATION PROCEDURES—Alan Rappaport, Ph. D.,** Cat. No. T3 — $ 9.95

4. **BREATHING AND MEDITATIVE TECHNIQUES—Judith Proctor,** Cat. No.T12 — $ 9.95

Appendix D

HEADACHE CENTERS AND PROGRAMS

1. Baltimore Headache Institute
   Brian E. Mondell, M.D., Medical Director
   Assistant Professor of Neurology
   The Johns Hopkins University
   School of Medicine
   Baltimore, Maryland

2. Baylor College of Medicine CBF Laboratory
   John Stirling Meyer, M.D., Professor of Neurology, Director
   VA Medical Center
   Houston, Texas

3. California Medical Clinic for Headache
   Lee Kudrow, M.D., Director
   Encino, California

4. Elkind Headache Center
   Arthur H. Elkind, M.D., Director
   Attending Physician, Mount Vernon Hospital
   Mount Vernon, New York
   Clinical Assistant, Professor of Medicine
   New York Medical College
   New York, New York

5. Headache Center at Thomas Jefferson University Hospital
   Dr. Stephen Silberstein, Director
   Philadelphia, Pennsylvania

6. Headache Research Foundation and John R. Graham Headache Centre
   The Faulkner Hospital
   Egilius L. H. Spierings, M.D., Ph.D., Director
   Assistant Professor of Neurology
   Tufts University School of Medicine
   Boston, Massachusetts

7. Head Pain Center-University of Mississippi Medical Center
   Dr. Donald Penzien, Director
   Jackson, Mississippi

8. Massachusetts General Hospital
   Michael Moskowitz, M.D., Director
   Associate Professor, Department of Neurology
   Harvard Medical School
   Boston, Massachusetts

9. The Menninger Foundation
   Joseph D. Sargent, M.D., F.A.C.P.
   Chief, Department of Internal Medicine
   Co-Director of the Headache Center
   Topeka, Kansas

10. Michigan Headache and Neurological Institute
    Joel R. Saper, M.D., F.A.C.P., Director
    Clinical Professor of Medicine (Neurology)
    Michigan State University
    Ann Arbor, Michigan

11. Michigan Headache and Neurological Institute
    Marjorie Winters, R.N., B.S.N.
    Clinical Coordinator and Research Associate
    Ann Arbor, Michigan

12. Montefiore Medical Center
    Seymour Solomon, M.D., Director—Headache Unit
    Professor of Neurology
    Albert Einstein College of Medicine
    Bronx, New York

13. Neurological Center for Headache
    Barry Baumel, M.D.
    Miami Beach, Florida

14. New England Center for Headache
    Frances M. Arrowsmith, N.P., M.P.H., Clinical Director
    Stamford, Connecticut

15. The New England Center for Headache
    Dr. Allan Rapoport, Director
    Stamford, Connecticut

16. New England Headache Treatment Program
    Fred D. Sheftell, M.D., D.A.B.P.N., Co-Director
    Greenwich, Connecticut
    Clinical Assistant Professor, Department of Psychiatry
    New York Medical College, New York, New York

17. New York Headache Center
    Dr. Alexander Mauskop, Director
    New York, New York

18. National Headache Foundation
    820 North Orleans, Suite 217
    Chicago, IL 60610

19. Organizations American Council for Headache Education
    19 Mantua Road
    Mount Royal, NJ 08061

20. Pain Control Center of Beverly Hills
    Gary W. Jay, M.D., Medical Director
    Beverly Hills, California

21. San Francisco Headache Clinic
    Jerome Goldstein, M.D., Director
    Associate Clinical Instructor in Neurology
    University of California
    San Francisco, California

22. Scripps Clinic and Research Foundation
    Donald D. Stevenson, M.D., Senior Consultant
    Division of Allergy and Immunology
    Chairman, Department of Medicine
    La Jolla, California

23. Speed Headache Associates, P.A.
    William G. Speed, III, M.D., F.A.C.P., Director
    Associate Professor of Medicine
    Johns Hopkins School of Medicine
    Baltimore, Maryland

24. Texas Headache Associates
    Dr. Robert Nett, Director
    San Antonio, Texas

25. UCLA Pain Management Center
    Steven B. Graff-Radford, D.D.S., Co-Director
    Head and Neck Section
    Anesthesia Pain Services
    Cedar-Sinai Medical Center
    Los Angeles, California

26. University of Missouri-Columbia Health Sciences Center
    James D. Dexter, M.D.
    Professor, Department of Neurology
    Columbia, Missouri

27. University of Texas Medical School
    Houston Headache Clinic
    Ninan T. Matthew, M.D., F.R.C.P. (C), Director
    Clinical Associate
    Professor of Neurology
    Houston, Texas

REFERENCES

1. Axlerod, J., Saavedra, J. M., "Octopamine", **Nature** (Volume 265, 1970): 501 – 504.

2. Barclay, Laurie, "Migraines More Common During Menstrual Periods", Web MD News, November 27, 2000.

3. Blanchard, E. B., Appelbaum, K. A., "Five Year Prospective Follow-up on the Treatment of Chronic Headache with Biofeedback and/ or Relaxation", **Headache** (Vol. 27, Nov.1987): 580 – 583.

4. Blau, J. N., Diamond, S., "Dietary factors in migraine precipitation: the physician's view", **Headache** (Volume 25(4), 1985): 184 – 187.

5. Blau, J. N., "Resolution of migraine attacks: sleep and the recovery phase", **Journal of Neurological and Neurosurgical Psychiatry** (Volume 45, 1984): 223 – 226.

6. Brainard, J. B., **Control of Migraine**, W. W. Norton and Company, Inc., New York, 1977.

7. Brody, J. E., **Jane Brody's Nutrition Book**, W. W. Norton and Company, Inc., New York, 1981.

8. Brown, B. B., Ph.D., **New Mind, New Body Biofeedback, New Directions for the Mind**, Harper and Row, New York, 1874.

9. Critchley, M., "Definition of migraine: in 3rd Migraine Symposium", Heinemann Medical Books, London, 1970: 181 – 182.

10. Dalessio, D. J., "Migraine Information for Patients", Scripps Clinical Medical Groups, La Jolla, CA, 1991.

11. Davis, Jeanie Lerche, "Does Exercise Trigger Your Migraines", Web MD News, July 2, 2001.

12. Davis, Jeanie Lerche, "New Drug Kicks 2nd Migraine Attack", Web MD News, June 25, 2002.

13. Davis, Jeanie Lerche, "New Hope for Migraine Sufferers", Web MD Medical News, April 24, 2000.

14. Davis, Jeanie Lerche, "Surgery for Migraines Looks Promising", Web MD News, December 30, 2004.

15. DeBakey, M. E., Gotto, A. M., Scott, L. W., Foreyt, J. P., **The Living Heart Diet**, Raven Press, New York, 1984.

16. De Noon, Daniel, "Kids' Migraines: Over-the-counter Drugs Best", Web MD News, December 28, 2004.

17. De Noon, Daniel, "Super-Sensitive Nerves Play Key Role in Migraine Pain", Web MD Medical News, April 27, 2000.

18. Dexter, J. D., Roberts, J., Byer, J. A., "The five-hour glucose tolerance test and effect of low sucrose diet in migraine", **Headache** (Volume 18(2), 1978): 91 – 94.

19. Diamond, S., and Dalessio, D. J., **The Practicing Physician's Approach to Headache**, Williams and Wilkins, Baltimore, Maryland, 1986.

20. Diamond, S., Prager, J., Freitag, F. G., "Diet and Headache: Is There a Link?", **Postgraduate Medicine** (Volume 79, Number 4, March 1986): 279 – 86.

21. Dietary Department, University of Iowa Hospitals and Clinics, "Recent Advances in Therapeutic Diets", (4th ed. Ames, IA), Iowa State Press.

22. Dietary Guidelines for Americans, U.S. Department of Agriculture and U.S. Department of Health and Human Services, Home and Garden Bulletin (2nd edition, No. 232, 1985).

23. **Diet, Nutrition and Cancer Prevention: A Guide to Food Choices**, U.S. Department of Health and Human Services, Public Health Service, and National Institutes of Health, National Cancer Institute, NIH Publication (No. 85-2711, 1984).

24. Drummond, F., "Hypnosis in the Treatment of Headache: A Review of the Last Ten Years", **Journal of the American Society of Psychosomatic Dental Medicine** (Vol. 28, No. 3, 1981): 87 – 101.

25. Drummond, P. O., "Scalp Tenderness and Sensitivity to Pain in Migraine and Tension Headache", **Headache** (Vol. 27, Jan. 1987): page 45 – 50.

26. Dudley, R., Rowland, W., **How To Find Relief from Migraines**, Beaufort Books, 1982.

27. Evans, P., **Mastering Your Migraine**, E. P. Dutton, New York, 1978.

28. Exchange Lists For Meal Planning, American Diabetes Association, American Dietetic Association, National Institute of Arthritis, Metabolism, and Digestive Diseases, and National Heart and Lung Institute (1976).

29. Fahrion, S. L., "Autogenic biofeedback treatment for migraine", **Mayo Clinic Proceedings** (Number 52, 1977): 776 – 784.

30. Friedman, H., Taub, H. A., "An Evaluation of Hypnotic Susceptibility and Peripheral Temperature Elevation in the Treatment of Migraine", **The American Journal of Clinical Hypnosis** (Vol. 24, No.3, January 1982): 172 – 182.

31. Gauthier, J., Lacroix, R., Cotie, A., Doyan, J., Drolet, M., "Biofeedback Control of Migraine Headaches: A Comparison of Two Approaches", **Biofeedback and Self-Regulation** (Volume 10, Number 2, June 1985): 139 – 59.

32. Ghose, K., Carroll, J. D., "Mechanisms of tyramine-induced migraine: similarity with dopamine and interactions with disulfiram and propranolol in migraine patients", **Neuropsychobiology** (Volume 12, Numbers 2-3, 1984): 122 – 126.

33. Ghose, K., "Tyramine pressor test: implications and limitations", **Methods and Findings** (Volume 6, 1984): 455 – 464.

34. Hanington, E., Horn, M., Wilkinson, M., "Further observations on the effect of tyramine", **Cochrane**: 113 – 119.

35. Haas, D. C., **Migraine Diagnosis**, International Headache Society, 1988.

36. Hass, F. J., Dolan, E. F., **What You Can Do About Your Headaches**, Henry Regnery Company, 1973.

37. **Headache: Hope Through Research**, National Institutes of Neurological Disorders and Stroke, National Institutes of Health, 1999.

38. **Healthy Food Choices**, American Diabetes Association, Inc. and The American Dietetic Association (1986).

39. Henderson, W., Raskin, N. J., "Hot-dog headache: individual susceptibility to nitrite", **Lancet** (Volume 2, 1972): 1162 – 1163.

40. Hitti, Miranda, "Melatonin May Help Prevent Migraines", Web MD Medical News, September 9, 2004.

41. Hitti, Miranda, "Migraine Headaches, Sex Hormone Linked", Web MD News, August 20, 2004.

42. Hughes, E. C., "Chemically defined Diet II, Use in the Diagnosis of Food Sensitivities", **Annals of Allergy** (Volume 40, 1978): 393.

43. Hughes, E. C., "Chemically defined diet in the Diagnosis of Food Sensitivities I: Hearing Impaired", **Trans American Academy of Ophthalmology, Otolaryngology** (Volume 15, 1970): 60.

44. Hughes, E. C., Gott, P. S., Weinstein, R. C., Binggeli, R., "Migraine: A Diagnostic Test for Etiology of Food Sensitivity by a Nutritionally Support Fast and Confirmed by Long-Term Report", **Annals of Allergy** (Volume 55, Number 1, July 1985): 28 – 32.

45. Hutchison, M., **Megabrain, New Tools and Techniques For Brain Growth and Mind Expansion**, Beech Tree Books, New York, 1986.

46. Ingles, D. L., Tindale, C. R., and Gallimore, D., "Recovery of biogenic amines in chocolate", **Chemical Industry** (Volume 12, 1978): 432.

47. JAMA-Migraine Information Center, 1988.

48. Karlins, M., Andrew, L. M., **Biofeedback-Turning on the Power of Your Mind**, J. B. Lippincott Co., Philadelphia, 1972.

49. Keefe, F. J., and Gardner, E. T., "Learned control of skin temperature: Effects of short and long-term biofeedback training", **Behavior Therapy** (Volume 10, 1979): 202 – 210.

50. Kewman, D., and Roberts, A. H., "Skin temeratrure biofeedback and migraine headache: A double-blind study", **Biofeedback and Self Regulation** (Volume 5, 1980): 327 – 345.

51. Kirchheimer, Sid, "Averting Migraines With Few Side Effects", Web MD News, December 31, 2002.

52. Kohlenberg, R. J., "Tyramine sensitivity in dietary migraine: A critical review", **Headache** (Volume 22, 1981): 30 – 34.

53. Lance, J.W., "What is migraine?", **Advances in Neurology**, Raven Press (Volume 33, 1982): 21 – 26.

54. Lovenberg, W., "Some vaso- and psychoactive substances in food: Amines, stimulants, depressants, and hallucinogens", **Toxicants Occurring Naturally in Foods, (2nd rev. ed.)**, Washington, D.C., National Academy of Sciences, 1973.

55. **Lowering Blood Cholesterol To Prevent Heart Disease**, National Institutes of Health Consensus Development Conference Statement (Volume 5, Number 7), Department of Health and Human Services, Public Health Service, National Institutes of Health (1985).

56. McCabe, B. J., "Dietary Tyramine and other pressor amines in MAOI regimes: A review", **Journal of the American Dietetic Association** (Volume 86, Number 8, 1986): 1059 – 1064.

57. Medina, J. L., Diamond, S., "The role of diet in migraine", **Headache** (Volume 18(1), 1978): 31 – 34.

58. Millichap, J. G., **The Role of Diet and Migraine Headaches**, Chicago, PNB Publishers, 2002.

59. Milne, G., "Hypnotherapy With Migraine", **Australian Journal of Clinical and Experimental Hypnosis** (Volume 11, No. 1, 1983): 23 – 32.

60. Moffett, A. M., Swash, M., Scott, D. F., "Effect of chocolate in migraine: a double-blind study", **Journal of Neurological and Neurosurgical Psychiatry** (Volume 37, 1974): 445 – 448.

61. Moffett, A. M., Swash, M., Scott, D. F., "Effect of tyramine in migraine: a double-blind study", **Journal of Neurological and Neurosurgical Psychiatry** (Volume 35, 1972): 496 – 499.

62. National Headache Foundation, **Alternative Therapies and Headache Care**, Chicago, Illinois, 1999.

63. **Nutrition Review**, "Nutrition Reviews: Headache, tyramine, seratonin and migraine", (Volume 26(2), 1968): 40.

64. Olton, D. S. and Noonberg, A. R., **Biofeedback: Clinical Applications in Behavioral Medicine**, Prentice Hall, Inc., Englewood Cliffs, New Jersey, 1980.

65. Osterwell, Neil, "Herb Holds Promise for Migraine Prevention", Web MD Medical News, April 30, 2000.

66. **Physicians' Desk Reference**, Barnhart, E., Publisher, Medical Economics Co., New Jersey, 1986.

67. Peatfield, R. C., Glover, V., Littlewood, J. T., Sandler, M., Clifford, R. F., "The prevalence of diet-induced migraine", **Cephalalgia** (Volume 4, Number 3, September 1984): 179 – 183.

68. Pennington, J. A. T. and Church, N. N., **Bowes and Church's Food Values of Portions Commonly Used, (14th ed.)**, J. B. Lippincott Company, Philadelphia (1985).

69. Perkins, J. E. and Hartje, J., "Diet and migraine: A review of the literature", **Journal of the American Dietetic Association** (Volume 83, 1983): 459.

70. Price, K. and Smith, S. E., "Cheese reaction and tyramine", **Lancet** (Volume 1, 1971): 130.

71. Schreiber, A. O., Calvert, P. C., "Migrainous Olfactory Hallucinations", **Headache** (Nov. 1986): 513 – 514.

72. Schutter, L. C., Golden, C. J., Blume, H. G., "A Comparison of Treatments for Prefrontal Muscle Contraction Headache", **British Journal of Medical Psychology** (Vol. 53, March 1980): 47 – 52.

73. Sen, N. P., "Analysis and significance of tyramine in foods", **Journal of Food Science** (Volume 34, 1969): 22.

74. Smith, J., Gordon, A. L., Harrington, E., "Studies of tyramine metabolism in migraine patients and control subjects", **Background to Migraine**, Heinemann Medical Books, London, England (Volume 34, 1973): 9.

75. Smith, W. B., "Biofeedback and Relaxation Training: The Effect on Headache and Associated Symptoms", **Headache** (Oct. 1987): 511 – 514.

76. Speed, W., Speed Headache Associates, Inc., Baltimore, MD.

77. Staff Writer, "Could Sleep Hormone Help Migraine", Web MD News, November 29, 2001.

78. Turin, A. and Johnson, W. B., "Biofeedback therapy for migraine headaches", **Archives of General Psychiatry** (Volume 33, 1976): 517 – 519.

79. Uzogara, E., Sheehan, D. V., Manschreck, T. C., Jones, K. J., "A Combination Drug Treatment For Acute Common Migraine", **Headache** (Volume 26, 1986): 231 – 236.

80. Waelkens, J., "Warning Symptoms in Migraine: characteristics and therapeutic implications", **Cephalalgia** (Volume 5, Number 4, December 1985): 223 – 228.

81. Wakefield, G., "Clinical feature of migraine, with special reference to the migraine aura", **Modern Topics in Migraine**, Heinemann Medical Books, 1975: 22 – 29.

82. Warner, Jennifer, "Acupuncture Eases Migraine Headache Pain", Web MD News, December 4, 2003.

83. Warner, Jennifer, "Genetic Link to Migraine Found", Web MD Medical News, February 26, 2002.

84. Warner, Jennifer, "Herbal Extract May Help Prevent Migraines", Web MD News, December 28, 2004.

85. Warner, Jennifer, "Migraines With Aura Magnify Stroke Risk", Web MD News, November 20, 2002.

86. Warner, Jennifer, "Taking the Pain Out of Migraine Treatment", Web MD News, December 4, 2003.

87. Wentworth, J. A., **The Migraine Prevention Cookbook**, Doubleday, 1983.

88. Whitbred, J., **Stop Hurting, Start Living-The Pain Control Book**, Delacorte Press, New York, 1981.

89. Wilkinson, M., **Migraine and Headache**, Arco Publishing Co., 1982.

www.ingramcontent.com/pod-product-compliance
Lightning Source LLC
Chambersburg PA
CBHW060000100426
42740CB00010B/1351

* 9 7 8 0 9 7 7 2 8 7 6 0 4 *